British Political Biography

Edited by
Chris Cook

BRITISH POLITICAL BIOGRAPHY

IAIN McLEAN

KEIR HARDIE

ALLEN LANE

British Political Biography
Edited by Chris Cook

Copyright © Iain McLean 1975
First published in 1975

Allen Lane
Penguin Books Ltd
17 Grosvenor Gardens
London SW1

ISBN 0 7139 0840 8 (cased edition)
ISBN 0 7139 0841 6 (paper edition)

Printed in Great Britain by
T. & A. Constable Ltd
Hopetoun Street, Edinburgh

Set in Monotype Modern Extended No 7
The title page illustration is reproduced
by kind permission of the Labour Party Library.

CONTENTS

ACKNOWLEDGEMENTS

Any work such as this must draw extensively on other men's labours. I should like to express my thanks to the librarians and archivists of many institutions where books and records of relevance to Keir Hardie are held: the Bodleian Library, Oxford, the British Library of Political and Economic Science, the Labour Party, the National Register of Archives, West Ham Public Library, Glamorgan County Record Office, Churchill College, Cambridge, and the National Library of Scotland. Without, I hope, making invidious distinctions, I should like to express special thanks to Newcastle University Library for a great deal of work arising out of inter-library loans; Nuffield College, Oxford and its library, for restful hospitality and a superb stack of books; and the Mitchell Library, Glasgow, for being a model for all a research student could ask of a library.

The work among old newspapers necessary in preparing this book was mostly done at the British Museum Newspaper Library at Colindale.

The Henry Demarest Lloyd papers are quoted by courtesy of the Wisconsin State Historical Society, Madison, Wisconsin.

I am very grateful to Surendra Patel for medical opinions, and to Hugh Berrington, Norman McCord, and Tony Badger, who read the manuscript in whole or in part, and whose comments were very valuable. The responsibility for what appears here is, of course, mine alone.

Finally, two special debts are to the Research Fund of the University of Newcastle upon Tyne for a generous grant for travelling expenses, and to Henry Pelling, who very kindly lent me his transcripts of a number of important papers relating to Hardie, particularly his correspondence with Bruce Glasier, the originals of which are not available to scholars at the time of writing. The study of these documents, coupled with the generous hospitality of St John's College, has left me with very warm memories of an enforced stay in strikebound Cambridge.

IAIN MCLEAN
Newcastle upon Tyne

1

EARLY YEARS

Like Ramsay MacDonald and Ernest Bevin, James Keir Hardie was an illegitimate child. He was the son of Mary Keir, a farm servant living in the small mining village of Laighbrannock (or Legbrannock) near Holytown in the Lanarkshire coalfield. On 15 August 1856 James was born here in an earth-floored, one-roomed cottage that had vanished long before his death; the site is now occupied by a cottage in the grounds of an ugly modern factory. The boy's father was later named in a paternity suit as William Aitken, miner. Later, a romantic and unsubstantiated story grew up that Hardie's real father was a prosperous doctor who paid Aitken to abscond when the suit was issued and thus appear guilty. Three years afterwards Mary Keir married David Hardie, a ship's carpenter by trade, and the boy took his stepfather's surname. The Hardies had eight other children – six sons and two daughters. Some died in infancy, but two of the boys, David and George, grew up to play modest roles in the labour movement.

When James* was about five, the family moved to Glasgow while David Hardie looked for shore work in the Clyde shipyards. Life was harder for the family than in Lanarkshire. Hardie's periods of employment were interspersed with illness, strikes, and lock-outs. As a result the family never achieved the modest security that a craftsman's household might have had. They had no settled home, but frequently moved on from one tenement 'single-end' in Govan or Partick to another. James never had any schooling in Glasgow, although his parents taught him to read. From the age of seven onwards he took various jobs running errands. Two or three attempts to get him apprenticed to a skilled trade all failed. The family could not afford to forgo the wages he got as a message-boy, and Hardie's mother would not let him go into the shipyards because the work was so dangerous.

When James was ten, and working as a baker's roundsman, there occurred an incident which has become one of the favourite morality tales of the British Labour movement. One morning, around Christmas 1866, James was late for work after spending most of the previous night looking after his mother, who was pregnant, and a sick younger brother. When he arrived at work, he was summoned to see his employer.

Outside the dining room door, a servant bade me wait till 'master had finished prayers'. (He was much noted for his piety.) At length the girl opened the door, and the sight of that room is fresh in my memory even as I write, nearly fifty years after. Round a great mahogany table sat the members of the family, with the father at the top. In front of him was a very wonderful coffee boiler in the great glass bowl of which the coffee was bubbling. The table was loaded with dainties. My master looked at me over his glasses and said, in quite a pleasant tone of voice, 'Boy, this is the second morning you have been late, and my customers will leave me if they are kept waiting for their hot breakfast rolls. I therefore dismiss you and, to make you more careful in the future, I have decided to fine you a week's wages. And now you may go.'

That night the baby was born, and the sun rose on the 1st of January 1867 over a home in which there was neither fire nor food.†

*During his childhood Hardie was called James or Jamie; when he started writing, he took his mother's surname as a Christian name. (Ramsay MacDonald did the same.) The same usage will be followed here.

† There are minor inconsistencies among Hardie's many re-tellings of this story. This version is from the *Merthyr Pioneer* of 26 December 1914.

The master's attitude was partly hypocritical, partly thoughtless – and probably partly punitive. A lock-out of shipyard workers was in progress, and David Hardie was one of the men locked out. So young Jamie's wages formed the household's only income. The family's poverty, therefore, was not due to 'respectable' causes, and there was no reason why humanitarianism should be allowed to override simple commercial principles. Shortly after this, probably as a result of the lock-out, David Hardie went back to sea, and his wife and family returned to the Lanarkshire coalfield. They went to live at Newarthill, only two miles from Legbrannock, where Mary Keir's mother still lived.

There was only one job for a boy in Lanarkshire who had failed to get an apprenticeship to a trade. James went off to work in a coal mine for the first time – and as he went, his stepfather comforted his worried mother: 'You hae this consolation at least, that sailors and colliers are the twa classes that ministers pray maist for – if that does ony guid.' It was Job's comfort; both parents had rejected Christianity and put no trust in ministers' prayers. James got a post as a trapper, a boy whose job was to open and close doors underground so as to control ventilation and allow traffic to pass. Though not physically hard, the work involved very long hours and considerable mental strain. But James was fairly well looked after, and soon progressed from trapper to pit-pony driver. At the age of twelve he was involved in a near-accident when a shaft closed in above the place where he was working with a number of hewers, entombing them. Rescue came fairly soon, but when the men got to the surface they found that young James was missing – so some of them had to go back down the half-closed shaft to look for him. They found him safe and well, but asleep beside his pony in its stable. This incident made a deep impression on Hardie, and he often retold it in later life.

In Hardie's late teens, the family moved across the Lanarkshire coalfield to the upland pit-village of Quarter, near Larkhall, about ten miles from Newarthill. Here Hardie progressed to become a hewer – as near as it was possible to get to a skilled and 'respectable' position in the Scottish pits of the period.

While working as a trapper at Newarthill, James had attended night school in Holytown near by. It was the only formal education he ever had. He used to practise the writing and shorthand he learnt there by laboriously writing out the characters on pieces of slate blackened with soot from his pit lamp during quiet moments underground. In his teens he started to dip into Scottish literature. The ballads and folk tales of the Borders and the south-west of Scotland introduced Hardie to the traditional values of rural Scotland: puritanism, respect for education, scorn for distinctions between man and man based merely on social status. The most enduring influences were the Covenanters, Burns, and Carlyle.

Hardie was to spend most of his adult life in the Ayrshire heartlands of the Covenanters. They were extreme Presbyterians of the seventeenth century, who became a persecuted minority in the reigns of Charles II and James VII and II – the 'Killing Times' during which the Covenanters, forbidden on pain of death to hold their services, held open-air 'conventicles' in the Ayrshire hills. As a matter of fact, the Covenanters were not nearly as admirable as Scottish folk tradition has always presented them as being; in power they were no more tolerant than out of power they were tolerated. But the picture of them as an incorruptible minority, unjustifiably persecuted for their religious beliefs, has always exercised a powerful sway over the Scottish imagination. It was a picture which influenced both Hardie and Ramsay MacDonald.

A figure from south-western Scotland who meant to Hardie even more than the Covenanters was Robert Burns. Hardie reacted instinctively to both the nationalistic and the democratic strains in Burns's poetry. Hardie never sat for a Scottish seat in Parliament; but he was in favour of Scottish Home Rule, and always returned when he could to his home in Scotland for rest and quiet. But it was the democrat in Robert Burns, the enthusiast for the French Revolution, who made the greatest appeal to Hardie. Hardie's socialism owed much to the author of 'A Man's a Man for a' that'.

> What though on hamely fare we dine,
> Wear hoddin grey, and a' that.
> Gie fools their silks, and knaves their wine,
> A Man's a Man for a' that.
>
> .　　.　　.　　.　　.
>
> For a' that, and a' that,
> Its comin yet for a' that,
> That Man to Man the warld o'er,
> Shall brothers be for a' that.—

In later life, Hardie admitted, 'I owe more to Burns than to any man living or dead.' But another literary influence on him at this time was again a writer from south-west Scotland: the 'Sage of Ecclefechan', Thomas Carlyle. In his teens Hardie was given a copy of Carlyle's first work, *Sartor Resartus* (written in 1831 and published in 1838). What a self-educated Lanarkshire pitman can have made of this obscure work written in Carlyle's leaden, Germanic, and (fortunately) unique style, it is difficult to imagine. Hardie read the book three times over, until, he wrote, 'the spirit of it somewhat entered into me'. One aspect of *Sartor Resartus* is the anarchic radicalism of Carlyle's early years – a point of view less obscurely expressed in his later *Chartism* and *Past and Present*. It was this that caught Hardie's attention, as we may judge from his underlined and annotated copy of the book. In a passage which made a deep impression on Hardie, Carlyle complains about the futility of war:

> To my own knowledge . . . there dwell and toil, in the British village of Dumdrudge, usually some five-hundred souls. From these, by certain 'Natural Enemies' of the French, there are successively selected, during the French war, say thirty able-bodied men. Dumdrudge, at her own expense, has suckled and nursed them: she has, not without difficulty and sorrow, fed them up to manhood, and even trained them to crafts . . . Nevertheless . . . they are shipped away . . . some two-thousand miles, or say only to the south of Spain; and fed there till wanted. And now to that same spot . . . are thirty similar French artisans, from a French Dumdrudge, in like manner wending: till at length . . . Thirty stands fronting Thirty, each with a gun in his hand. Straightway the word *Fire* is given . . . and in place of sixty brisk useful craftsmen, the world has sixty dead carcasses, which it must bury, and anew shed tears for. Had these men any quarrel? Busy as the Devil is, not the smallest! . . . How then? Simpleton! their Governors had fallen out; and, instead of shooting one another, had the cunning to make these poor blockheads shoot.

Hardie also noted how Carlyle's fictional Professor Teufelsdröckh spoke of the 'two men I honour, and no third. First, the toilworn Craftsman, . . . second . . . [the] Artist; not earthly Craftsman only, but inspired Thinker, who with heaven-made Implement conquers Heaven for us.' Carlyle was not a conventional radical, and later in life he became a violent reactionary. But his story of Dumdrudge put into picturesque language the creed of the radical Liberal opposed to all war. These views Hardie acquired, and kept all his life.

Imbued with the puritan ideals of the Covenanters, Hardie soon took the first step down the road trodden by so many British working-class leaders: he became a temperance organizer, and a leading member of organizations like the Good Templars and the Band of Hope dedicated to opposing all alcoholic drink. His upbringing and attitudes were in many ways typical of those of an earnest Victorian working man, although they had some unusual features. Hardie's mother and stepfather had abandoned their religious beliefs by the time he was in his formative years. But if Mary Keir was an agnostic, she was unmistakably a Scottish Presbyterian agnostic. Early in his journalistic career Hardie wrote about his mother in one of his occasional Scots dialect articles. 'Her idea o' Heeven seemed tae be that it was a great big farm whaur ye could get workin' on frae year's end tae year's end withoot stoppin'.' This reflected the 'Protestant ethic' of Scots Calvinism: work was inherently morally virtuous, and laziness and drink were deadly sins. Hardie inherited these views, and he came to think that many of the miners' problems were brought upon themselves by indolence and addiction to drink. Referring to the argument of the statistician Robert Giffen that the real income of the poor had doubled in fifty years, Hardie asked himself why the working class seemed to be as poor as ever. 'To my mind,' he wrote in 1884, 'the answer is as clear as the noonday sun: the people are pouring it down their throats in intoxicating drinks.'

Hardie's self-conscious teetotalism set him apart from most of his fellow miners. Nevertheless, his progression from spokesman for Good Templary to spokesman for the miners' grievances was a natural one, and can be paralleled in the early careers of a number of other British labour politicians, such as Hardie's later colleagues Philip Snowden and Arthur Henderson. Temperance work gave a man self-confidence and abilities in public speaking which could easily be put to use elsewhere.

During the 1870s, when Keir Hardie first became a hewer, miners' wages were under severe pressure, after a brief boom caused by the Franco–Prussian War of 1870 which disrupted coal-mining in Europe. The Scottish miners had never been able to form a stable trade union, largely because they could never control entry to the pits. Any attempt at a strike or at restriction of output could easily be broken by importing strangers – often Irishmen – who were not particular as to where and how they worked. In the early 1870s the Lanarkshire County Miners' Union, such as it was, had collapsed. So in the absence of a union the miners looked for men to represent their grievances locally. Hardie was an articulate man whose temperance work had given him experience in speaking, writing, and the conduct of business; he was the inevitable choice of his colleagues. And the outcome was not unexpected. In about 1878 Hardie was dismissed from his employment at Quarter. 'We'll hae nae damned Hardies in this pit,' said the manager as the cage Hardie had been in was wound back to the surface instead of going on down to the workface. He never worked in the pits again. No coalmaster would employ a dangerous agitator. He had to move again, this time to Cadzow, on the outskirts of Hamilton, the principal town of the Lanarkshire coal and iron manufacturing area. Here Keir Hardie earned a precarious living by opening a tobacconist's shop and writing his first journalism as the local correspondent of a Glasgow radical paper, the *Glasgow Weekly Mail*. The *Weekly Mail* and its stable companion the *North British Daily Mail*, owned by a Liberal M.P., were the only papers circulating in the area which gave sympathetic coverage to miners' affairs. Fortunately his parents did not depend on his earnings. His mother had opened another shop and his stepfather got a steady job after years of uncertainty and insecurity. He became a joiner at Quarter Iron Works – so evidently not every 'damned Hardie' was boycotted.

In June 1879 Keir Hardie, now twenty-two, married Lillie Wilson, a girl he had met during his temperance work in the county. Already most of his life was taken up with public affairs, and his involvement was barely even interrupted by his marriage – not that there was any question of a newly married Victorian workman going away for a honeymoon. A month later a mass meeting of Lanarkshire miners invited Hardie to be their Corresponding Secretary, and in early August he became Miners' Agent. Thus he came face to face with the problems that were to be his central concern for the next seven years. For a year in Lanarkshire, followed by six years in Ayrshire, Hardie struggled with very little success to build a miners' union. In the circumstances of the 1880s there was only one strategy open to miners who wished to protect or raise their wages. This was restriction of output, known in the west of Scotland as the 'wee darg'.* If across a whole county – or, better still, the whole of Scotland – the miners could be persuaded not to produce more than an agreed quantity of coal per shift, this would protect the wages of those who, at the time, were working at 'hard places', where the coal was difficult to extract. More ambitiously, it was hoped that a widespread adoption of the 'wee darg' would make it impossible for the coalmasters to reduce piece-rates at any pit, and would even, by raising the price of coal, benefit the whole industry, masters and men alike.

This was the objective towards which union organizers strove. But there were several difficulties in its way, any of which would have been severe; combined, they were disastrous. First, the managements were a good deal more united than the men. The mines of Lanarkshire and Ayrshire could be divided into 'sale pits', whose produce was sold on the open market for domestic and industrial use, and the iron companies' pits, whose coal went straight to the ironworks of the Bairds of Gartsherrie and the other great iron companies of the district. In the sale pits, whose ownership was fairly fragmented, there was some hope that unions might be able to gain concessions by playing off one

---

* 'Darg': Scots dialect term for 'day's work'.

inst another; in the ironworks pits, there was very little.
re, the 'salemasters' had no particular objection to restrictions in production which might lead to higher coal prices; but the ironmasters emphatically did object, as their own costs were affected. Therefore the ironmasters acted together on miners' wages – and they were under heavy pressure to keep them down, because Lanarkshire iron was fast losing its competitiveness in the market. Local iron-ore reserves were becoming exhausted, whereas in new iron and steel areas like Tees-side new ironstone mines were being opened on the doorsteps of the foundries. And Lanarkshire iron-owners had failed to keep up a proper level of investment in their plant; in particular, they had not re-equipped it for the new Bessemer steelmaking processes. The only direction in which the ironmasters could try to gain a competitive advantage was through cutting labour costs – including costs in the collieries where their coal was mined. Thus miners' wages were reduced by 6d. a day in the ironworks pits in October 1879. It was an inauspicious time and place for Hardie to start his union career.

Other difficulties facing the policy of the 'wee darg' were even more basic. It could work only when an effective federal union had been formed; but how to set about forming one? Neither Hardie nor anyone else was able to do this in the 1880s, and Hardie's appointment as 'National Secretary of the Scottish Mineworkers' as early as October 1879 represented aspiration, not achievement. No union leader could ever make Quarter act in the interests of Newarthill, still less Lanarkshire in the interests of Fife or South Wales. The most ambitious aim of the 'wee darg' was to create a scarcity of coal. Since consumers would still need coal, the result ought to be a rise in coal prices. If this reasoning was sound, the 'wee darg' could be effective only if it spread from its place of origin to the farthest place from which coal could be economically moved. But there was no chance of this happening. Restriction in one pit or area meant increased demand in another, and the miners always seized the opportunity to profit in times of plenty, whatever their leaders might say. In 1882, for example, when Lanarkshire miners accepted a forty-hour working week in return for a promise not to restrict output, Hardie wrote bitterly, 'They are getting fat aff the meesery o' ithers. Were it no that 5,000 miners are on strike in North Wales at present tae resist a reduction the pat widna be boilin' sae brisk here.'

Even within a pit, it was not always easy to inculcate trade-union solidarity. The Scots miners tended to blame the Irish for this, although doubtless they were not the only culprits. Ill-feeling between

native Scots and Irish in Scotland was to play its part in holding back
Hardie's political career. But he joined in the attack.

Nothing angers the miner so much during a time of restriction, than
[*sic*] to find a fellow working at a stoop where the requisites are a big
shovel, a strong back, and a weak brain, said fellow having a few weeks
before been busy in a peat bog or a tatie field, but who is now producing
coal enough for a man and a half, and . . . to hear him say, 'Och, I'll fill as
many as I loike.'

Unlike many occupations in which trade unionism had been established before 1880, colliery work did not demand a formal apprenticeship. Since mining did not have any rules regarding apprenticeship,
miners lost a vital lever of influence available to some of their contemporaries such as the engineers or the carpenters and joiners: they
had no control over entry into the pits. Hardie was himself a beneficiary of this, since none of his relations (disregarding his presumptive
father) had worked in the pits. But by the same token, the miners had
no way of preventing blacklegs or Irishmen from entering the pits to
break strikes or ignore restrictions – often, as Hardie's own comment
shows, out of pure self-interest, not any form of collusion with the
mineowners.

These, then, were the gloomy circumstances in which Hardie began
his career in mining trade-unionism. In the autumn of 1879 the miners
of the Hamilton area held meetings in protest at the proposed wage
reductions in the ironmasters' pits, and were addressed by Hardie and
Alexander Macdonald. Macdonald, who was the founder of mining
unionism in Scotland, was one of the first two working men to become
an M.P. (he became Liberal member for Stafford in 1874). He was a
very popular speaker among the miners, and an advocate of extreme
caution. But even he could not hold their union together. At this
period Hardie shared Macdonald's basic views on the need to be
sparing in the use of the 'wee darg'; but the younger man inevitably
seemed more impetuous than the elder statesman. Hardie fell out with
Macdonald because of his part in the Lanarkshire miners' strikes in
1880. The first of these took place early in the year, in protest against
the wage cuts in the ironmasters' pits. The second started in August,
lasted for six weeks, and involved all the mines in Lanarkshire. Neither
strike could be called a success, although the ironmasters did raise
wages in January. The main importance of these strikes was that they
introduced Hardie to Ayrshire, which was to be his home for the rest
of his life. In August 1880 he went around north-eastern Ayrshire
attempting to spread the Lanarkshire strike; and later that month we
find him described, for the first time, as 'secretary and miners' agent

for Ayrshire'. He was also nominally secretary of the Lanarkshire Miners' Association. Of course, neither a Lanarkshire nor an Ayrshire miners' association actually existed, and these were largely self-imposed titles indicating that Hardie was trying to create a miners' organization in both places.

In the autumn of 1880, after the end of the Lanarkshire strike, Hardie finally decided to migrate to Ayrshire. It was not entirely a free choice. The Lanarkshire strike had left behind a legacy of debts owing to friendly shopkeepers who had supplied miners' families with goods on credit. Alexander Macdonald indicated that he could use his influence to raise money to settle these debts – but only on condition that Hardie ceased to be secretary of the Lanarkshire miners. Another reason for the move was that the iron companies were rather less dominant in the Ayrshire coalfield than in Lanarkshire. There were more sale pits, which, for reasons we have already explored, were more amenable to union organization. Again, the Ayrshire coalfield was a new one, which made industrial relations run more smoothly. The mines were more profitable, so that the owners did not have to lean so heavily on their employees' wages to cut costs, and there were fewer 'hard places' where coal was difficult to get. Since hewers were paid on piece rates – so much per ton of coal mined – 'hard places' were one of the most fruitful sources of dispute in the coal industry for the whole of Hardie's lifetime.

One drawback of the Ayrshire coalfield was that many of the mining villages such as Auchinleck, Muirkirk, or Annbank were 'company towns': new settlements where the coal company owned all the houses and could add the threat of eviction to its other anti-strike weapons. But Hardie was able to settle in one of the old-established and independent towns in the area, namely Cumnock. Here he eventually bought a substantial red-sandstone house called Lochnorris, with the aid of an interest-free loan from a philanthropist called Adam Birkmyre. In Lochnorris, which still stands on the edge of the town, Hardie settled down to life as a journalist and trade-union leader.

Soon after arriving in Cumnock, Hardie became first a correspondent for, and later editor of, the *Cumnock News*. This was a local off-shoot of the *Ardrossan and Saltcoats Herald*, one of the leading Liberal weekly papers in the west of Scotland. From 1882 to 1886 he contributed a regular column, called *Black Diamonds, or Mining Notes worth Minding*,* to the parent paper. (This column, full of political and industrial advice to the miners, is the earliest of Hardie's writings

* 'Mind' is here used in the Scottish sense of 'take note of'.

on politics to have survived. It is valuable for what it reveals of his political views at the time.) Meanwhile, Hardie settled down to the life of a superior working man and a pillar of the community. Reacting against his parents' agnosticism, he became a member of the local Congregational church. He later recorded in a fragmentary diary entry that he was 'converted to Christianity in 1878'. Later, he was one of a number of members of the Church who seceded to form a branch of the Evangelical Union, a liberal offshoot. What spare time he had from journalism and attempts at forming a miners' union was spent in worthy local activities: church meetings, the Cumnock Junior Liberal Association, the local lodge of the Independent Order of Good Templars. Hardie was in many ways a typical trade unionist of his time: a devout teetotaller and a devout Liberal. An amusing insight into the cast of his mind at the time is given in a fragment of his diary that has survived:

Thursday, 21 February 1884. Lodge meeting tonight, read Essay was Burns Drunkard and concluded he was not. Conclusion open to question, even in own mind, but always like to be charitable.

Hardie had been brought up to revere Robert Burns's poetry; he was now living in Burns's native county – but he could not in honesty deny that his idol might have had feet of clay.

More seriously, Hardie threw himself into politics. Like most Victorian working men who had risen through temperance and self-help, he was a strong Liberal. At no time before the 1886 general election could his loyal Liberalism have been called into doubt. On hearing of a Conservative plan to run working-class candidates, he wrote scornfully in *Black Diamonds*, 'When once the working-man is found who is a Conservative from honest intelligent conviction, he should either be sent to Barnum for exhibition, or he should be stuffed and put under a glass case in the British Museum.'

In some parts of the country, the Liberalism of trade unionists was put under severe strain by the fact that their employers, even the most resolutely anti-union, were also Liberals. In the Lancashire cotton industry, for instance, this led to the emergence of 'Conservative-Labour' trade unionists like James Mawdsley, the secretary of the Cotton Spinners, who fought an election in Oldham as a Conservative. But there was no such problem for Ayrshire miners. Coal-owners were as likely to be Tory landowners as Liberal capitalists; and above all, the most hated figures in the industry, the royalty owners (who levied fees called 'royalties' on coal extracted from their ground) were almost all landowners and Tories. The industrial situation strengthened

Hardie's Liberalism; it did not undermine it as it might have done elsewhere.

In 1884 he saw the importance of the Liberal Government's Franchise Bill. Disraeli's Reform Act of 1867 had given most men the vote in boroughs, but had left the areas outside boroughs untouched. The 1884 Bill proposed to extend the same franchise to the counties. This was of great importance for miners, most of whom lived in areas that, though towns in all but name, were too new to belong to traditional borough constituencies. Two miners had been returned to Parliament in 1874, but both sat for borough seats: Stafford and Morpeth. Miners living inside the boundaries of Morpeth town could vote in 1874, but those outside could not. The next General Election after the 1884 Act would, therefore, be the first at which miners' votes could be polled to their full strength. Hardie spent a lot of his spare time in 1884 and 1885 on voter registration work and on building up the Liberal Party. During 1884 new Liberal Associations were formed at New Cumnock and Auchinleck, two mining settlements a few miles on either side of Cumnock; by the autumn of 1885 2,670 claims for electoral registration were before the local authorities in Ayr. In the summer of 1885 Gladstone's Liberal ministry, which had failed to fulfil its early promise, resigned; it was replaced by a minority Conservative Government under the Marquess of Salisbury. A General Election was inevitable before long, and was in fact called for November 1885.

Hardie was a radical Liberal. In using the word 'radical' about the politicians of this time, we must take great care, because radicalism had two, increasingly divergent, components. A well-known Liberal slogan was 'Peace, Retrenchment, and Reform'. Peace and Retrenchment belonged to an older radicalism which preached avoidance of wars and entanglement in Europe or the Empire, and the minimum possible public expenditure. 'Reform' originally implied matters like franchise reform, but came to incorporate demands like more stringent factory inspection and statutory restriction of the working day. Many politicians who strongly believed in the old radicalism had grave doubts about the new; some who were interested in reform were uninterested in the campaigns of the older radicalism. Since this distinction constantly recurs in the ideologies of politicians of this era, we ought to give names to the two tendencies. 'Individualist' and 'collectivist' radicalism are clumsy terms, but they are the best available.

Looking at the speeches and manifestoes which Keir Hardie addressed to the Ayrshire miners in 1885 and 1886, we can see that he was preaching both individualist and collectivist radicalism. On the one hand, he demanded a reduction in the cost the country had to pay to support the Queen and the aristocracy. On the other, he called for free primary education and for reforms in the system of official colliery inspection. Earlier generations of radicals would have called these matters none of the state's business: a comforting doctrine for industrialists, less so for working men. After the election had been announced, Hardie printed a list of miners' demands for the reform of the Regulation of Coal Mines and Employers' Liability Acts; he announced that the Liberal candidate for South Ayrshire had agreed to support these demands, and urged miners in the constituency to vote for him. On the eve of poll Hardie issued his manifesto. It is a somewhat sententious document: 'When in the quietness and secrecy of the polling booth you stand alone with God, and with no eyes to see you but His alone, cast your vote for Home, Freedom, and Country, in favour of the Liberal candidate.'

The Liberals won both of the county seats in Ayrshire from the Conservatives, and Hardie attributed the Liberal gain in the southern division to the newly enfranchised miners. Overall, the election resulted in stalemate. The Liberals had a majority of 86 over the Conservatives, but the independent Irish Party also had exactly 86 members. They could keep either party out, but could put only the Liberals in. As was the custom at the time, Salisbury did not resign until defeated soon after Parliament first met early in 1886, when Gladstone formed his third ministry. By now it had become known that he favoured Home Rule for Ireland as the only viable solution to the vexed Irish question. Not only the Conservatives but also a section of the Liberals revolted against this; popular support for the revolt derived largely from anti-Irish feeling which was widespread in urban and mining areas. The Liberal Party was split; Gladstone's Home Rule Bill was defeated, and he called another election in the summer of 1886. The dissident Liberals, under Joseph Chamberlain and the Marquess of Hartington, fought as 'Liberal-Unionists'. Eugene Wason, the Liberal elected for South Ayrshire in 1885, wavered between Gladstone and Chamberlain, but eventually came down on Gladstone's side. Hardie again threw himself wholeheartedly into electioneering on behalf of Gladstonian Liberalism. Again he issued a manifesto to the miners of Ayrshire, but this time it concentrated entirely on Home Rule. However, Home Rule was an issue to split, not to rally, the Ayrshire miners. As we have seen, many miners including Hardie himself accused the Irish of undermining trade unionism in the collieries by blacklegging and failing to observe restriction of output. It is very likely that some working-class voters deserted the Liberals to contribute to the defeat of the Liberal M.P. by the extremely narrow margin of 6,123 votes to 6,118.

Throughout this period there is no evidence that Hardie was anything other than an orthodox Gladstonian Liberal. His conversion to more advanced views was closely connected with some developments in trade unionism, to which we must now return. The Ayrshire Miners' Union and the National Union of Scottish Mineworkers had kept up a precarious existence during 1881 and 1882. In August 1881 all the Ayrshire miners had struck for a ten per cent increase in wages. It is not clear how much of this was Hardie's doing, for it was in large measure a spontaneous outburst of indignation. Late summer was a propitious time for a strike. The miners could live off potatoes given or sold on credit by friendly farmers, and the strike, like other autumn miners' strikes, became known as the 'tattie strike'. But winter was less happy, and the miners had to go back to work after ten weeks on strike. Shortly afterwards a wage rise was conceded. But it was a pyrrhic victory. The miners' organization, such as it was, collapsed bankrupt as a result of the strike. Shortly afterwards the Scottish Mineworkers' National Union followed the Ayrshire organization into extinction. The Scottish miners, Hardie complained, had expected too much for too little. Durham miners paid 6d. a week to the union; their death benefit (always the most important benefit offered by Victorian friendly societies) was £5. The Scots had expected to get £6 death benefit for only 1½d. a week.

Hardie had now to rely on his journalism as his sole source of income as he tried to rebuild the Ayrshire Miners' Union. Time after time his efforts failed. It was not difficult to get the miners in an individual pit to take an 'idle day' to hear a speech (or go to Ayr races). Indeed, Hardie was more often persuading them not to than encouraging them to do so. What was far more difficult, for reasons we have examined already, was to get miners in different collieries to unite so that others did not profit from, and thus defeat the purpose of, the 'idle day' or 'wee darg' decided on at one pit. The first real sign of success was a conference in Kilmarnock on 21 August 1886, for the purpose of linking up 'at least half-a-dozen district unions'. This marked the real foundation, or re-foundation, of the Ayrshire Miners' Union. By October, Hardie was able to report that 'in all the sale districts, and also in some of the ironworks, men are joining the Ayrshire Miners' Union freely'. As ever, the sale pits were easier to organize than the mines belonging to iron companies. At the same time another Scottish Miners' Federation was formed and Hardie became its secretary. From the Ayrshire Miners he drew a salary of £75 per annum, and from the Scottish Miners the generous sum of £3 15s.

The Scottish Miners' National Federation was not a success. Its aim was that which Hardie had always preached: to federate county unions in order to make restriction of output effective across the country.

> What is wanted [said Hardie in his first Annual Report as Secretary] is the adoption of a policy which will bring the supply of coal going into the market well within the demand. Thus and thus only can wages be got up . . . What we aim at meanwhile is to get all the miners of the United Kingdom to be idle for a fortnight or so all at the same time.

But the Fife miners refused to join the Federation precisely because they thought they were doing nicely, and were not their Lanarkshire brothers' keepers. Furthermore, the Chairman of the Federation was Chisholm Robertson of Stirlingshire, whom Hardie disliked throughout their association. This was not a matter of policy, as Hardie and Robertson held very similar views on political and industrial issues. Rather, it was a question of simple personal antagonism between two ambitious men. The National Federation did not really survive a strike in Lanarkshire in January and February 1887, when the iron companies managed to impose an agreement that 'no workman should consult with any other' about restriction of production. (This was a formula designed to exclude permanent union officials from any right of negotiation.)

Developments in Ayrshire were more promising. The Ayrshire Miners' Union was at last firmly established, and in January 1887 Hardie started a monthly paper of his own called *The Miner*. During the two years it was to be published, it would mirror the hardening of Hardie's attitudes to the conventional Liberalism of his political upbringing. The two main springs of his disillusionment with Liberalism were the reluctance of the Liberal Party to support working-class candidates and his own disappointment at the behaviour of the existing working-class Liberal M.P.s – the 'Lib-Labs' as they were known. Hardie no doubt felt that his efforts on behalf of Liberalism in South Ayrshire from the passing of the Franchise Act in 1884 to the 1886 election had been inadequately recognized by the middle-class leadership of Ayrshire Liberalism. The general dissension in the party following the Home Rule split in the summer of 1886 and the Liberals' consequent loss of the 1886 election possibly made it easier for Hardie to carry his resentment to the stage of practical action. In May 1887 he announced with delight that 'the Ayrshire miners have at length made a move in connection with the representation of their calling in

the House of Commons'. This took the form of a resolution accepting
the need for a miners' candidate for Parliament, to be put up by the
Ayrshire miners themselves. And by the end of the month Keir Hardie
himself had been nominated as the miners' candidate for the North
Ayrshire division. This constituency had no Liberal candidate, because the Liberal elected in 1885 had become a Liberal Unionist, and
had been returned unopposed under that label in the 1886 election.
The nomination of Hardie did not in itself imply any disagreement
between him and the Liberals; but it put him outside the pale at once.
For the first time in his political career, he was attacked in the Radical
papers. The *Glasgow Weekly Mail* thought that his candidature was
being paid for by Tories to split the Liberal vote. No charge was to be
more frequently hurled at Hardie during his political career, and once
or twice it was to be true, in an oblique fashion. But this time it was
certainly untrue. The *Ardrossan and Saltcoats Herald* editorially
attacked its own Cumnock correspondent. 'It will be the duty of the
Liberal Association', it said angrily, 'to resent any usurpation of their
undoubted right of fixing upon the candidate who is to contest the
division at the next election.' The Association needed no encouragement. In November 1887 Sir William Wedderburn was adopted as
prospective Liberal candidate for North Ayrshire. The *Ardrossan and
Saltcoats Herald* recorded what happened next.

Mr Clelland asked if the Executive had any communication with Mr
Hardie regarding his candidature for North Ayrshire.
The chairman said they had no communication directly with Mr Hardie.
The statement he made on one occasion, that he was prepared to stand in
spite of the association, was sufficient in his mind to preclude the Execu-
tive from ever thinking of Mr Hardie. (Loud applause.)

Hardie ought to have anticipated that his action would have this
angry result. In other parts of the country, trade unionists were
trying, with a certain amount of success, to persuade Liberal associations to adopt working-class parliamentary candidates. From first
to last Hardie made no attempt to approach any Liberal organization
in this way. Why did he, instead, strike out boldly on his own?
Several possible answers might be suggested. The first, and most contentious, would be that by the middle of 1887 Hardie was no longer a
Liberal, but had become a socialist. Whether or not this is true can
only be decided in the light of a study of Hardie's writings and
speeches at the time, which will be considered later. But independently
of this, two other reasons may be put forward. Hardie was a stubborn
and at times a vain man. One reason for his action was undoubtedly
that he felt slighted. He was as good a man as the upper-crust Liberals

of North and South Ayrshire, and had done a good deal more for the
party than they had. By standing, entirely on his own initiative (for
any political resolution passed by the Ayrshire Miners' Union was
obviously no more nor less than an expression of Hardie's views) as a
miners' candidate, he would shake them out of their complacency.
The possible loss of an opportunity to recapture the seat from
the Unionists, because of a split in the Liberal vote, would be the
price the Liberal Association would have to pay for ignoring Keir
Hardie.

Another reason for Hardie's independent action was probably that
he disapproved of the tactics of the existing Lib-Lab M.P.s. There
were about a dozen of them in 1887 – quite an advance on the two
working-class M.P.s of 1874. But Hardie did not have a high opinion
of them. This was partly a consequence of the impatience of a young
man at the seeming inability of older men to get anything done – impatience which had been shown in the disagreement between Hardie
and Alexander Macdonald in 1880. But it went deeper than that. The
Lib-Lab M.P.s had been raised, as Hardie had been, in the orthodoxy
of Gladstonian economics, which taught that no interference, however
well-intentioned, with the free workings of the market was in the best
interests of any of the parties. Labour, it was held, benefited as much as
capital from freedom of contract and minimal government interference
in industry. These doctrines were part of what we have called the creed
of 'individualistic radicalism' and were devoutly believed by mid-
nineteenth-century Liberals. But some of the Lib-Lab M.P.s carried
the doctrine to what Hardie regarded as paradoxical and absurd
lengths. His anger came to be concentrated on the views of the existing
miners' M.P.s, such as Thomas Burt and Charles Fenwick of Northumberland and William Abraham ('Mabon') of South Wales. In the
summer of 1887 a bill was promoted to restrict the maximum of hours
worked by boys in the mining industry to eight per day. It seemed a
modest enough measure, and precisely the sort of thing that miners'
M.P.s had been sent to Westminster in order to support. But Burt
was at best half-heartedly in favour of it, and Mabon actually spoke
against the measure. Hardie bitterly pointed to the sectional self-
interest that bolstered this attitude. Northumberland had already
won a six-or seven-hour day at the coalface for hewers – and if boys
were allowed to work long hours, say ten or eleven a day, on ancillary
tasks such as trapping, one shift of boys could act as helpers to two
shifts of hewers. Since hewers were sometimes subcontractors who
paid boys' wages out of their pockets, they stood to lose from any reduction of boys' hours and consequent increase in the cost of boys'

labour. For these local reasons Northumberland failed to support the measure. Here Hardie met with the same attitude which had for five or six years defeated all his own attempts to build a union in the west of Scotland: the resolute refusal of one district to inconvenience itself on behalf of another. There is a noticeable cooling off of Hardie's attitude to the Lib-Lab M.P.s, as judged by his successive comments about them in the *Ardrossan and Saltcoats Herald* and the *Miner* from 1886 onwards. The change was undoubtedly connected with Hardie's growing feeling that more than an obstinate attachment to outworn economic attitudes underlay the miners' M.P.s' conservatism. In the autumn of 1886 Hardie wrote mildly, 'I would be half inclined to join issue with Mr Burt when he says that Trade Unions have no power to raise wages, all they can do being to enable the worker to get the full market value for their [*sic*] labour ... Trade Unions ... have the power to raise the market value of his [the worker's] labour.' In January 1887 Hardie was still on sufficiently good terms with Burt to get him to write an introduction to the first issue of the *Miner*, but events in the summer of 1887 changed Hardie's attitude. A miners' delegation, of which Hardie was a member, went to Westminster to lobby M.P.s in favour of legislation for a compulsory eight-hour day for all miners, not just boys. The lobby had some success. The Liberal member for Kilmarnock proposed, and the Conservative member for South Lanarkshire seconded, an amendment in favour of an eight-hour day to the Mines Bill being passed through the Commons. But the Lib-Lab miners' M.P.s actually opposed the amendment, which was lost by 159 votes to 104. Their argument was that statutory regulation of hours was pernicious and unnecessary. For instance, Charles Fenwick, the member for the Wansbeck division of Northumberland, said: 'The regulation of the hours of labour is a matter of organization, and the miners do not require the intervention of Parliament.' This, to Hardie, was insufferable complacency, not to say hypocrisy. The miners' leaders of Northumberland were not simply enunciating trite views about wages and parliamentary organization: they were expressing complacent pride about the strength of their union organization and contempt for the weakness of the miners' unions in Scotland. As Hardie saw it, Fenwick's comment was a scarcely disguised sneer at the efforts of people like himself. If Keir Hardie had been as competent a union organizer as Charles Fenwick he would not be bleating about the need for a statutory eight-hour day – his union's negotiating strength would have secured it. Angered by these imputations, Hardie went off, as delegate from the Ayrshire Miners' Union, to the 1887 meeting of the Trades Union Congress at Swansea. His mood of political bitterness was deepened by personal tragedy: he had just lost an infant daughter, who died in August 1887.

At Swansea, Hardie made himself known for the first time to an audience outside his native west of Scotland. In his determination to make an impact, he spoke five or six times, which in itself antagonized many delegates: what right had a young member of a newly affiliated union, paying its very small affiliation fee for the first time ever, to seek for himself such a large share of the T.U.C.'s time? Henry Broad-hurst, a prominent Lib-Lab who was secretary of the T.U.C., made a point of complaining about this: 'Mr Hardie was there taking a share – and no small share – on the platform erected by the trade-unionism of the country, towards which Mr Hardie had not contributed a single farthing.' Broadhurst was responding in kind to an outspoken attack on him by Hardie, who had raised two main issues. First, why had Broadhurst spoken and voted against the Eight-Hour Day amendment put forward to the Coal Mines Bill? Second, why had Broadhurst made speeches in the 1886 election campaign on behalf of prominent Liberal industrialists whose workers suffered very bad conditions? (This was a reference to Sir John Brunner, the chemical magnate, who was Liberal M.P. for Northwich. The ammunition for Hardie's attack had been provided for him by R. B. Cunninghame Graham, the very left-wing Liberal member for North-West Lanark.) Broadhurst's reply was a contemptuous dismissal of Hardie – and because most delegates had regarded Hardie's speeches as unwarranted personal attacks on Broadhurst, the latter was able to reply in kind without spending very long on defending his actions.

Some of the bitterness was caused by the fact that Hardie and Broadhurst were men of opposite temperament. Broadhurst was an elder statesman of the Labour movement, the ex-stonemason who had worked his way up to be a close confidant of Francis Schnadhorst (the *eminence grise* of the Liberal Party who was responsible for its electoral organization) and an acquaintance of Mr Gladstone himself.

---

* Broadhurst has often been accused of distorting Hardie's interventions in the debate, in order to make a fool of him. A study of the text of the discussion shows that the charge is not entirely fair. Where, asked Broadhurst, had Hardie been in the 'struggle which had lifted labour up from the position it was in fifty years back, when Odger, Howell, and all the other champions of labour were fighting their battles?' Hardie: 'I was not born.' Broadhurst: Hardie was an 'exceedingly forward infant' if he had not been born ten years ago. Despite Broadhurst's loose construction, his original sentence clearly referred to the 1850s and 1860s, when George Odger and George Howell were among the leading figures in the revival of trade unionism. When Hardie mistakenly took him to be saying 'Where were you fifty years ago?', he was fair game for Broadhurst's sarcastic reply.

He had attained the dizzy height of Under-Secretary at the Home Office in the short administration of 1886. He was also, according to Hardie, the only one of the Lib-Lab M.P.s who was not a teetotaller. Broadhurst was of the Establishment; Hardie was an angry young man attacking it – and to make matters worse, he came from a new and puny union which was sending its delegate to the T.U.C. for the first time. But, aside from all this, the debate shows that there were real differences between Hardie and the trade-union leadership of the day. Hardie was an advocate of greater independence of labour from its bonds to the Liberal Party than were some of his opponents, such as Broadhurst. He was, one might say, a 'labourist'. But was he a socialist? It is important to see that the two views are distinct and that neither entails the other. 'Labourism' is a name one might give to the view that more energetic steps should be taken towards working-class representation in Parliament in order to redress working-class grievances. 'Socialism' could be variously defined, but any definition would have to include some belief in collective ownership of means of production as a way to greater social justice. We ought to look closely at Hardie's intellectual development up to 1887 in order to see whether his views could warrant being called 'socialist'.

One difficulty is that socialism is usually thought of as being an economic doctrine; but Hardie was never an economist, and in later life always denied that his socialism had its roots in economics. In his early years the economic views he occasionally expressed were strictly within the framework of classical economics – hardly surprising, since a self-taught Lanarkshire miner in the 1870s would have had no access to Marxist or other critical economic doctrines. Thus, for example, he was prepared to admit that restriction of output – the 'wee darg' – 'violates the laws of political economy', and could only argue that, bad though it was, the miners had no alternative open to them. There is no indication that Hardie ever deviated from these orthodox views before 1886. He still thought the working class would be emancipated if and only if they ceased drinking alcohol.

There is striking evidence that Hardie was not at all a socialist as late as April 1886. In his column in the *Ardrossan and Saltcoats Herald* for 23 April 1886, Hardie wrote an approving review of an American novel called *The Stillwater Tragedy* by T. B. Aldrich. This is a detective story with a strongly anti-trade-union bent. The villain belongs to the Marble Workers' Association, which is crippling the local marble works by restricting the number of apprentices that may be taken on. The hero, who is courting the boss's daughter, breaks a strike and forces the union to abandon its restrictive policy. That Hardie should have approved of this is most remarkable. In the particular passage to which he drew attention in his review, a socialist trade-union leader is making a speech explaining how wealth will be equally distributed around the whole population under socialism. One of his supporters adds, 'When it comes to a regular division of lands and greenbacks in the United States, I go in for the Chinese having their share.' This appals his hearers, and it appalled Keir Hardie.

Later in 1886 Hardie visited London, where he met members of Britain's first socialist party, the Social Democratic Federation founded by a former stockbroker called H. M. Hyndman. This may have helped to bring about a distinct change in Hardie's economic views. The Rules of the Ayrshire Miners' Association were drafted by Hardie in 1886, not long after he had been condemning socialism because it involved sharing our property with the Chinese. The preamble to the rules ran:

All wealth is created by Labour. Capital is part of this wealth which, instead of being consumed when created, is stored up and used for assisting Labour to produce more wealth . . . Capital, which ought to be the servant of labour and which is created by labour, has become the master of its creator.
The principles of trade unionism . . . aim at a reversal of this order of things.

The obvious inference to be made from these lines would be that Hardie had become a Marxian socialist; nevertheless, the inference ought to be resisted. As we have said, Hardie was no economist; he simply acquired these Marxian views without shedding the orthodoxy he had earlier preached. As late as December 1887 we find Hardie writing an article in which the new hostility towards capitalism nestles side by side with the old view that trade unions cannot upset the market mechanism of supply and demand.

There ever has been, and must ever be, war between the capitalist and the labourer, so long as they continue to exist side by side . . .
Demand and supply regulates the wages of labour, and . . . the labourer should therefore take good care never to let the supply exceed the demand. Trades Unions cannot of themselves keep up wages; but Trades Unions can secure for the workmen the highest value the market affords for their labour.

In the light of this, it seems unlikely that it was conversion to Marxist economics which led to Hardie's disenchantment with Liberalism in 1887. Another explanation has been put forward, and was indeed proposed by Hardie himself in later life. This is that he was converted by the American land reformer Henry George, who visited

Ayrshire on his second visit to Britain in 1884. George thought that all economic ills sprang from private ownership of the land: nationalize the land, and poverty would no longer exist in the midst of plenty. This was a doctrine which appealed to many radicals of the day, especially those sympathetic to the new 'collectivist' radicalism; it often led them on to more orthodox socialism (which George never embraced). Furthermore, if landowners had no title to the land, they had *a fortiori* no right to demand royalty payments when minerals were extracted from it. This implication of George's doctrines was eagerly seized upon by a number of radicals, who tried to get the miners' support for a concerted campaign for the abolition of royalty payments to landowners. One of these men was William Small, a Lanarkshire draper who was interested in mining affairs and was trying to re-form the Lanarkshire Miners' Union. Small wrote to Hardie in Cumnock to ask for his support in a campaign against mineral royalties. But Hardie, who probably regarded Small as a middle-class meddler, replied brusquely, 'I fail to see . . . that the miners could gain anything at present – even though royalties were abolished.' When Henry George himself visited Ayrshire during his 1884 tour of Britain, the visit excited no interest; his audience at Kilmarnock was the smallest he had had in Scotland.

Thus it is clear that Hardie was no immediate convert to George's ideas. Nevertheless, he warmed to them later. Relations between Hardie and William Small improved in 1886 because of their common interest in promoting the Scottish Miners' National Federation. Soon Hardie took up George's enthusiasm for land nationalization. In November 1886 he persuaded the Cumnock Debating and Literary Society that 'the legislation of the future must advance on the lines of Socialism until the People are in possession of the land'. This quotation shows that socialism did not mean the same thing to Keir Hardie in 1886 as to us today. In Hardie's mind, socialism was linked with a Georgeite campaign for land nationalization; the word had no particular implications about attitudes to industrial organization. By 1887 Hardie's economic views were a rather confused mixture of *laisser-faire* orthodoxy, Marxism, and Georgeism. He was certainly a collectivist radical and would have been regarded as very 'advanced' by his contemporaries. But collectivist radicalism is not the same thing as socialism. It would be wrong to describe Keir Hardie at this time as a socialist as that word is generally understood. From 1888 to 1893 Hardie's closest political associations were to be with Georgeite radicals rather than socialists.

In all this, however, the point should not be lost that socialism, however defined, meant much less to Hardie than what we have called 'labourism', and a misleading impression may be gained from excessively detailed study of Hardie's passing remarks on economic principles, which were not his main interest. It was essentially his disillusionment with the Liberal Party and the Lib-Lab M.P.s over the issue of the miners' eight-hour day which pushed Hardie into his candidature for North Ayrshire; any evolution in his economic views was secondary. Less than a year later the dispute was to come to a head. As it turned out, however, the battle would be fought not in North Ayrshire but in the towns and villages surrounding Hardie's own birthplace: the constituency of Mid-Lanark.

2

MID-LANARK
TO
WEST HAM

   In March 1888, Stephen Mason, the Glad-
stonian Liberal M.P. for Mid-Lanark, announced that he was retiring
from Parliament on grounds of ill-health. Mid-Lanark was one of the
new constituencies created after the enlargement of the franchise in
1884. It contained much of the Lanarkshire coalfield, including all the
places Hardie had worked in during his career as a miner, together
with the burgeoning iron and steel towns like Motherwell and Wishaw.
It seemed a more appropriate constituency than North Ayrshire for a
showdown between Hardie and the forces of traditional Liberalism.
Immediately the vacancy was announced, Hardie put himself forward
as a candidate. The six weeks of extremely confused negotiations

B

which followed can only be understood in the light of the very complex and fluid position of Scottish Liberalism in the wake of the Home Rule split of 1886.

The split had serious consequences for the party all over Britain. In Scotland, however, the question of Home Rule was intertwined with a number of others, and the aftermath of the split was both more complex and more damaging to the Liberal Party than elsewhere. Since the Party had reigned supreme in Scottish politics ever since the Great Reform Act of 1832, the rifts in the party were much more momentous even than in England. Before the Home Rule crisis broke out, the unity of the party had been under threat from the proposal to disestablish the Church of Scotland. English politicians did not understand Scottish ecclesiastical politics. In England the Conservative Party was the party of Anglicanism, and in favour of established state churches; the Liberal Party was the party of nonconformity, the party which had disestablished the Anglican Church of Ireland, and could be presumed to have similar designs in Wales and Scotland. But in Scotland the links between religion and voting behaviour were quite different from those in England. The established Church of Scotland was presbyterian, not Anglican; its supporters tended to vote Liberal, not Conservative, but their loyalty would be strained by any proposal to disestablish the Scottish Church. For a long time Gladstone refused to express any opinion on Scottish disestablishment (he finally pronounced himself in favour of it in 1889), but it was obvious to Liberal Churchmen that the tide of party opinion was moving in favour of the proposal. Therefore when the Liberal Party split over Home Rule, the Liberal-Unionists were strengthened by the accession of Church of Scotland members who had abandoned the Gladstonian wing on the question of disestablishment. This meant that Liberal-Unionism became especially strong in urban areas, where the established church was strongest, and among professional and middle-class supporters. At the same time, working-class Liberal voters were divided. Most of them remained faithful to Gladstone – although, according to one local observer, 'not, I fear, so much because they have thought the matter out . . . as because their affection for the Grand Old Man [Gladstone] and their faith in him are as kindly and as blind as the Tory enmity is bitter and odious'. On the other hand, there was a substantial backlash of anti-Irish sentiment. Working-class anti-Irish feeling in the 1880s had similar origins to hostility to coloured Commonwealth immigrants in the 1960s. It had a cultural dimension, a feeling that the Irish were men of an alien religion and different eating habits. But it also had a strong economic dimension, rooted in the feeling that the Irish were taking jobs away from the native working class, and were bringing down the general level of wages by being prepared to work for longer hours and lower wages than anybody else. We have already observed these resentments at work in the Ayrshire coalfield in the 1870s and 1880s.

Besides disestablishment and Home Rule, a third issue served to weaken Scottish Liberalism, though it had more effect on local party leaders than on the electorate as a whole. This was the 'crofters' revolt'. Following the example of the militant land agitation by rural tenants in Ireland in the early 1880s, crofters in north-west Scotland had staged a revolt in protest against the insecurity of their tenure, which was aggravated by the enthusiasm of landlords for clearing arable and pasture land to create deer forests. In the crofting counties this resulted in the return of five 'Independent Crofter' M.P.s against official Liberals in the 1885 election. The crofters' cause generated a good deal of emotional sympathy in other parts of Scotland. Hostility to absentee landlords living in England and Georgeite enthusiasm for land reform blended to form a predominantly middle-class radical movement with nationalist overtones. Two political organizations owed their strength to this reaction to the crofters' revolt: the Scottish Land and Labour League, and the Scottish Home Rule Association. Both were to play a part in advancing the next stage of Hardie's political career.

The political scene, then, at the announcement of the Mid-Lanark vacancy, was thus extremely complex, but four main challenges to the traditional Liberal dominance could be discerned. There was the threat from the Unionists, allied to anti-Irish feeling; the threat from the Churchmen and opponents of disestablishment; the threat from the crofters and their lowland sympathisers; and, lastly, the threat from labour, in the shape of Keir Hardie. It would have taken a political clairvoyant of rare powers to see that the last and apparently least significant of these revolts was the one which spelt most danger of all to Liberalism. Liberalism was under attack from every quarter at once; perhaps this is why the Liberals in Mid-Lanark were in no mood to placate Keir Hardie.

On 15 March 1888 Hardie put his name forward to the Mid-Lanark Liberal Association for consideration as a possible Liberal candidate. This was probably mostly for show. In the light of the North Ayrshire Liberals' reaction to Hardie's activities, he can scarcely have expected a hearty welcome from their counterparts in Mid-Lanark. He withdrew his name again on 21 March. It is unlikely that the Liberal executive ever considered it, as they had many other problems to deal with, arising out of the complex fracturing of Liberal support. At one stage no less than three Liberal candidates apart from Hardie were in the field, and the merits and claims of each were being extensively discussed in the local Press which was keenly interested in the by-election. Meanwhile, away from all the controversy, the 'Constitutional and Liberal-Unionist Association' in the constituency adopted as its candidate the unsuccessful Conservative nominee in the 1885 election.

By the beginning of April Hardie had recruited to his side one of the most important politicians in the West of Scotland. This was John Ferguson, a Glasgow councillor and magistrate who, despite being a Protestant, was the unchallenged leader of the local branches of the Irish National League. The I.N.L. (later called the United Irish League) was the organization which worked to deliver the votes of the Irish resident in Britain to candidates who were certified to be reliable friends of Ireland and Home Rule. In many districts it was the most efficient electioneering organization in existence – such being the special genius of Irish politicians outside Ireland – and it was much respected by politicians of other parties.

Ferguson wrote to the local papers suggesting a plebiscite among the electors of Mid-Lanark. His proposal was in effect for a 'primary' in which the voters would be invited to choose a candidate from the various Liberal contenders, including Hardie. By this time a quite new claimant had appeared in the person of J.W.Philipps, a London barrister of Welsh origins, who neither had nor claimed the slightest knowledge of the constituency or its problems. 'With regard to mining questions', he was reported as saying, 'he did not profess to know technically what would be best, but if returned to Parliament he would follow men like Mr Burt and Mr Fenwick.' Such a proposition was hardly likely to mollify Hardie's feelings.

By this time, possibly as a result of Ferguson's intervention, Hardie's campaign had the support of the Labour Electoral Association. This was a body formed as the result of a resolution from the 1887 Congress of the T.U.C., to coordinate the work of local bodies promoting working-class Liberal candidatures. Its secretary, T.R. Threlfall, came to Mid-Lanark to speak on Hardie's behalf; the L.E.A. offered to contribute £400 to his election expenses. Hardie announced that he was prepared to withdraw only in one set of circumstances: that Ferguson's proposal of a test ballot was adopted, and one of the candidates other than Hardie won it. This condition was never met, but two attempts were made to get Hardie to withdraw.

The first was organized by Threlfall. According to Hardie's later account,

... One evening Threlfall ... turned up at the hotel bubbling over with excitement. 'I've settled it,' he cried excitedly. 'I've been in conference with them all the evening, and it's all fixed up.' 'In conference with whom, and settled what?' I asked. 'In conference with the Liberals,' he replied, 'at the George Hotel, and you've to retire.' I don't quite know what happened then, but I remember rising to my feet and Threlfall ceased speaking. Next morning he returned home to Southport.

Naturally, the Labour Electoral Association withdrew its offer of money for Hardie after this incident. The financial difficulty which this caused was partly resolved by H. H. Champion. Champion was a maverick upper-class socialist, once described as 'patrician to the finger tips ... yet emitting red-hot revolution in the placid accents of clubland'. He had a special ability at getting money from wealthy Conservatives to pay for labour candidates in parliamentary and local elections – the objective of the donors, of course, being to ensure that the Liberal vote was split in order to let the Conservative in. Champion made no attempt to conceal these activities, and he had a quite open contempt for most working-class politicians. He was one of those who could appropriately be charged with loving the proletariat in the abstract, but not any actual members of it. In the next two years this erratic figure, very different from the Liberals and Lib-Labs from whom most of Hardie's prominent supporters were drawn, was to do his cause much more harm than ʝood, but for the moment his assistance was welcome.

After the failure of Threlfall's attempt to secure Hardie's withdrawal, another was made by Francis Schnadhorst, the Liberal election mastermind, who was busy behind the scenes. He visited Hardie and his supporters, accompanied by Sir George Trevelyan, who had held the newly created post of Secretary for Scotland in Gladstone's 1886 ministry. Clearly the Liberals, in sending such a high-powered team to negotiate with Hardie, were worried by the electoral threat he represented. Not surprisingly, different versions of what went on at these unsuccessful negotiations have been preserved. According to Schnadhorst, they failed because 'the Labour party wishes to impose conditions as to the future which Mr Schnadhorst had no authority, in the interests of other constituencies, to accept'. But Ferguson, who had been helping the relatively inexperienced Hardie in this horse-trading, claimed that Hardie had allowed him to propose a weaker version of the earlier 'primary' offer. This would have been a proposal that Hardie should retire in favour of Philipps (who was now, after much dissension, the official Liberal candidate), and that the Liberal Association should afterwards take a plebiscite to see which Liberal candidate – Philipps or Hardie – would be preferred, presumably at subsequent elections. Hardie himself recorded that Trevelyan offered him a seat elsewhere and £300 a year salary as an M.P. if successful, on condition that he withdrew from Mid-Lanark.

At any rate, no satisfactory terms could be got, and Hardie fought on. He received a letter of support from Ramsay MacDonald, who at the time was the secretary (in London) of the Scottish Home Rule Association. The letter is very interesting, not only because it is the earliest known item of correspondence between the two Scotsmen who were to dominate the Labour Party in its first fifteen years, but also because it makes no reference to socialism, and a great deal to injured nationalist and radical feelings. MacDonald wrote:

Dear Mr Hardie,

I cannot refrain from wishing you God-Speed in your election contest. Had I been able to have gone to Mid-Lanark to help you – to do so both by 'word and deed' – would have given very great pleasure indeed. The powers of darkness – Scottish newspapers with English editors (as the *Leader*), partisan wire-pullers, and the other etceteras of political squabbles – are leagued against us.

But let the consequences be what they may, do not withdraw. The cause of Labour and of Scottish Nationality will suffer much thereby. Your defeat will awaken Scotland, and your victory will re-construct Scottish Liberalism. All success be yours, and the National cause you champion. There is no miner – and no other one for that matter – who is a Scotsman and not ashamed of it, who will vote against you in favour of an obscure English barrister, absolutely ignorant of Scotland and of Scottish affairs, and who only wants to get to Parliament in order that he may have the tail of M.P. to his name in the law courts.

I am, Dear Sir,

Yours very truly,

J. Ramsay MacDonald.

However heartwarming this might be, the Scottish Home Rule Association, like many fervent nationalists of other generations, was not based in Scotland. It could not deliver the votes of Mid-Lanark electors to Hardie. The Irish National League could; and Hardie did what he could to get Irish support. Ferguson was firmly on his side. So was Michael Davitt. Davitt was the most radical of the leaders of the Irish Party, who had organized the militant land campaign among peasants in the West of Ireland in the early 1880s. He was also the only one of the Irish Party Leaders who cultivated British working-class politicians, and Hardie was an early beneficiary. He got further help from another leader of the Glasgow Irish, Richard McGhee. In addition Hardie sought the support of the Home Government Branch of the League in Glasgow, one of the largest and most radical branches. He wrote:

I venture to solicit your help in winning the Mid-Lanark election for Home Rule and Labour . . .

Should I be returned to Parliament I will vote with the Irish party on all questions relating to Ireland, even though such vote should be against the Liberal party . . .

In all other matters I am a Democrat of a very advanced type, so much so that I would support every measure curtailing the power of Royalty, aristocracy, and snobocracy with a view to their ultimate abolition.

Hardie got the branch's endorsement – but it came from Glasgow, not from the constituency. And the majority of the local branches of the League, backed by the leaders of the Irish Party in London, decided to support the Liberal candidate instead. Hardie got the worst of both worlds. Few of the local Irish working-class electors supported him, but he also suffered from the anti-Irish backlash in parts of the constituency. The large steelmaking town of Wishaw, for instance, was always a stronghold of Orangeism. It was particularly stony ground for Hardie, and he had one very embarrassing meeting there. When, at the end of the meeting, the chairman moved a vote of confidence in Hardie (a conventional procedure at Victorian election meetings) only six people out of a large audience voted in favour of it.

In the light of all these obstacles the result of the election – the first ever at which an independent Labour candidate had stood against both the main parties – was by no means discreditable to Hardie. The figures, announced on 24 April 1888, were:

	1888 By-election	1886 (General Election)
Gladstonian Liberal (Philipps)	3847	(3779)
Unionist (Bousfield)	2917	(2909)
Independent Labour (Hardie)	617	—

The special place of the Mid-Lanark by-election in the history and mythology of the British Labour movement, together with its sheer complexity, makes an accurate appraisal of Hardie's real motivation very hard. His relationship with official Liberalism was still highly ambivalent. On the one hand, he announced before the election in the *Miner* that, whether or not the Liberals selected a working-class candidate, a Labour candidate should be put forward. 'Better split the party now, if there is to be a split, than at a General Election, and if the Labour party only make their power felt now, terms will not be wanting when the General Election comes.' This position marks a clear advance on that of the Lib-Labs, who would be quite happy to endorse a Liberal candidate so long as he was a working man. But it should be noted that Hardie, in 1888, still saw the matter in terms of tactical advantage, not ideological conviction. His quarrel with, say, Threlfall was not that Hardie was a socialist and Threlfall was not. It was simply a matter of tactics: how best to force the Liberal Party to endorse a higher proportion of working-class candidates for Parliament? Hardie insisted during his campaign, perhaps not very convincingly, that 'he was a lifelong Liberal, and did not desire to do anything to injure the Liberal Party'. His election manifesto dealt mostly with the radical issues of the day. Besides supporting the Liberal Party's programme in full, he announced that he was in favour of a miners' eight-hour day, government regulation of mines, nationalization of mineral royalties, and taxation of land values. His programme thus incorporated both individualist and collectivist radicalism, and it conveyed more than a hint of Henry George, but it had nothing to do with socialism as we would understand the term. The same is true of Hardie's views as presented for Irish consumption to the Home Government Branch of the I.N.L. Hardie was attacked in *Justice*, the organ of the Social Democratic Federation, for failing to make any mention of socialism in his election campaign.

The disagreement between Hardie and the Labour Electoral Association was in fact over a very narrow front. Hardie's well-known account, from which I have quoted, of the negotiations between Threlfall and the Liberals suggests that Threlfall was a rather foolish and subservient tool of the Liberal caucus. This is not so. Within the labour movement Hardie and Threlfall were on the same side, ranged against the old trade-unionist Lib-Labs like Broadhurst, Burt and Fenwick on the side of much greater independence of labour from the Liberals. At the T.U.C. in 1887 Threlfall had persuaded the delegates to support the linking up of local Labour Electoral Associations into a national body. 'I am a hearty advocate', the Congress report records him as saying, 'of a genuine and distinct labour party . . . and one in which all workingmen, whatever their general politics, may unite. . . . The time has arrived when the labour party must cut itself adrift from the great parties of the country.' This was the same message as Hardie's, although much less flamboyantly preached. The adoption of Threlfall's resolution was probably more important than Hardie's spectacular clash with Broadhurst at the same Congress. It showed that rank-and-file delegates were well ahead of their leaders in the demand for labour representation. Congress was basically sympathetic to the sort of message Hardie wished to convey, even though it did not support Hardie's attack on Broadhurst. And at the by-election the real issue between Hardie and Threlfall was this: how stiff should Hardie make his terms for forcing concessions from the Liberal leadership? Hardie was prepared to keep playing beyond the stage at which Threlfall advised him to quit with his substantial winnings (namely the promise of a seat at the next General Election). Hardie, it is true, was less keen than most of his supporters to regard the issue in such instrumental terms, and more inclined to think that a principle was at stake. But it was none the less a principle of tactics, not of ideology.

Within a month of the Mid-Lanark by-election Hardie had helped to found the Scottish Labour Party – the first time the phrase 'Labour Party' with a capital P had ever been used in Britain. After a further abortive attempt by Threlfall to reach a Liberal-Labour agreement about candidatures in Scotland, a meeting was held in Glasgow on 19 May 1888 for the establishment of a new Labour Party. The title was perhaps a misnomer. Of all the founders of the new party, only Hardie and John Ferguson had any links with organized industrial labour. The snub to labour administered by the Liberals at Mid-Lanark was by no means the only grievance rankling in the minds of the new party's founders.

To be sure, the President of the party was R. B. Cunninghame Graham, the somewhat erratic aristocratic radical M.P. for North-West Lanark. He drew his credentials as a labour leader from his rude remarks about his fellow Liberal M.P.s, and from the fact that he and an up-and-coming working-class politician called John Burns had been sentenced to six months' imprisonment for their part in 'Bloody Sunday'. This was a riot in Trafalgar Square in 1887, which occurred when Graham and Burns tried to lead a large body of demonstrators into the square in defiance of troops and police, who were trying to enforce a government ban on the use of the square by demonstrators. But, unlike Hardie, Cunninghame Graham had nothing in common with the ordinary working-class elector, loyal to Mr Gladstone and Liberalism. Graham, a descendant of the Marquess of Montrose and of 'Bonnie Dundee', was more an upper-class romantic than a serious politician, and he lacked staying power. He was more interested in travelling in South America, where he was known as 'Don Roberto', than in day-to-day Labour politics. After being badly defeated in the

1892 General Election he disappeared from British domestic politics, to reappear in the late 1920s as a Scottish Nationalist.

The rest of the new party's leaders were mostly connected with the land-reform movement. There was Dr G. B. Clark, one of the leaders of the crofters' revolt, who was elected M.P. for Caithness in 1885, and there was J. Shaw Maxwell, one of the leading Glasgow supporters of the crofters' agitation. These people were held together by their grudges against the Liberal Party, but they had no real mass appeal to the urban worker. Their ideology was one of protest, but it was still essentially rural radicalism spiced with the doctrines of Henry George, not radicalism designed to appeal to the urban working class. Hardie's mining interests combined with the Georgeite enthusiasm of the crofters' leaders to emphasize nationalization of land and mining royalties as the main plank of the party's platform.

Once formed, the Scottish Labour Party busily set about further attempts at pacts with the Liberals, alternating with attempts to impress them with its strength by putting up independent candidates at by-elections. In April 1888, before the party was set up, Hardie had threatened that 'the Labour party' would contest every Scottish Liberal-held seat with a majority of under 500. Unfortunately no Scottish Labour Party candidatures succeeded. An attempt to run J. G. Weir, the local miners' secretary, at a by-election in West Fife in 1889 failed. Later in the same year the prospects for independent labour seemed to be improving as John Burns announced his intention of fighting a by-election in Dundee. Burns was a Londoner of Scottish origins, who was rapidly rising to fame as one of the organizers of the great London dock strike of 1889 – the first industrial revolt by un-skilled workers, as distinct from the craftsmen who had hitherto been the bulwark of trade unionism, to catch public attention. But in the event Burns succumbed to the offer from the Liberals which Hardie had refused: he withdrew from Dundee in return for a promise of no Liberal opposition if he stood in Battersea at the next election – a promise which was honoured when the 1892 election came round.

In spite of the failure of the Scottish Labour Party to produce any effective threat to the Liberals' electoral position, the Liberal Scottish Whip did offer the S.L.P. a pact in 1890: if the Labour Party kept out of a forthcoming by-election it would be given a free run in three Scottish working-class seats. This pact failed – for the predictable reason that the Liberal Associations in the seats it was proposed to hand over to Labour candidates angrily refused to withdraw their own candidates in what the Whip said was the party's interest. At the same time the Labour Party was weakened by the withdrawal of the support of Davitt and Ferguson, and the radical section of the Irish Party, and also by a further row between Hardie and Chisholm Robertson. It was probably strengthened by the departure of Champion, who retreated to Aberdeen to form an independent Labour party of his own, which had little electoral impact. When the General Election of 1892 came round, at the end of the six-year Unionist administration under Salisbury, the Scottish Labour Party put up five candidates, and four or five other labour candidates of one variety or another stood in Scotland outside its auspices. None was successful, but Cunninghame Graham, who was one of them, resigned his former constituency of North-West Lanark to stand for a Glasgow seat. The ensuing split in the Liberal vote was probably responsible for a Unionist victory.

Long before the election, however, Keir Hardie's interests had shifted from a Scottish to a national – or even international – scale, and his own electoral activity was far away from Scotland and the Scottish Labour Party. Hardie's campaign in Mid-Lanark and his activities in the T.U.C. made his name known outside Scotland. In the T.U.C. over the years, Hardie's faction made steady progress, although Hardie's own abrasive methods of debate probably did his side more harm than good. The rows between Hardie and Broadhurst reached a peak at the Congress of 1889 in Dundee, but only eleven votes were cast against a vote of confidence in Broadhurst. In 1890 Broadhurst was succeeded as secretary by Charles Fenwick, whose opposition to legislation enforcing the eight-hour day was well known. None the less, Congress came over to the side of the statutory eight-hour day in that year, and Hardie assiduously pressed for changes in the T.U.C. executive committee. Indeed, he overreached himself in 1891, when the Standing Orders Committee of Congress confiscated a leaflet being circulated by Hardie which called on delegates to vote for a slate of candidates whom Hardie named as 'all eight-hours men'.

These activities no doubt brought Hardie to the attention of a number of left-wing activists in West Ham; in April 1890 his name was first put forward as a possible parliamentary candidate there. Radical politics in this dockland borough in East London had been transformed by the emergence of new personalities connected with the 'new unionism' – the movement of unskilled workers symbolized by the dock strike of 1889. It would be wrong to suppose that 'new unionism' produced a great upsurge of radical feeling among unskilled workers. But it possibly mobilized many of them for the first time, prodding them into some sort of political awareness. And it produced a new breed of local political leaders. The two 'new unions' at the head of the movement were the Dockworkers and the Gasworkers. Both of these were occupations well represented in West Ham, which was the home of Will Thorne, the founder and leader of the gasworkers' union. Throne was a nominal member of the Social Democratic Federation, although his political views were more realistic than the intransigent and doctrinaire socialism preached by H.M.Hyndman, the founder of the S.D.F. Thorne became one of the leading backers of Keir Hardie after a somewhat unexpected opportunity arose to take advantage of the splits in Liberalism to Labour's benefit.

West Ham South had been one of the dozen English working-class constituencies to return a Lib-Lab M.P. in the 1885 election. In 1886, however, this M.P., Joseph Leicester, had been defeated in a straight fight with a Conservative. As elsewhere, this defeat combined with the 1886 split to demoralize and antagonize local Liberals, and the party soon split into two factions. A wealthy Liberal manufacturer, Hume Webster, set up a personal machine to bolster support for himself as official Liberal candidate. Then, in 1890, his rival as prospective candidate, J.S.Curwen, withdrew. The opportunity was opened for radicals and socialists to press for the adoption of Keir Hardie. A rather curious report in one of the local papers, the *Stratford Express*, implies that Hardie and his friends were doing some careful scheming. At a meeting in April 1890, ' ... a Working Man asked to be permitted to move a resolution adopting Mr Keir Hardie as their candidate, but he was stopped by the Chairman. Mr Hardie said that the wooing was going on nicely, they did not want to hurry matters or frighten the people whom they were trying to woo, but he thought it would be out of place if they made any announcement that night.' Nevertheless, Hardie did allow an official adoption meeting to take place in May 1890. But he seemed to be still slightly diffident about his position; at all events he was reported in September 1890 to have proposed a 'primary' where the 'Liberal electors of the constituency' could choose between himself and Hume Webster, and that if Webster won the primary, Hardie would retire and give him every assistance. It is by no means clear who would have won such a primary. The only, inadequate, information we have is the local press's reporting of the activities of each candidate, which would appear to credit them with approximately the same degree of support.

There was no primary, however, and the rival candidatures proceeded side by side. At this stage there was no reason to suppose that Hardie might win the seat; the most likely prognosis would have been for the Conservatives to retain the seat on a split Liberal vote. Matters changed dramatically, however, when Hume Webster unexpectedly committed suicide on 22 January 1892. (Many years later, Hardie alleged that he did it 'to save himself from prison'.) This placed the Liberals of West Ham South in an acute dilemma. The Government was nearing the end of its term, and a general election was likely during the course of 1892. What were Liberals to do ? The radical wing of the party argued that Keir Hardie should be given a straight fight with the Conservatives. Thus, for instance, a stormy meeting was held in February 1892 of 'Liberal, Radical, and Home Rule electors' to decide on a replacement for Hume Webster. The pro- and anti-Hardie factions were both out in force. A letter stating 'that Mr Keir Hardie had been selected two years ago and was the only Radical candidate before the constituency was read amid a storm of cheers and hisses'. Hardie's supporters pointed out that he had publicly announced his adherence to the Newcastle Programme – the radical manifesto drawn up by the National Liberal Federation at a conference in Newcastle which was regarded as a sort of unofficial Liberal election programme. But they narrowly failed to get the meeting to support him.

Hardie's opponents in the Liberal camp spent several months feverishly looking for a candidate to put up against him. One name after another was confidently whispered in the local press, only to be dropped again after a couple of weeks. Eventually an approach was made to Joseph Leicester, the former M.P., who agreed to stand as a Lib-Lab. Leicester's campaign was not a success. Everybody knew that he was only the fourth or fifth choice of the local party, and the friends of the manufacturer Hume Webster did not think much of an elderly artisan who had once been a glassworker. Leicester was harried by Hardie's camp. At least one of his meetings was taken over by a large band of Hardie supporters, headed by Will Thorne, who put himself in the chair and elicited a pledge of support for Hardie. Leicester's attempt to secure for himself the temperance vote was countered by Hardie, who solicited testimonials from elderly Scottish ministers who had known him in his youth, and published them in the West Ham papers as evidence of his sobriety and respectability.

Eventually Leicester withdrew, in June, when it was known that the general election was to be in July. He had run out of money, and he had completely failed to get any official Liberal support for his campaign. In fact, he was advised by Schnadhorst to retire, after pro-Hardie Liberals had impressed Schnadhorst with the strength of Hardie's following. Hardie gave an account of a meeting he had had with Schnadhorst, who had asked him what he wanted the Liberals to do. 'Nothing', retorted Hardie, 'only leave us alone to fight the battle.' 'That is exactly what we intend to do,' replied Schnadhorst.

Before 1918, general election campaigns were spread over a period of a fortnight or more, and in 1892 the West Ham results were among the first to be declared. Hardie was in – he had won with 5,268 votes against 4,036 for his Conservative opponent. This was a heavy increase in the poll since 1886, suggesting that many more voters had been registered in the intervening period. In other parts of the country Hardie's lead in Mid-Lanark had encouraged a number of Labour candidates to fight the election, with varying degrees of success, more or less independently of the two main parties. Two others besides Hardie won their contests. John Burns won Battersea, having had the clear run from the Liberals he had earlier been promised; and Havelock Wilson, the energetic and controversial founder of the National Sailors' and Firemen's Union, won Middlesbrough in a three-cornered fight.

One very great difficulty in the way of independent working-class politics was the cost of elections. In Hardie's day candidates had to share out between them the Returning Officer's expenses in all elections, a sum which could be around £200 or £300 per candidate. This was why the problem of financial support was so critical, and sometimes explosive, for Labour candidates. No working man, and no trade union other than the strongest and best-established craft unions, could make more than a token contribution to a candidate's expenses. Candidates like Hardie had therefore to rely largely on middle-class sympathizers, often of a rather eccentric kind – or even on people whose donations were based on expediency rather than principle. The Mid-Lanark campaign, for instance, had been financed by the Tory socialist Champion and by an eccentric Scottish lady novelist who wrote under the name 'John Law'. The published accounts of Hardie's 1892 election fund tell a similar story. Although Hardie had said when he first came to West Ham that he would be paid £200 by the Ayrshire Miners, he never actually got any money from them. It is most unlikely that they would have had enough; and, in any case, Hardie had resigned from the post of their secretary in 1891. In 1892, therefore, he had to look elsewhere. £293 was raised, of which no more than £25 came from working-class sources. There were a number of donations from radical M.P.s, including G. B. Clark, and also one from J. S. Curwen, who had retired in Hardie's favour in 1890. But the main sources of money were two donations of £100 each. One nominally came from the *Workman's Times*, a new Labour paper in Bradford. This was actually money raised by Champion, often from Conservatives who gave money to foster Labour candidatures which might help to split the Liberals. Tory gold was wasted in West Ham South, since there was no Liberal whose vote could be split. Nevertheless the source of Champion's money, and his dubious personality, were well known to many Liberals and Lib-Labs, whose estimation of Hardie did not improve as a consequence. Hardie's other £100 donation came from an even more unlikely source – Andrew Carnegie, the Scots-American philanthropist. Carnegie was scarcely in sympathy with Hardie's views, being a champion of rugged individualism at whose steelworks trade unionism was brutally suppressed. But G.B.Clark successfully canvassed him, during one of his visits to Scotland, for funds for Hardie. His willingness to give Hardie money perhaps arose out of a typically Scottish admiration for the very Victorian virtue of 'self-help'. (Samuel Smiles, the popularizer of that phrase, was also a Scotsman.) Hardie, like Carnegie himself, was a poor Scot who by his own efforts had achieved a prominent position in public life, and was therefore worthy of support.*

In 1892 no working-class aspirant could have become a truly independent Labour M.P. without outside support. It was simply financially impossible. Hardie depended for money on people fundamentally opposed to his aims, and on the action of Schnadhorst in discouraging Liberal opposition to him. Burns, as we have seen, depended on the sort of pact that Hardie had spurned at Mid-Lanark. Of the three 'independent' M.P.s, Wilson had the best claim to genuine independence in this regard – being middle-class, he could afford it – but he was very rapidly absorbed into the Liberal ranks. In the real world of electoral politics it was very difficult for Hardie to maintain the rigorous independence from other parties which he energetically propounded. On the other hand, the support Hardie had got came without strings. It implied no obligation, not even moral obligation, towards the older parties. As if to emphasize this, Hardie's first act on being elected – before the elections were over – was to go up to Newcastle to attack John Morley, one of the leading radical Liberals, because of his opposition to eight-hours legislation. Of contemporary politicians, Morley was the best example of an individualistic radical who refused to accept collectivist radicalism. The eight-hours issue was what had originally set Hardie apart from Broadhurst, Burt, and Fenwick, and his attack on Morley was bitter. After the election was over, it was clear that the Liberals, with Irish support, had won narrowly, and Gladstone set about forming his fourth and

---

* Hardie later claimed that he privately sent the Carnegie money back. It is not clear, in this event, what replaced it to pay Hardie's share of the returning officer's expenses.

last government. Morley was to be a member of it. As the law stood at the time, this meant that he would have to resign his seat and fight a by-election before he could take office as a Minister. Hardie therefore renewed his attack on Morley. If the Conservatives did not oppose him, Hardie argued that Labour should, in the person of Cunninghame Graham; if the Conservatives did stand, Labour should not run, but independent Labour supporters should 'concentrate all their efforts in bringing about Morley's defeat'.

In the event, Morley won his Ministerial by-election, but only just, in a close fight with a Liberal-Unionist. Hardie's attack naturally angered many Liberals and Irish voters who had earlier supported him. Of all the leading Liberals, none was more closely identified than Morley with the cause of Irish Home Rule: what did Keir Hardie think he was doing when he stirred up opposition to John Morley? How was this compatible with Hardie's own claim, both at Mid-Lanark and at West Ham, that he would do everything to forward the interests of the Irish? These questions were to rankle all the time Hardie was to sit for West Ham. For the time being, however, the discontent caused by Hardie's attack on Morley was as nothing compared to the righteous indignation expressed by virtuous middle-class persons everywhere at Hardie's first appearance at Westminster as M.P. for West Ham South, in August 1892. Lib-Lab M.P.s had treated Parliament with exaggerated deference, and had been careful to dress in a manner befitting their very great dignity: gossip columnists used to remark that Thomas Burt had the most scrupulously polished top hat at Westminster. Hardie would have none of this. 'Gie fools their silks, and knaves their wine, A Man's a Man for a' that.' The maxims of Burns were reinforced by Cunninghame Graham, who (somewhat theatrically, seeing how far he was from being a working man himself) said that working men should enter the Commons in their ordinary working clothes, carrying a bag of tools, and thus show their contempt for the flummery that surrounded Westminster. Hardie needed no such encouragement. He went to Parliament in his ordinary clothes: a tweed suit, soft shirt, red tie, and the deerstalker hat (often wrongly referred to as a cloth cap) which was to become his trademark in public life. Furthermore, a number of his West Ham supporters hired a two-horse charabanc equipped with a trumpeter to escort their Member of Parliament to Westminster. This probably provoked more hostile comment than anything Hardie had previously done since he entered politics. Even John Burns, who by no means shared the Lib-Labs' fondness for frock coats and top hats, described Hardie's dress as 'the kind of thing you saw going to Epping Forest, an old deerstalker cap

and knickers of check, you could have played draughts on them'. It is
unlikely, however, that many of Hardie's constituents considered the
manner of his arrival to be an insult to the dignity of the Mother of
Parliaments.

There was one unfortunate loser in this famous incident. Before the
election, the National Clothing Stores of Stratford East had offered to
supply a free pair of trousers to each of the M.P.s elected in the
Borough of West Ham. They were extremely discomfited at the awful
rebound of this advertising gimmick, as the news spread around that
Keir Hardie had entered Parliament in a pair of 'yellow check trousers'.

As this attire has, and will cause a great amount of speculation and
criticism . . . [we] wish to impress upon the Public that the aforemen-
tioned and much-derided trousers were not those presented to the honourable member on his election by the above firm, and the only conclusion
arrived at is that Mr Keir Hardie intends to wear them on some future
occasion. . . No mention being made of Mr Archibald Grove's Trousers
implied a pleasing and foregone conclusion that they gave every satisfaction to the wearer and newly-elected House of Commons.*

The years 1888 to 1892 are marked by Hardie's final abandonment of
the Liberal Party and by some evolution of his views from 'labourism'
to socialism. His contacts in the socialist movement widened dramatically after the Mid-Lanark by-election. By 1889 he was exchanging
letters with Friedrich Engels, the co-founder of Marxism. Engels had
outlived Karl Marx and was trying at this time to encourage the
growth of socialist movements, both in London and internationally.
But Hardie's correspondence shows that he was mainly concerned with
specific objectives and impatient with ideological generalizations,
especially when they came from middle-class socialists like Champion
and H.M.Hyndman. Hardie wrote sternly to Engels:

Social democracy [i.e. Marxist socialism] as an organised force in Scotland is nowhere. . . We are a solid people, very practical, and not given to
chasing bubbles. Mr Graham's Eight Hour agitation has made more progress here in six months than the S.D.F. has made in six years or could
make in sixty years.

Evidently Hardie's contacts with the S.D.F. had not succeeded in
converting him to their political point of view. Indeed, as late as
December 1889 Hardie could write in terms which were purely
'labourist': which gave no hint at all that the writer was a socialist.
Lord Randolph Churchill, the erratic Conservative M.P. (father of Sir

* Advertisement in *West Ham Herald*, 13 August 1892. Original punctuation
and syntax. Grove was the Liberal M.P. for West Ham North.

Winston) had gained something of a reputation as a social reformer, and Hardie invited him to come and speak to the Ayrshire Miners on the 'labour question'. 'We are not party politicians in the ordinary sense of the word', wrote Hardie; the Ayrshire Miners would support any candidate who desired the 'shortening of the hours of labour and the general social elevation of the masses'. The invitation was pressed on Churchill to come 'if only to show that the social question is not the exclusive property of any political party'. (An earlier draft was more outspoken: Hardie denied being a party politician 'in any sense of the word', and invited Churchill to speak 'if only for the sake of breaking down the absurd prejudice which exists towards that party' – meaning the Conservatives.)

Churchill declined the invitation, though adding that he was generally in favour of the eight-hour day, and that 'the prohibition of immigration into this country of foreign paupers' would be a pre-requisite for its success. The real importance of the correspondence, however, is in what it shows us of Hardie's views, and when all due allowance is made for the circumstances in which he was writing, his letter does seem to confirm that he was by no means a committed socialist by 1889. What clearly had happened, however, was an abandonment of Hardie's former loyal Liberalism in favour of a belief in what the Fabian Society called 'permeation' – that is, the view that reforms should be pursued by convincing politicians of whichever party was convenient. Perhaps Hardie's experience in Cumnock had been a catalyst of this change. Hardie and his friends, in the guise of the 'Social and Political Reform Club' of Cumnock, had written to leading politicians of the day to find out their views on the eight-hour day. They found that Liberals like Gladstone were against it, while Conservatives like Randolph Churchill were in favour. Gladstone, like Morley, was an old-fashioned individualistic radical. He favoured Home Rule for Ireland, but could not bring himself to believe that the law should intervene in contracts between employer and employee. Many Liberals were not sympathetic to the collectivist radicalism of Hardie and those who thought like him, and this certainly hastened his drift away from Liberalism. It does not necessarily follow, however, that he automatically became a socialist.

Until the 1892 election Hardie remained strikingly unwilling to display any socialist convictions on the public platform. At his first public meeting in West Ham in 1890, for instance, he explained that the aim of the 'labour party' would be 'to introduce into life more sunshine, beauty, and happiness than could be said to pervade it at the present time'. This noble but undeniably vague ideal predominated in all his speeches in the constituency up to the election. 'Speaking to a large open-air gathering at Beckton Road on social matters, Mr Hardie said that they desired that the lives of the people should be, so far as possible, beautiful and free from tendencies that dragged them downwards.' It is difficult to imagine any member of Hardie's audience disagreeing with such sentiments. He put himself forward as 'a *bona fide* representative of the working-class interests . . . in addition to being a Home Rule Liberal'. He advocated a Georgeite land programme, but the only specifically socialist proposal in his election manifesto was a relatively mild suggestion that the government or local authorities 'might with advantage' take over public utilities, mines, and banks.

If, then, we describe Hardie as a socialist in 1892, we must do so with reservations. The first is that he was very reluctant to display his socialism on the public platform. There were very good reasons for this. Indeed, if Hardie had described himself as a socialist on the hustings at West Ham, he would have risked losing the important Irish Catholic vote. Because socialist parties in continental Europe were pronouncedly anti-clerical, the Roman Catholic hierarchy was inflexibly opposed to socialism. With a different political tradition, British socialism was in no way anti-clerical, but this would not have deterred Catholic parish priests from denouncing from the pulpit any candidate who was suspected of socialism.

Therefore the extent to which Hardie was prepared to admit to socialist beliefs varied according to the audience he was addressing. Not surprisingly, his firmest declarations of socialist principle came in the *Miner*, and in the *Labour Leader*, which succeeded that journal after 1889. 'The socialisation of land and capital is the aim of the Socialist', Hardie wrote firmly in an early issue of the *Labour Leader*. But when it came to practical applications, this clear principle became mixed up with Hardie's own political preoccupations: 'Liberalism is one thing,' he wrote, 'Socialism is another, and the new Labour Party is Socialistic. It is this which marks the dividing line, and the outward and visible sign of it at present [1889] is the Eight Hours Question.' Socialism was not a matter of the collective ownership of the means of production; it was a matter of statutory restriction of the working day – a component of what we have called 'collectivist radicalism'.

We may, perhaps, conclude that Hardie had become a socialist, but that socialism was not yet the driving force behind his political activities. As a miner he was more interested in the eight-hours agitation; as a Parliamentary candidate he was concerned with the plight of the poor and unemployed. He did not fight West Ham as a socialist, nor was he returned as one. This does not diminish the importance of his achievement, still less of the consequences that arose from it. Less than a year after the election which took Hardie to Westminster there existed in Britain for the first time ever a socialist political party with real hopes of electoral success.

3

MEMBER FOR
WEST HAM SOUTH

Hardie's performance in Parliament after his spectacular arrival there was an inevitable anti-climax, for reasons which were largely beyond his control. In the leisurely way in which politics operated at the time, the Parliament of 1892 opened in August with Salisbury's Conservative Government still in office, although the Liberals and Irish had won a narrow victory at the polls. The rising young lawyer H. H. Asquith moved the Liberal amendment to the address on the Queen's Speech. This was seconded by Burt, who had attained a position of some standing in the Liberal ranks, and was carried, Hardie voting with the Liberals. Not until this point did the Conservative administration resign, and Parliament stood adjourned until February 1893. Parliament was still a spare-time occupation for gentlemen, not a full-time business for professional politicians.

All this had happened before Hardie had had a chance to get his parliamentary bearings, and when he made a request for an autumn session to deal with unemployment, the Speaker ruled that the request could not be entertained, as no Ministry was in existence to deal with it. It was not until the leisurely process of forming a Liberal Government was complete, and the Liberal Ministers had won the by-elections entailed by their appointments, that Hardie had any opportunity of making an impact on the Commons. His first speech was on 7 February 1893. It was not in Hardie's nature to observe the convention that a maiden speech should be a decorous affair full of well-turned compliments to one's colleagues and one's constituency, but empty of any controversial matters. Hardie proposed an amendment to the Address on the Queen's Speech, in which he regretted that the Government's programme contained no proposals for the relief of unemployment. It was an unflamboyant, rather plodding speech; it contained nothing which might give even the most sensitive Conservative the impression that Hardie was a dangerous revolutionary. It was not even very obviously socialist in tone. Only once in his first spell as an M.P. did Hardie claim in Parliament that socialism was the only solution to the unemployment problem. More often, as on this occasion, he was content to talk about unspectacular palliatives. The government should ban overtime in workshops it controlled; it should refuse to give contracts to foreign firms; it should reduce the legal maximum of hours worked by transport and postal workers; it should encourage 'home colonies' where the unemployed could work on improving poor-quality agricultural land by intensive cultivation. (This last was, as Hardie possibly knew, a direct evocation of Feargus O'Connor's Land Scheme, put forward in the Chartist era fifty years earlier as a solution to unemployment.)

It was scarcely the stuff of revivalist politics; but it no doubt earned Hardie a more respectful hearing in the Commons of 1893 than he would have gained by seeking converts to socialism. A large part of his parliamentary activity was directed, through questions to ministers, at raising the industrial grievances of various workmen, and at exposing collusion between magistrates, industrialists, and the police in labour disputes. This was the era of what has been called the 'employers' counter-attack' in industrial relations. Worried by the strength of craft unions and the growth of 'new unions' such as the dockers and the gasworkers, employers in some areas took a leaf from the book of their American counterparts, and determined to suppress trade unionism among their employees. One of the employers' associations which rose to prominence was the Shipping Federation, which wished to curb the power of the dockers' and seamen's unions. Hardie and Havelock Wilson conducted an active campaign, mostly by means of parliamentary questions, designed to show that it was the Shipping Federation, through the local magistrates, which had ensured that troops were brought in to try to end a strike of dockers at Hull in the summer of 1893. Hardie and Wilson got as far as securing an adjournment on the activities of the Federation, although no parliamentary action followed.

In the latter part of his term Hardie again took up the problem of unemployment. This time, he tried a new tack. He turned to the Local Government Board, and by means of a persistent series of parliamentary questions elicited from that rather sluggish department information as to the power possessed by Boards of Poor Law Guardians to start public works in their district in order to relieve unemployment. After lengthy harassment by Hardie, the Government eventually agreed to empower local authorities to acquire land to enable land colonies of the unemployed to be established. It was Hardie's only legislative success in the Parliament of 1892 to 1895, and hardly any local authorities responded. But it would have been quite unrealistic for Hardie to have expected anything more. He was a one-member party in a Parliament where the Liberal Government was fighting for its political life in trying to get its proposals for Irish Home Rule through the overwhelmingly Conservative House of Lords, and coping with the succession problem to Gladstone when he eventually retired in 1894 at the age of eighty-four. Labour questions were low on the Government's agenda.

Hardie's most striking contribution to parliamentary discussion in these years, however, was nothing to do with labour, unemployment, or the Shipping Federation. It was a memorable and courageous speech made on the occasion of the birth of a son to the Duke and Duchess of York (the future King George V and Queen Mary) in the summer of 1894. A year earlier Hardie had protested against parliamentary time being wasted on a motion of congratulation at the Duke of York's marriage instead of a discussion of unemployment. But his protest of 1894 was much more dramatic. It drew its emotional force from the fact that the Government had refused a request from Hardie to propose a motion of condolence for the relatives of 250 miners who had been killed in a colliery explosion in the Merthyr valley in South Wales a few days earlier. In a *Labour Leader* editorial pulsing with anger and emotion, Hardie wrote, 'The life of one Welsh miner is of greater commercial and moral value to the British nation than the whole Royal Crowd put together, from the Royal Great Grand-mama down to this puling Royal Great Grand-child.' A little later, on 28 June, the resolution for 'an humble Address' of congratulation to the royal couple was proposed and seconded by the leading Commons members of both parties. Hardie attacked it in a furious outburst of outraged Scots puritan radicalism:

Mr Speaker, on my own behalf and those whom I represent, I am unable to join in this public address. I owe no allegiance to any hereditary ruler [Interruption] – and I will expect those who do to allow me the ordinary courtesies of debate. The Resolution . . . seeks to elevate to an importance which it does not deserve an event of everyday occurrence . . . When we are asked as the House of Commons representing the nation to join in these congratulations, then in the interests of the dignity of the House I take leave to protest.

Hardie went on to protest about the indignity of the procedure whereby a Government Minister was required to be present at the birth to ensure that no commoner was substituted for the royal infant. Hardie complained rather prudishly about the impropriety of this. Interrupted by a shout of 'Rot!', he retorted, 'If those hon. Gentlemen mixed as freely as I do with the common people they would know their opinions on this question.' Warming to his theme, Hardie asked rhetorically 'what particular blessing the Royal Family has conferred upon the nation that we should be asked to take part in this proceeding today'. Undeterred by the interruption of the honourable and gallant member for Armagh, who demanded that Hardie should be silenced, he went on to examine the record of the Prince of Wales (later King Edward VII).

The 'fierce white light' which we are told 'beats upon the throne' sometimes reveals things in his career it would be better to keep covered. Sometimes we get glimpses of the Prince at the gaming table,* sometimes on the racecourse. His Royal Highness is Duke of Cornwall, and as such he draws £60,000 a year from the Duchy property in London, which is made up of some of the vilest slums – [cries of 'Question!'].

Mr Speaker: The hon. Gentleman is not now speaking to the Resolution before the House.

* This was a reference to the 'baccarat scandal' of 1890 and 1891. The Prince of Wales had had to stand in the witness-box for a week during a suit for slander brought by an army officer accused by the Prince's companions of cheating during a game of baccarat. A large sector of public opinion thought (probably mistakenly) that the Prince was the real culprit, and that the army officer was being victimized to protect him.

Mr Keir Hardie: I will bow to your ruling, Sir, and proceed to the subject of the Resolution . . . From his childhood onward this boy will be surrounded by sycophants and flatterers by the score – [cries of 'Oh!, Oh!'] – and will be taught to believe himself as of a superior creation. [Cries of 'Oh!, Oh!']. A line will be drawn between him and the people whom he is to be called upon some day to reign over. In due course, following the precedent which has already been set, he will be sent on a tour round the world, and probably rumours of a morganatic alliance will follow† – [loud cries of 'Oh!, Oh!' and 'Order!' and 'Question!'] – and the end of it all will be that the country will be called upon to pay the bill . . . The Government will not find an opportunity for a vote of condolence with the relatives of those who are lying stiff and stark in a Welsh valley, and, if that cannot be done, the motion before the House ought never to have been proposed either. If it be for rank and title only that time and occasion can be found in this House, then the sooner that truth is known outside the better for the House itself.

Hardie's protest was solitary. He was a republican out of his time. Only ten years earlier the Commons had not wanted for critics of royalty, and in particular of the total withdrawal of Queen Victoria from public life after the death of the Prince Consort. But the Queen's Jubilee of 1887 had surrounded her in a warm glow of romantic affection, which could be conveniently extended to cover the alleged misdeeds of her son and heir. Even in 1894 there had been one radical revolt against a vote of a substantial allowance to one of Queen Victoria's relatives who had succeeded to the throne of a German duchy. But Hardie's protest was too strong meat even for contemporary republicans such as Henry Labouchere. No member, not even another Labour member, was prepared to join Hardie even though he was merely expressing in public what many radicals still thought about the Royal Family.

The Royal Baby speech (as Hardie always called it) and his persistent nagging on behalf of the unemployed established Hardie's parliamentary reputation by 1894. But the real strength of his reputation arose from activities outside Parliament. In the years 1892 to 1895 Hardie became a national figure. The crucial step was taken back in 1893, with the famous conference in Bradford which founded the Independent Labour Party (I.L.P.) The immediate impetus for the conference came from a socialist propagandist called Joseph Burgess, who in 1892 was the editor of the *Workman's Times*, a labour paper circulating mainly in Bradford and the West Riding woollen district. Burgess was one of the leading lights of the Bradford and

† This was the most prophetic statement Hardie ever made. The baby in question grew up to be the globe-trotting Prince of Wales, and later, for a short period, King Edward VIII.

District Labour Union, a local labour party which had attracted wide-spread working-class support because of resentment at the behaviour of Liberal employers during a notable mill strike in 1891. In the summer of 1892 Burgess proposed through the columns of his paper an arrangement for putting local supporters of independent labour representation in touch with one another, so that in due course they could form local Labour Parties which would be able to send delegates to a conference to constitute a national Labour Party. Hardie assisted Burgess in his preparations by arranging a meeting at the 1892 Congress of the T.U.C. which set up an Arrangements Committee to supervise the summoning of the national conference, which eventually took place in Bradford on 13 and 14 January 1893.

The conference attracted quite a lot of attention from the press. Although the T.U.C. had been established for over twenty years, the idea that working men should be capable of running a political organization of their own without any guidance from experienced middle-class politicians was decidedly novel. The delegates to the I.L.P. conference were very largely working-class, and their geographical distribution gave a clear indication of where the strength of independent labour sentiment lay. In spite of Burgess's arrangements, the bulk of the delegates came from places where local parties had already existed before his initiative. The West Riding itself was heavily over-represented; the Scottish Labour Party sent a deputation; Manchester, under the leadership of the brilliant but erratic socialist journalist Robert Blatchford, was present in strength. Mining districts like Northumberland, Durham and South Wales had few or no delegates: confident of their ability to get Liberal nominations when they wanted them, the miners were not as yet supporters of an independent Labour party. London was also poorly represented, and that largely by self-appointed pundits such as Edward Aveling, the disreputable paramour of Karl Marx's daughter Eleanor, and Bernard Shaw, whose credentials as a delegate from the Fabian Society were acrimoniously challenged.

This was an accurate foretaste of the I.L.P. as it was to be: essentially a provincial party, at its best in the strongholds of that puritanical radicalism with which it had so much in common. It was always weak in London, where none of its appeals to the working class could strike home. There was much more casual labour, instability and unemployment in London than in the great industrial centres of the North and Scotland. This was not, as might have been expected, a source of strength to ths I.L.P. but one of weakness. The established craft trade unions were weak in the capital, and the 'new unions' like

the dockers who had made such an impressive showing in 1889
fluctuated rapidly with the rise and fall of unemployment. 'New
unionism' had undoubtedly helped Hardie win West Ham in 1892,
but it could not provide the sort of solid electoral and financial support which, for instance, the miners' unions could give to their
Lib-Lab M.P.s in Northumberland, Durham and Yorkshire. Furthermore, the overlap between nonconformist evangelism and the I.L.P.
style was an asset in the West Riding, but no help in London. The
rising star of socialism in the West Riding was a young clerk called
Philip Snowden, who had been crippled by a childhood illness and
whose drawn, almost emaciated appearance went well with his style
of evangelist oratory. Snowden swept the West Riding with fervent,
if vague, descriptions of the better life to come under socialism. His
views, expressed in pamphlets like *The Christ that is to Be* and platform
speeches whose style was known to his friends as 'Philip's Come to
Jesus' were put over in the manner of a religious revival. In a less
dramatic way, Hardie had something of the same manner. Hardie
and Snowden made an immediate appeal to the nonconformist
craftsman or the Scots Presbyterian miner that was lost on other
sections of the working class.

The first I.L.P. conference, then, met in the heartlands of the movement, at the Bradford Labour Institute. The events of the conference
have often been described. Hardie was appointed chairman, and under
his influence the 120 or so delegates steered a careful path between the
Scylla of Lib-Labbery and the Charybdis of sectarianism. On the one
hand, the proposal to call the party 'Independent Labour Party' was
carried almost unanimously against 'Socialist Labour Party' (which
had been favoured by the Scottish Labour Party). Hardie supported
the majority view, which he had to defend, neither for the first nor for
the last time, against the sea-green incorruptibles of the S.D.F. who
argued that it was treachery to the cause to drop the title 'Socialist'
from the party's masthead. Hardie realized, as the sectarian S.D.F.
never did, the importance of getting across to working-class opinion-
formers, such as trade-union leaders. To these people 'socialism' was
still a dubious foreign import much beloved of eccentric middle-class
intellectuals. Nevertheless, although the I.L.P.'s socialism was not
flaunted in its title, socialist objectives were firmly written into the
party programme from the very beginning. It was proposed that the
statement of the party's objectives should start 'To secure the collective and communal ownership of all the means of production, distribution, and exchange.' An essentially Lib-Lab amendment to this
was moved: 'To secure the separate representation and protection

of Labour interests on public bodies.' But the amendment was lost by 91 votes to 16, after which the original statement was put as a substantive motion and carried almost unanimously. Thus a significant section of the British labour movement took up for the first time the socialist commitment to public ownership which even yet, in almost the same words, forms Clause IV, part iv, of the Labour Party Constitution.

Here again Hardie sided with the majority. His views had advanced from the days of Mid-Lanark, or even from the time of his election at West Ham, if we are to go by his public statements at that time. He now wholeheartedly embraced socialism – socialism in the mainstream sense of public ownership of resources, and not in any of the rather offbeat senses in which Hardie had previously used the word. Furthermore, his differences with conventional Lib-Labs were no longer merely tactical. Although, unlike the S.D.F., he never lost sight of the importance of 'labourist' objectives – protecting working-class interests on public bodies – he now thought firmly that 'After all has been said, we "maun gang oor ain gait".'* For this there were two reasons, both in their different ways compelling although seemingly difficult to reconcile. In the first place, an independent party without links to the Liberals could appeal as no Lib-Lab could to the Tory working man. The strength of this argument was recognized not only by Hardie but even by some of the Lib-Labs themselves, who came to support the idea of a party which put the working-class view on what they called 'labour questions' (like the miners' eight-hour day) while steering clear of what were regarded as 'purely political questions' (like disestablishment of the Church of Wales). Contemporary analysts alleged that the independent Labour candidates in 1892 had taken almost as many votes from the Conservatives as from the Liberals. Ordinary working-class voters had probably never been so firmly committed to the Liberal Party as had their leaders. In any case, the Liberal split of 1886 almost certainly boosted the Conservative working-class vote, as voters who disliked Home Rule for Ireland abandoned the Liberals in favour of the Unionists. But not only might the I.L.P. tap the votes of Tory working men, it ought to be able to develop a distinctly socialist programme which went far beyond Liberalism, even the radical Liberalism of the Newcastle programme.

These two reasons for the independence of the I.L.P. were probably less incompatible than they might appear, if only because the belief-systems of ordinary voters did not necessarily resemble those of the

* 'We must go our own way.'

political elite. To the sophisticated it might seem incongruous to woo the Tory working man with promises of socialism. But the incongruity depends on the belief that there is a continuum of political ideologies, of 'packages' of political views: that the most dedicated Conservative voter is the one least likely to support socialism. But there is no evidence that the mass electorate has ever thought in terms of the bundles of beliefs which have formed political parties' programmes. Just as, in the 1960s, a loyal Labour voter might be in favour of restricting coloured immigration, so in the 1890s a working-class voter, moulded by a Liberal environment, might none the less be unmoved by Welsh disestablishment, and perhaps hostile to Home Rule. The achievement of Hardie and the other early Labour leaders was that they put together a credible package which a mass working-class electorate eventually came to support. In the long run it made very good sense to detach 'labour questions' like factory legislation and restriction of hours from a Liberal programme in which they took, at best, a very poor second place to the politics of organized Nonconformity. There was no reason why the Liberal and the Tory working man should not both be recruited to a programme which put labour questions first, and which was underpinned by a definitely socialist ideology.

For the moment, at any rate, it was inopportune to make the boundaries too distinct. Having resoundingly declared its independence of the old parties, the infant I.L.P. proceeded to blur the implications of independence by refusing to accept a resolution banning members of other parties from membership of the I.L.P., and preferring a comfortably vague formula: 'No person opposed to the principles of the party shall be eligible for membership.' Hardie had said, when the same question had come before the Scottish Labour Party, 'I was a member of a Liberal association for eighteen months after I was connected with the Scottish Labour Party, and if a resolution of this kind had faced me at the beginning it is hard to say what might have happened.'

Again, Hardie warned the new party against becoming too dogmatic too soon over the issue of the so-called 'Fourth Clause'. This was to become a hardy annual at I.L.P. conferences and an occasion for bitter disputes between Hardie and Robert Blatchford. The fourth clause of the constitution of the Manchester District Independent Labour Party bound its members to abstain from voting in every election in which there was no socialist candidate. Blatchford and his colleagues tried unsuccessfully to make this the policy of the national I.L.P. But Hardie had a much better understanding of political realities than Blatchford. He argued that a dogmatic commitment

like this gained the socialists no advantage; it was in any case un-
enforceable, and would only make the socialists look foolish if it was
patently unenforced.

This attitude was typical of the undogmatic pragmatism with which
Hardie kept the sectarians at bay; if nothing else, it made for a fairly
low-key, harmonious conference which concluded in great warmth
and amity. Keir Hardie had a rich and powerful bass voice, in which
he led the delegations in the singing of 'Auld Lang Syne', coaxing
along some of the English delegates who were not very sure of the
words; and so the conference dispersed. The I.L.P. was an accom-
plished fact.

The first conference set up a weak party executive – indeed the word
'executive' was shunned, perhaps because it suggested undemocratic
elitism, and the party's central committee was always known as the
National *Administrative* Committee, or N.A.C. The first N.A.C. was
elected on an unwieldy regional basis, which was probably the result
of an attempt to find an appropriate equivalent to the trade-by-trade
election of members of the executive of the T.U.C. Surprisingly,
Hardie was not a member of this first N.A.C. The secretary was Shaw
Maxwell, an old stalwart of the Scottish land-reform movement whom
we have already met in the Scottish Labour Party. With this moder-
ately encouraging start, the I.L.P. was launched into the British
political scene.

The initial arrangements for the organization of the I.L.P. were
found to be clumsy and ineffective. The unwieldy fifteen-member
N.A.C. met only twice between the first two annual conferences, more
frequent meetings being ruled out on grounds of expense. At the
second conference of the party, in January 1894, the position was
regularized. The idea of a regional executive was dropped, and a compact nine-member N.A.C., drawn very largely from Lancashire and
Yorkshire, was appointed. Hardie accepted the position of President
of the party, which he retained (although the title was soon changed to
Chairman) until 1900. This was only fitting. Whatever the contribution of Burgess and others, the I.L.P. was unmistakably Keir
Hardie's party, and he was its unquestioned leader. He took a pro-
prietorial pride in the party. From early 1894 he had at his service a
weekly paper, the *Labour Leader*. This had had a chequered career.
After two years of running the *Miner*, in 1887 and 1888, Hardie had
tried to spread the appeal of his paper beyond the mining community
by renaming it the *Labour Leader* and ceasing to concentrate on mining
topics. This first *Labour Leader* was not a success, but the paper re-
emerged as a slim monthly, the organ of the Scottish Labour Party.

By the end of 1893 Hardie had managed to collect enough financial backing (one of his most useful abilities) to be able to promise that the paper would soon be converted into a weekly, published in London and Glasgow. The first number of the weekly *Labour Leader*, owned and edited by Keir Hardie, came out at the end of March 1894.

Even at the outset, Hardie faced complaints that the paper ought to be made the official organ of the I.L.P. and not remain his private property. This was to become, until the party eventually did take over the paper in 1904, something of a sore point. Hardie was often to be accused of running the paper badly – at any rate dully, compared to the sparkling *Clarion*, edited by Blatchford – or, more seriously, of using it as a vehicle for his own views without giving enough prominence to those of others when they disagreed with him. There is some substance in these charges; but it is only fair to Hardie to point out that it was his incessant work and the finance he raised which enabled the paper to survive at all. Often, especially in the early years, Hardie wrote virtually the entire paper himself, from the political commentary to the children's serial. With the aid of a devoted, though not always very efficient, staff, the paper staggered on from crisis to crisis, without ever quite being forced to close. In terms of sheer output, Hardie was one of the most prolific political writers of his day. He would send in articles written in draughty, uncomfortable railway carriages and waiting-rooms while he was stumping the country addressing socialist meetings – and would then have to rush back to London to make up the paper and see it through the press.

The pioneering years of the British socialist movement were marked by papers which rose from obscurity, survived a few weeks or months or even years, but as surely slid back to obscurity. Apart from journals whose losses were subsidized by wealthy eccentrics like Hyndman or Champion, only two socialist papers came near enough to financial viability to have staying power: Blatchford's *Clarion* and Hardie's *Labour Leader*. They were essential to the success of the early socialist movement, which needed them to reach a larger public than could be touched by even the most intensive programme of public meetings. Only one later socialist paper, Tom Johnston's *Forward* (first published in Glasgow in 1906, and rising to national fame because of its suppression by Lloyd George in 1916) ever had anything like as great an influence on the growth of the I.L.P.

It is very hard to recapture, and still harder to distil into print, the atmosphere in which the I.L.P. was to grow in its first three or four years. As a consequence it is difficult to give Hardie the full credit for his incessant activities. In the 1890s the age of mass communications had not dawned. Not only was there no radio or television, there was not even a popular press with a national circulation. *The Times* or the *Morning Post* might cover the whole country; but the working class did not read them. The *Daily Mail* and the *Daily Express* were new-born and rather sickly infants. It was the heyday of the local weekly, which was the staple diet of most newspaper readers. In these circumstances much of Hardie's work inevitably consisted of going round from town to town and village to village, making speeches in all weathers and to all sorts of audiences on behalf of socialism. These speeches, reproduced at length – often word for word – in the tiny print of a yellowing local newspaper, may inspire no emotion (unless boredom) in the modern reader at all. But very few speakers are inspiring in print – a glance at the speeches of Gladstone or Lloyd George should confirm this – and it is impossible now to re-create the effect which Hardie had on his audiences. He was a dour and rather humourless speaker, but he carried his audience with him – especially in northern England and Scotland – by the force of his personality, his determination, directness, and sincerity. He treated all his audiences with the same directness as the Lanarkshire pitmen among whom he had first learnt public speaking. His audiences were never 'Gentlemen', always 'Men'.

Hardie's life during these years was an unending round of speeches, railway journeys, trips to London for Parliament and the *Labour Leader*, and infrequent journeys to Cumnock to see his family. (Mrs Hardie, like Mrs Lloyd George, was a stay-at-home housewife who refused to settle in London.) Because Hardie was a missionary, a revivalist, and not an economist or any sort of precise or analytical speaker, many of his writings and speeches have not worn well, but this does not detract from their undoubted impact at the time. Hardie's style was precisely right for bringing the I.L.P. to life.

As an example of what Hardie expected to appeal to his audiences, it is interesting to look at a booklist he contributed to the *Labour Leader* in the summer of 1894 under the heading of 'Texts for Speakers: A Few Hints'. Hardie wrote:

As a basis on which to develop a Socialistic system of thought, let me recommend the first four books of the New Testament, Carlyle's *Sartor Resartus* and *Past and Present*; Ruskin's *Crown of Wild Olives* and *Unto This Last*; Mazzini's *Thoughts on Democracy* and *Faith into the Future* ... As textbooks take Nunquam's *Merrie England*, Hobson's *Problems of Poverty* and Morrison Davidson's *The Old Order and the New*.

Of all these authors, only one – the unorthodox Liberal J. A. Hobson – was an economist. Hardie accurately sensed that the I.L.P. would respond to ethical appeals and to critics of the self-confident complacency of Victorian industrialism (such as Carlyle and Ruskin) far more readily than to economic analysis. Apart from Carlyle, Hardie's list of authors would have been both easier to read and far more immediately appealing to the self-educated working-class socialist than the texts of Marx and Engels which the S.D.F. set their branch members to read.

Of the books on Hardie's list the most influential was one which had only just been published. 'Nunquam' (the Latin for 'never') was the pen-name of Robert Blatchford, and his *Merrie England* had an immense sale – over a million copies. Its success is not easy to understand at first. It is a woolly-minded and incoherent jumble, marked by xenophobia and somewhat primitive views on economics. Blatchford thought that the solution to the problems of industrial pollution and unemployment was for Britain to turn her back on world trade and become a self-sufficient agrarian country. It was not intelligent economics, nor was it practical politics; but it was marvellous propaganda. Blatchford's appeal to John Smith of Oldham to abandon factory life and turn to intensive agriculture and water-powered home cotton-spinning struck a sympathetic chord. The Lancashire mill towns, like the Yorkshire woollen towns, were still surrounded by unspoilt Pennine countryside. Open moorlands and mountains could be seen at the end of even the most depressing street. It was only natural for reflective working men in the dismal Lancashire cotton towns to look about them, and to come to believe in the myth of an agricultural Golden Age before the industrial revolution. Blatchford was only echoing an appeal made by many previous radicals in revolt against industrialism, such as William Cobbett, Feargus O'Connor, and for that matter Hardie himself, with his belief in 'home colonies'. There is no doubt that, for all Blatchford's superficiality, he was second only to Hardie as a 'recruiting-sergeant' – his own description – for the I.L.P.

The party's progress in the years leading up to the General Election of 1895 can best be shown in two spheres – its election results, and its influence on the rest of the labour movement, particularly the T.U.C. From 1892 onwards a number of independent labour candidates began to win seats on local authorities. Halifax was a notable early I.L.P. stronghold. Bradford was another, where Fred Jowett was first elected to the town council in 1892 and had become an alderman by 1896. In a number of other centres I.L.P. members were elected, and turned to the Fabian tracts being written by Sidney and Beatrice Webb and their associates for advice as to municipal reform.

c

The party also fought a number of by-elections and, on the whole, did very well. John Lister, described as the 'Squire of Shibden Hall', a prosperous landlord who was the first treasurer of the I.L.P., won 3,028 votes at a by-election in Halifax on 9 February 1893. This was between a quarter and a third of the poll; the successful Liberal got 4,620 and the Conservative 4,251. In the spring of 1894 J.W. Philipps, who had beaten Hardie in Mid-Lanark, resigned the seat, and the I.L.P. decided to fight it. The candidate was an old friend of Hardie's: Robert Smillie, secretary of the Lanarkshire miners' union. He did not get any Irish support – although Davitt and Ferguson hinted obscurely that they might support Labour at an ensuing General Election. With 1,221 votes, Smillie doubled Hardie's total of 1888, but received only about one-seventh of the votes cast.

The most significant by-election, however, was the contest in the Attercliffe division of Sheffield. Attercliffe was a solidly working-class constituency, Liberal by a comfortable majority in 1892. When a by-election was announced in 1894 the President of the local Trades Council, who was a prominent member of the Labour Electoral Association, was put forward as a potential Liberal candidate; local labour leaders thought the Liberal Association had agreed to give him a clear run against the Conservatives. The association, however, nominated a local manufacturer to fight the seat and the President of the Trades Council retired hurt. At this, the I.L.P. decided to contest the division, and put up, for what was to be the first of many unsuccessful contests, Frank Smith, a close friend of Hardie's.

Smith's route to socialism had been through the Salvation Army. In 1894 he was a rather precise-looking, spry man in his thirties, a former cabinet maker who had become a small businessman. He was a Progressive member of the new London County Council which had been set up in 1889. (The Progressives were an alliance of Liberals and Labour men – and even some Conservatives – whom the Fabians regarded as a much more promising instrument of social and municipal reform than the I.L.P.) Smith was giving Hardie rent-free accommodation in London while he was in Parliament. For the rest of Hardie's life Smith was to be his *eminence grise*, to whom Hardie often had to turn for financial help. It is clear that Smith was better as a backroom boy than as a fighter in the front line for socialism, and his fight at Attercliffe produced 1,249 votes, a little more than an eighth of the votes cast.

The result at Attercliffe mattered much less than the moral. Here was further evidence that the L.E.A. approach was inadequate. Liberals were not showing any tendency to hand over working-class seats to working men who asked nicely. One who was convinced of this moral was Ramsay MacDonald, who had spent four years as private secretary to a radical Liberal M.P. He wrote to Hardie:

My dear Hardie,
 I am now making formal application for membership of the I.L.P. I have stuck to the Liberals up to now, hoping that they might do something to justify the trust we had put in them. Attercliffe came as a rude awakening, and I felt during that contest that it was quite impossible for me to maintain my position as a Liberal any longer . . .
 Between you and me there never was any dispute as to objects. What I could not quite accept was your methods. I have changed my opinion. Liberalism, and more particularly local Liberal Associations, have definitely declared against Labour, and so I must accept the facts of the situation and candidly admit that the prophecies of the I.L.P. relating to Liberalism have been amply justified. The time for conciliation has gone past and those of us who are earnest in our professions must definitely declare ourselves.

Here was no Damascus road conversion. MacDonald, like Arthur Henderson nine years later, joined the forces of labour out of cool, self-interested calculation and political analysis. The slightly wary tone of the letter shows how MacDonald held Hardie at arm's length. This was always the case. Hardie and MacDonald had very similar backgrounds. MacDonald was also the illegitimate son of a Scots farm servant, from Lossiemouth in the north-east. But he climbed up the social ladder at an earlier age than Hardie. He was never a manual worker, and had none of Hardie's trade-union associations. Despite a political association that lasted until Hardie's death, the two were never really close friends, and their relationship was at times stormy.

There were two further Labour candidates during the Parliament of 1892–5, one of which was sponsored by the I.L.P. In August 1894 there was a double by-election in the two-member constituency of Leicester, when both Liberal members retired. The Liberals put up two candidates, one of whom was Henry Broadhurst, who had lost his seat against the tide in 1892. The Conservatives fielded only one candidate, and Joseph Burgess went forward as an I.L.P. candidate. It might have been an ideal situation for the Labour candidate to profit from the votes of Conservative working men who might give their second votes to Burgess. But he was bombastic and self-important – not a very good candidate. In the event he did well but not spectacularly: he got 4,402 votes as against 9,464 for Broadhurst and 7,184 for the other Liberal. 2,072 voters 'plumped' for Broadhurst and Burgess, and only 707 for Burgess and the Conservative candidate. A more remarkable by-election took place in Bristol East in March

1895, where the sole opponent of the Liberal was H. H. Gore, a Christian Socialist. The I.L.P. urged its members to support Gore, who came very close to winning the seat. He got 3,558 votes to his opponent's 3,740.

The socialist movement seemed also to be making great strides in the T.U.C. As Hardie grew up from the angry young man of 1887 to the experienced politician of 1894, his views became more and more influential in the T.U.C. There were lapses – as at the Congress of 1891, when, as already mentioned, Hardie got into trouble for circulating a leaflet containing his slate of approved candidates for the executive. But by 1894 Hardie's influence on the T.U.C. had reached a peak. The Parliamentary Committee (the old-fashioned name, in use till 1921, for the executive, now called the General Council) had stonewalled on a resolution from the previous Congress to promote an organization for independent labour representation; and Charles Fenwick, secretary of the committee, had once again voted against the Miners' Eight-Hours Bill. These failings were more than recompensed by the congress. Fenwick was displaced as secretary by Sam Woods, M.P., of the Lancashire Miners (only later did this prove to be a pyrrhic victory.) More strikingly, Hardie intervened on a resolution calling for the nationalization of mineral royalties to move an amendment demanding the nationalization of the 'whole of the means of production, distribution, and exchange'. Amid loud cheers Hardie's amendment was carried by 219 votes to 61. Broadhurst supported it, as did most of the miners: John Burns spoke in favour of it. 'Henceforth', rejoiced the *Labour Leader*, 'socialism is the accepted creed of Trade Unionism in this country.' Broadhurst was sitting next to Hardie during the voting and said to him quite affably, old sores having healed somewhat, 'Hardie, this is the most significant vote ever recorded by Congress.'

Of course, it was nothing of the sort. The Parliamentary Committee had no intention of taking any steps in favour of nationalization. The resolution was a purely expressive demonstration of feelings. Even at that, however, it represented an immense step forward from the situation at Hardie's first Congress, only seven years earlier. However nominal the T.U.C.'s commitment to socialism, it was nevertheless down on record, and Congress never went back on it.

Nevertheless, the socialists' triumph was the prelude to disaster. Hardie had never been popular with Congress; neither had the 'new unions' representing the unskilled workers, and many of the more conservative delegates regarded Hardie and the new unionists as merely two aspects of the same undesirable phenomenon. As Hardie noted during the 1894 congress, 'the votaries of the "old" are using every available influence to maintain their grip upon the machinery of the Trades Union Congress'. What perturbed craft unionists was, as one of the engineers' delegates put it, that 'the semi-skilled and unskilled bodies, backed by the political and Socialist bodies, should be able to swamp the skilled trades at a Trades Union Congress'. The anti-socialist faction on the Parliamentary Committee staged a re-markable coup during the winter of 1894 and 1895. Seizing on an innocuous instruction from the 1894 Congress to revise standing orders for the conduct of business at Congress, they proposed impor-tant restrictions on the eligibility of delegates. Trades Councils were to be excluded – nominally because their inclusion led to dual repre-sentation of some union members, actually because they were thought to be hotbeds of socialism; and union members were to be eligible to be Congress delegates only if they were either full-time officials of their union or actually working at their trade. This was a proposal aimed straight at Hardie and some of the leaders of the new unions, although it also excluded Broadhurst and John Burns. Burns's role in the affair was quixotic. So intense was his dislike of Hardie that he became joint sponsor, with the Conservative cotton-spinner James Mawdsley, of the proposal which excluded himself as well as Hardie. Ben Tillett, one of the leaders of the 1889 dock strike and a strong (though erratic) supporter of the I.L.P. wrote furiously to the *Labour Leader* to de-nounce the new standing orders, which he attributed to the weakness of the new chairman. He ended by lamenting the absence of the 'robust frankness and genial sturdiness of Charles Fenwick', the un-seating of whom had been thought to be a socialist triumph only three months earlier.

At the Congress of 1895 the vote on the acceptability of the new standing orders was taken according to the new standing orders. Not surprisingly, since those who would have disapproved were excluded from voting, they were carried. This elegant piece of gerrymandering, worthy of the politics of Tammany Hall, ensured that Hardie never again attended the T.U.C. as a delegate. Fortunately he had long ceased to require the T.U.C. as a platform for his views, although the conversion of the T.U.C. to his view of strategy was as important as ever.

Before the 1895 Congress took place, however, another General Election had come and gone. The Liberal Government appointed in 1892 had never been strong. It was Gladstone's last Government, and that indomitable statesman had become Prime Minister for the fourth time at the age of eighty-three, more intent than ever on passing Home

Rule for Ireland. In any case, the Government depended on the Irish Party for its parliamentary majority. But the House of Lords was now overwhelmingly Conservative. This was already true before 1886, but became even truer after the split in the Liberal Party had driven many Whig and Liberal peers into the arms of the Conservatives. So the Lords threw out Gladstone's Home Rule Bill of 1893 by 419 votes to 40. Gladstone resigned, to be succeeded by the ineffectual aristocrat Lord Rosebery, who was better at breeding Derby winners than at running the country. The Liberal Government, rent by conflicts of personality between Rosebery and the disappointed aspirants to Gladstone's succession, such as Sir William Harcourt, limped on until July 1895. It then collapsed after the 'cordite vote' – a rather trivial vote of censure arising out of alleged inadequacies in army supplies.

For the ensuing General Election, the I.L.P. put up twenty-eight candidates. The party entered the election campaign with high hopes. Not only was the East Bristol by-election an extremely encouraging pointer, but membership figures were healthy. The party claimed to have 35,000 members paying contributions to Head Office, and many more not doing so (an agreeably anarchic situation). An urgent appeal for funds went out in the *Labour Leader* and the *Clarion*. Allied to an appeal to middle-class sympathisers, it raised enough to fight the election.

The results were a severe disappointment in the light of the party's expectations, though by no means disgraceful for a new party fighting its first General Election. The twenty-eight candidates polled between them some 44,000 votes, rather more than thirteen per cent of the total poll in the seats they fought. But no progress was made in the constituencies which had appeared to hold out the best prospects for the I.L.P. In Halifax, John Lister failed to advance his vote from the by-election percentage in 1893; in Bradford Ben Tillett did less well than in 1892; in Bristol East the Liberal beat his Labour opponent by a margin of three to one. Worst of all, Keir Hardie lost his own seat to the Conservatives by 4,750 votes to 3,975 in a straight fight. In a number of ways this was not a surprising result. Hardie had not been a good constituency M.P. Inevitably he had been preoccupied with national affairs during the previous three years, and was able to spend very little time in West Ham, even during the election campaign itself. By contrast, his Conservative opponent was immersed in local affairs, and was far better equipped than most Conservatives to take Liberal and radical votes, as he was a Progressive member of the local school board. Some signs of hostility to Hardie had been evident during his tenure of the seat. For example, an open-air meeting at Plaistow in

1894 ended in some disorder, when a vote was alleged to have resulted in a majority calling upon Hardie to resign forthwith, and the cart on which he was standing was hijacked by his opponents (though fortunately they went only a few yards with it). Even the local radical paper, the *West Ham Herald*, which had been loyal to Hardie ever since 1890, admitted on the eve of the election that the dissatisfaction of his supporters with him had 'sometimes been very deep'. Perhaps the clinching factor was the attitude of the local Irish organizations. They had still not forgiven Hardie for his attacks on John Morley in 1892, which were an enormous blunder from the point of view of Hardie's electoral fortunes. All the Irish voters in South-West Ham were advised to support Major Banes, Hardie's Conservative opponent.

Hardie's loss of his seat was welcomed, and not only by Conservatives. The I.L.P. was perhaps unlucky, because the major current of opinion in the 1895 election was a substantial swing from the Liberals to the Conservatives, and the small party probably merely suffered the fate of the Liberals, with whom it was willy-nilly associated. But it had had grandiose plans, and its apparent humiliation caused barely concealed pleasure to many in the labour movement who were no friends of Keir Hardie. The Fabians, for instance, placed much more trust in their policy of 'permeation' of the older parties than in the independent policy of Hardie and the I.L.P. Beatrice Webb noted, not without satisfaction, 'The I.L.P. has completed its suicide. Its policy of abstention and deliberate wrecking is proved to be futile and absurd.' With Hardie out of Parliament, the I.L.P. faced a stern test of its coherence and resilience.

4

OUT OF PARLIAMENT

The I.L.P. had had a somewhat exaggerated sense of its own importance prior to 1895. Socialists would discuss politics mostly with other socialists, or would address hundreds of enthusiastic electors (and non-electors) without reflecting on the political views of the tens of thousands of others who did not attend their meetings. So the 1895 election result was a rude shock, especially as it did not bear out the prognosis of by-elections such as Halifax and East Bristol. (Not even the most sophisticated political commentator in 1895 was aware of the very common phenomenon of a swing against the Government of the day, from which third parties often benefit in by-elections. Such a swing has certainly operated in every inter-election period since 1886, and has usually been followed by a rallying of support for the main parties as a General Election approaches.) Naturally, much of the recrimination fell on Hardie's shoulders. Ramsay MacDonald, for instance, was evidently worrying whether his marriage of convenience to the I.L.P. was not a mistake. He wrote to the up-and-coming young Liberal Herbert Samuel, 'Hardie by his own incapacity lost his seat and none of us – being scapegoats – got in . . . Meanwhile the party of progressive ideas is being so badly handled that it is almost suicide to join it.' Beatrice Webb was not the only person who thought that 'Keir Hardie has probably lost for good any chance of posturing as M.P. and will sink into the old place of a discredited Labour leader.' Often between 1895 and 1900 Hardie himself virtually despaired of the movement and thought his chances of a return to Parliament were slim. Fortunately for himself and the British labour movement, he never gave up in disgust as those with less staying power, such as Blatchford, Champion and Hyndman were wont to do from time to time.

The immediate aftermath of the 1895 election was a trip to America. In all his journeys abroad Hardie had an infallible knack of turning something intended for his relaxation into an occasion for acute physical and sometimes mental strain. This first American trip was no exception. With his faithful *alter ego* Frank Smith, Hardie sailed from Liverpool in August 1895, having been given a rousing send-off by the local branches of the I.L.P. Hardie and Smith toured New York, Chicago, San Francisco, and a number of places in the American Mid-West. Immediately, they found themselves enmeshed in the tangled web of American radical politics.

The industrial scene was readily comprehensible, if somewhat gloomy. American industrial workers had been involved in violent clashes with bitterly anti-union employers, one of whom was Andrew Carnegie. Socialism was making some progress among the American working class (although as in Britain there was tension between the pragmatists and the sectarians). One of the purposes of Hardie's visit was to attend the Chicago Labour Congress. Nevertheless, all this activity was really only on the fringe of the American political scene. In proportion to its population, America was much less industrialized than Britain, and American radicalism was still primarily rural radicalism, similar to the crofters' revolt which had coincided with the beginning of Hardie's own political career. The coming man of American radicalism was William Jennings Bryan, soon to be the Democratic candidate for the Presidency, who led the popular cry for 'free silver'. Debt-ridden farmers, suffering from the low prices they received for their crops in a period of deflation, blamed a conspiracy of East Coast bankers who insisted on a currency based on the gold standard. The farmers sought inflation as a remedy, and believed that their prices would rise if the currency was increased by the provision of a joint gold and silver standard. Thus originated the radical plea for bimetallism, or 'free silver'. Another radical campaign was the 'anti-trust' agitation, directed against capitalists who were trying to create huge monopolies in some sectors of the economy, such as steel and railways, and were not particular as to how they did it: this was the era of the 'robber barons'.

It was a leading anti-trust campaigner, Henry Demarest Lloyd, who was responsible for the invitation to Hardie. Lloyd kept up a busy correspondence with many European radicals. Of Hardie he thought 'I do not believe he has John Burns's genius but I believe he has . . . unswerving integrity.' During his tour Hardie was on familiar ground when, for instance, he met the railwaymen's leader and pioneer socialist Eugene Debs, in prison on an absurd charge of 'conspiring to interfere with the U.S. mails and interstate commerce' arising out of a recent strike. He was on much less familiar ground when he constantly encountered issues like bimetallism on labour platforms. He expressed his regret that American reformers were so preoccupied with 'such side issues as the silver question'. The most striking incident of the tour occurred in San Francisco, where Hardie and Smith were offered $100,000 – just over £20,000 at the then current rate of exchange–if the I.L.P. would come out publicly in favour of bimetallism. (A few campaigners in Britain were beginning to advocate bimetallism at this time.) Needless to say, Hardie treated the idea with ridicule, to the pained and uncomprehending astonishment of his hosts.

Their surprise would have been even greater if they had known of Hardie's financial straits. Within two days of this meeting Hardie and Smith were down to their last dollar, and they had to be temporarily bailed out by the proceeds of an impromptu meeting summoned by a Scots expatriate playing the pipes. The tour would have been quite a considerable strain even without financial worries; as it was, Hardie and Smith were dogged by problems of organization and money throughout. Lloyd sent them off on their travels with a hardly over-generous allowance of £100 for their expenses. Within ten days Hardie was writing back ruefully to Lloyd to note that 'organization is not a strong fort of the laboring people [sic]', and before long he was pleading with Lloyd's friends for more money. The idea of a politician – even a working-class politician – without private means of one sort or another was presumably strange to these well-heeled American radicals, for they received Hardie's appeals with a bad grace. The sorry end of the affair, according to one of Lloyd's correspondents, was that Hardie and Smith had to sell some of their personal possessions in order to pay their remaining expenses.

Thus Hardie returned to a bleak winter at the end of 1895. The authority of the I.L.P. was faltering; so was Hardie's own standing in the party, because of his long absence; the *Labour Leader* was in financial difficulty. The first sign of any revival came with a by-election in North Aberdeen in May 1896, when Tom Mann, the Secretary of the I.L.P., lost by only 430 votes to a Liberal in a poll of nearly 5,400. It was, however, no consolation to Hardie personally. Possibly under the influence of H. H. Champion, the local independent labour supporters had refused to have him as a candidate. At the same time there came the first hints of moves to oust him from his candidature in West Ham South.

The whole party was cheered up, however, by the affair at Boggart Hole Clough, which started in the summer of 1896 and dragged on until the autumn. This delightfully named spot was an open space in the northern suburbs of Manchester which the local branches of the I.L.P. had habitually used for a number of years for public meetings. In June 1896, however, the local Stipendiary Magistrate, acting in collusion with local councillors, determined to oust the I.L.P., fined a number of I.L.P. speakers on trumped-up charges of obstruction at Boggart Hole Clough – even though no evidence could ever be produced that any user of the park had actually been obstructed. Two of the men fined went to prison for a month each after refusing to pay. The I.L.P. promptly announced that their next speaker would be Mrs Emmeline Pankhurst, the wife of a prominent radical lawyer who had just been elected to the National Council of the I.L.P. They correctly guessed that the magistrates would not dare to press charges against a woman. A summons was taken out against Mrs Pankhurst, but immediately adjourned: whereupon the I.L.P. promptly stated that she would speak again at Boggart Hole Clough the following weekend, this time accompanied by Keir Hardie.

By this time, public interest was thoroughly aroused, and the *Labour Leader* claimed that Hardie and Mrs Pankhurst spoke to an audience of 50,000. The summonses out against Mrs Pankhurst were again adjourned, as Manchester Corporation, by now looking very foolish, hastily tried to rush through a by-law banning public meetings in Boggart Hole Clough. This required the consent of the Home Secretary, who, however, refused to give it, and the I.L.P. was left with a moral victory in which it had the support of almost all liberal opinion. The affair brought Hardie and Mrs Pankhurst into contact for the first time, and it no doubt gave her a taste for the limelight which she was later to exercise in much more dubious ways.

The farce of the Manchester magistrates and Boggart Hole Clough was paralleled by the farce of the London congress of the Socialist International, which met in July 1896 while the Manchester affair was still in progress. The Second International, as it became known, was founded in 1889, a revival of the International Working-men's Association which Karl Marx had sponsored in 1864. Dedicated to the international brotherhood of the working class, it immediately split into two warring factions. Hardie had attended one of their rival conferences back in 1889, and in one of his three surviving letters to Friedrich Engels he wrote of his hopes for a reconciliation between the factions, but added that 'Hyndman & Co. are doing their little best to make that all but impossible'.

Seven years later nothing much had changed. True, this time the whole British Labour movement from the trade unions to Hyndman's stage army from the S.D.F. was represented. But the fact that there were 177 trade-union delegates, 112 from the I.L.P. and 118 from the much smaller S.D.F., boded ill for the success of the conference. In the event, the first three days of the five-day conference were exclusively occupied by multilingual recriminations over delegates' credentials as the international working class assembled in a seedy hall in London. The first session dissolved in slapstick disorder after one delegate pushed another off the platform, while the hall owner was vainly trying to throw out everybody, as the workers of the world had omitted to book his hall for a long enough period. On the second day, Hardie ruefully noted, almost everybody, led by Hyndman and the S.D.F., 'shouted pretty constantly, except the Russians, who would have done if they had known what the matter was'. Voting took place nation by nation, Dr Aveling solemnly passing himself off as the accredited representative of the working class of Australia. Even when the conference did get down to business, there were difficulties. On the last day, the meeting was summoned for 9.30 a.m., 'but the delegates [noted the *Labour Leader* reporter], although prepared to establish any number of proletarian armies and fight for the revolution . . . were not prepared to get up so early in the morning for it'. So, when they did turn up, business had to be rushed through. It concluded with a report from the British I.L.P.er Bruce Glasier, on behalf of the Miscellaneous Commission, on 'things in general, including a universal language'. No doubt the need for a universal language had been shown in the previous four days.

It says much for Hardie's resolute faith in socialist internationalism that it survived untarnished by these utterly farcical proceedings. But any hope of keeping the allegiance of the British trade unions, who had been so painstakingly allured to the congress, had of course vanished beyond recall. The conference cast grave doubts, or should have done, on the notion that the International had any authority at all. Even if it had discussed matters of greater importance than the eligibility of anarchists to be delegates or the need for a universal language, what powers had it to convince the workers of the world, whom it nominally represented, or to get them to do anything? The answer, of course, was absolutely none, but Hardie could not or would not see this. He continued to regard the International as an important force for peace and socialist brotherhood. In the circumstances, this was a triumph for faith over evidence.

The serious business of Hardie and the I.L.P. remained in British politics. The I.L.P. felt it had to take action when the Bradford East constituency fell vacant in October 1896. It was not as promising a seat as Bradford West, but it lay in the I.L.P. heartlands, and the I.L.P. had to fight. Hardie himself was chosen as the candidate, and accepted rather reluctantly: 'not as one would, but as one must', he said. It seemed an excellent opportunity to do well at the expense of the Liberals, who were at the nadir of their fortunes. Not long after the party's election defeat, Rosebery had resigned as leader, and the party was hopelessly split. So demoralized were the Liberals in East Bradford that they took several weeks to find a candidate, before coming up, with only a few days to go to polling day, with a former M.P. who had been defeated in 1895. This should have been an opportunity for the I.L.P. to dig deep into the Liberal vote, but it was not so. Hardie got 1,953 votes to the Conservative's 4,921 and the Liberal's 4,526 in a high poll. As ever, Hardie's public reaction was a stern refusal to be discouraged: 'Defeat is not in the Socialist dictionary.' But it was not a good result, and Hardie knew it. With the party's leader and best-known personality as candidate, the I.L.P. had done much less well than with unknown candidates in the by-elections it had fought before 1895. Furthermore, a bill for election expenses of £700 – a truly monumental sum – was more than could be raised from the party's funds, and there was considerable dissension within the I.L.P. about it. (Some of the ill-feeling may have been due to hostility to Frank Smith, who had been Hardie's agent, on the part of other leading figures in the I.L.P.)

At this time, Hardie was issuing frequent and strident warnings against any pact between the I.L.P. and the Liberals. Such warnings

can only have been occasioned by a desire within the I.L.P. to give up
the unequal struggle for independence. But as Hardie aptly, though
scarcely encouragingly, put it: 'The one thing we have to lose is our
Independence.' Matters were not improved by a further West Riding
by-election, this time again at Halifax, which fell vacant in February
1897. The I.L.P. put up a powerful candidate in Tom Mann, the fiery
leader of the 1889 dock strike, who had been secretary of the party for
three years, and who had already done well in the North Aberdeen by-
election. The Liberal candidate was the somewhat shop-soiled ex-M.P.
who had failed to retain Bradford East. For all that, the result was
considerably worse than that of the previous Halifax by-election of
1893. The Liberal won with 5,664 votes, the Liberal-Unionist was not
far behind, and Mann got precisely 2,000. In just over four years, the
Independent Labour share of the votes cast had actually declined,
from 25·5 to 15·5 per cent. This was not an encouraging progression.

The third important by-election was at Barnsley, in the autumn of
1897. In this mining division, again in the West Riding of Yorkshire,
the I.L.P. had high hopes of capturing the miners' votes, even though
the Yorkshire Miners' Union, under its veteran leader Ben Pickard,
M.P., was strongly opposed to the I.L.P. The I.L.P. candidate was
Pete Curran (his Christian name was Patrick, but for some reason he
was always known as 'Pete'). Curran was a mercurial Irishman who
had been one of the founders of the Gasworkers' and General
Labourers' Union – perhaps not the most tactful choice of candidate
in a constituency dominated by the 'old union' aristocracy of labour
in the shape of the Yorkshire Miners. The campaign was a very long-
drawn-out one, and very expensive for the I.L.P. It was also pecu-
liarly bitter. The Liberals assiduously spread the story that Curran
had deserted his wife and was living with another woman – an alle-
gation that was to turn up in every election campaign Curran ever
fought. (It may well have been true.) Miners' union leaders went to
quixotically extreme lengths to conceal the fact, constantly harped on
by Hardie, Curran and the I.L.P., that the Liberal candidate was a
coal merchant who had become rich by supplying Durham coal to
Yorkshire when Yorkshire miners were on strike. Union leaders who
would sooner see a strike-breaking capitalist than a trade union
organizer for their M.P. made a heartbreakingly depressing sight. But
so bitter did the campaign become that more than once I.L.P. can-
vassers were violently ejected from pit-villages by stone-throwing
crowds. In the end the Liberal won easily from the Conservative, and
Curran got a paltry 1,091 votes – 9·7 per cent of the votes cast.

Hardie was nearer to despair after Barnsley than at any other time in his political career. He wrote to his friend David Lowe (the Scots assistant editor of the *Labour Leader*), 'Barnsley altogether is the worst thing we have yet done.' Financial wrangles continued on the N.A.C. for months afterwards, during which it became clear that a great deal of money which the I.L.P. could ill afford had been wasted at Barnsley – at a time when the debts from the previous year's by-election at Bradford had still not been paid off. For two years, the I.L.P. fought no further by-elections, the reason given by Hardie to I.L.P. Conferences being that it was still trying to pay off the debts incurred in the Bradford and Barnsley campaigns.

Hardie had his back to the wall during these years. His leadership was under attack from those who thought he was too intransigent. 'Considerable dissatisfaction prevails with the lead of Mr Hardie,' the *Manchester Guardian* commented in February 1897, 'who is thought to be lacking in tact, and indeed to be too extreme to bring about any practical results.' The I.L.P. conferences of 1896, 1897 and 1898 were marked by petty, bad-tempered bickering and sterile debate on subjects like fusion with the S.D.F. – which would have been the kiss of death for British socialism if it had ever taken place. By the spring of 1898 Hardie was complaining that 'the whole movement . . . seems to have gone back to the academic stage. There is no definite object round which the movement is gathering.' Furthermore, Hardie was in serious financial trouble. He had no regular source of income, and he did not wax fat on the fees paid to him for speaking at I.L.P. meetings.

Thus the I.L.P. was not in a healthy state to meet the next crisis which faced it – the Boer War. In September 1899 Britain went to war with the Boer republics in South Africa over the treatment of British settlers in Transvaal by President Paul Kruger's government. The I.L.P. was in no doubt as to the real cause; the N.A.C. immediately protested against the aggressive attitude of the British Government towards the Transvaal Afrikaners. The I.L.P. never wavered from a policy of downright hostility to the war, even while the whole country was gripped by a war fever that now appears pathetic and degrading. Of course, there was something in the I.L.P. temperament that relished this situation. The early-Christian feeling of martyrdom could be psychologically very satisfying, and members of the I.L.P. were probably bound closer to one another by putting up a united front to a hostile world. Nevertheless, the persecution of the 'pro-Boers', as the opponents of the war were called, often extending to mob violence, frightened off weaker brethren and made electoral success for the I.L.P. seem even less likely. Even the Socialist movement was by no means united on the anti-war platform. Not all British socialists shared Hardie's view that Kruger was a saintly peasant whose peaceful regime was aggressively attacked by British imperialists. The Fabians were split, but some of them approved of the war, on the grounds that it would improve national strength and efficiency. Hardie's (by now) inveterate opponent Robert Blatchford was also an enthusiast for simpler, atavistic reasons: as an ex-soldier himself he thrilled to the thought of British soldiers killing Boer peasants.

The I.L.P. appeared to be at the lowest point of its fortunes in 1899 and 1900. It seemed to have lost its chances of making any electoral impact; and in its views on the Boer War it found itself in a tiny minority joined only by a few pro-Boer Liberals such as John Morley and Lloyd George. Hardie, although only in his early forties, was beginning to show the strain. A delegate noted that he looked 'grey and worn' in 1900; his hair was fast greying and giving him the Old Testament patriarch appearance familiar to us in photographs. Even a hostile witness like John Burns had to admire his staying power: 'Hardie is a dour, dogged fellow. If I were a general I would give him a lonely outpost that should be held to the death.' But the lonely outpost of the I.L.P. imposed a great mental strain on its commander. He wanted to give up the chairmanship of the party in 1899, but his colleagues on the Council refused to accept the idea; however, he did give it up in 1900, to be succeeded by Bruce Glasier.

Of the three Scots who did so much to set up the I.L.P. Glasier is the least remembered. Born in Glasgow, he became an unsuccessful poet and slightly more successful architect who embraced the I.L.P. at about the same time as he fell in love with, and married, a blue-stocking convert to socialism, Katherine St John Conway. Though something of a late-Victorian romantic, he had at least one foot in the real world and his surviving correspondence with other I.L.P. leaders indicates a sufficiently shrewd and realistic mind. After Frank Smith, Bruce Glasier was probably the nearest Hardie had to a close political friend.

By 1900, in fact, better times for the I.L.P. were not far off, even though this must have been difficult to observe in the dark days of the South African War. The catalogue of misery having been exhausted, we should look at the factors which kept Hardie and the I.L.P. afloat and in due course led to revival. A number of these factors were present even during the unfolding of the gloomy events just described.

For one thing, there was Hardie's journalism. The *Labour Leader*, as already noted, was not a particularly exciting journal, but when

Hardie's moral feelings were outraged he could rise to inspired moments of denunciation which certainly kept him in the public eye. An interesting example occurred early in 1896. Hardie was appalled by a case proceeding through the Glasgow courts which involved a fashionable brothel in the West End of the city. The brothel-keeper had been brought to trial; the prostitutes who worked for her, mostly poor working-class girls, were identified by name in court, but their prosperous middle-class clients were not. Hardie was outraged by the unpleasant class discrimination involved, and he set out with rare ruthlessness to track down the men concerned. Indeed, he was so keen to pursue his quarry that he wanted to join in the sleuthing expeditions of his staff, who had to point out that this would be impossible, as everybody would know who he was. Before long, his sleuths started bringing in their reports.

A shipbuilder from Port-Glasgow seems to have been a leading light. Just to show him that we are not bluffing, I may mention that we are on the trail of 'Mrs Captain Norton', alias Miss Watt; of Mrs Stewart, of poor Susie, and several others of his flames, including the one who died in Dundee after an illegal operation.

Hardie went on to name others. There were, for instance, 'Mr W, a bluff young clergyman, recently ordained, who told funny stories . . . another young W and his uncle M, a member of Free St Matthew's Church . . . a Member of Parliament for one of the divisions of Glasgow . . .'. In tones of naïve self-congratulation the *Labour Leader* of 22 February noted, 'Newsagents say our leap to the front is *the* miracle in the history of their trade.'

Hardie's ruthless streak came out again in his much better known attack on Lord Overtoun in 1899. J. Campbell White was a Glasgow business man who waxed rich on the family chemical works at Shawfield, on the south-eastern corner of the city. He was a leading Liberal, and a notably pious benefactor of the Free Church of Scotland, who favoured compulsory piety by others as he campaigned against entertainments being open on the Sabbath Day. In a word, he was the baker who had dismissed the young Keir Hardie all over again. He was created Lord Overtoun in 1893 in recognition of his services to the Free Church and the Liberal Party.

In the spring of 1899 some of the workers in Overtoun's chemical works went on strike, and asked the *Labour Leader* staff to assist them. The most appalling circumstances immediately came to light. Labourers at Shawfield worked for twelve hours a day, seven days a week. (As a devout Free Churchman, Overtoun had petitioned Glasgow Corporation to close its museums and shut down its tramways on Sundays.) The men were liable to contract horrible skin diseases from the chemicals they touched or inhaled, and the cartilages of their noses were sometimes destroyed by fumes. The sanitation in one part of the works consisted of two earth privies with no doors, each with a bench seat to accommodate between four and six men. Labourers were paid 3d. an hour; furnacemen 4d. On 17 April 1899 (Hardie recorded without comment), Lord Overtoun presided over a meeting of the United Evangelistic Association, sitting under a text hanging on the wall: 'Come unto Me all ye that labour and are heavy laden, and I will give you rest.'

Much to the chagrin of his many friends in business and the evange-listic movement, Overtoun took no steps to rebut the allegations, though he immediately shortened the hours worked at Shawfield and abolished Sunday work. A number of evangelical ministers and others therefore undertook to defend him against Hardie's allegations, and Hardie counter-attacked with unparalleled fury. Reading Hardie's articles and pamphlets which, seventy-five years later, still seem alive with hatred of Overtoun's hypocrisy, we may easily understand the impact they had in the Glasgow of 1899, and realize why the *Labour Leader* had to change its printer in the middle of the Overtoun cam-paign. The Rev. Mr Paterson having obtained an interdict against one of Hardie's pamphlets which said of him, 'Clergymen living separated from their wives should be very chary in their reference to scandals', Hardie rounded on him with an undisguised threat of blackmail: 'From the day when he somewhat hurriedly married the Kirkcaldy schoolmistress down to the present time there are some interesting facts connected with his career, all of which may not be known to his congregation.' No more was heard from the Rev. Mr Paterson. Like many others with a well-developed sense of moral indignation, Hardie was sometimes extraordinarily ruthless, to the point of unscrupulous-ness, when aroused.

The Overtoun campaign was short, sharp, and spectacular. Behind the scenes, changes had been taking place in the attitudes of the trade unions to labour representation which were of much greater impor-tance, although they took several years to mature. In 1895, as we have already seen, the T.U.C. slammed the door on the socialists and 'new unionists'. But events during the following four years went a long way towards weakening the traditional allegiances of many craft unionists. In 1897 the Engineering Employers' Federation mounted a head-on attack on the engineers' union, the Amalgamated Society of Engineers (A.S.E.) In their own words, the federated employers wanted 'to obtain the freedom to manage their own affairs which has proved so beneficial to the American manufacturers'. This was extremely ominous. Observant British trade unionists had watched with concern the union-busting activities of a number of large American employers, which had occasionally culminated in violent strikes – and violent suppression of strikes. They decided that the process must be stubbornly resisted in Britain. The engineers' lock-out of 1897 and 1898 was therefore very bitter on both sides. The Federation actively coerced non-federated employers who did not wish to lock out their men. Naturally, the I.L.P. supported the engineers. Referring to them, Hardie wrote in terms of uncontrollable bitterness at Christmas 1897, 'The thoughts and feelings which pertain to the Christmas season are far from me . . . A holocaust of every Church building in Christendom tonight would be as an act of sweet savour in the sight of Him whose name is supposed to be worshipped within their walls.' Early in 1898 the engineers had to go back to work, virtually on the employers' terms. This was a grim warning to trade unionists. One of the oldest and strongest unions had been broken by a determined attack by the employers. Could anyone any longer trust the old Lib-Lab doctrine, much beloved of the Northumberland miners' leaders, that working men should achieve their political aims through cooperation with their employers and, failing that, through applying their industrial strength – and not through trying to influence legislation? Besides, if Liberal constituency associations were to select by-election candidates, as at York in January 1898, who were active members of the Engineering Employers' Federation, what was the point of traditional Lib-Lab political activity?

One union which had long realized the importance of parliamentary action was the principal railway union, the Amalgamated Society of Railway Servants. Railway companies were among Britain's most anti-union employers. Of all the large companies only the North-Eastern Railway was prepared to recognize trade unionism among its employees. But a series of accidents in the 1870s and 1880s had brought railway companies' staff affairs uncomfortably into the lime-light. A number of categories of railwaymen, especially signalmen, were found to be working scandalously long hours. Parliament, therefore, had already intervened with the support of public opinion to ban railways from forcing their employees to work excessive hours. The campaign had uncovered some unsavoury behaviour by railway companies, the worst offender being the Cambrian Railway in Wales, which dismissed a stationmaster for having given evidence to the House of Commons Select Committee on railwaymen's hours. The A.S.R.S. had the satisfaction of seeing two Cambrian directors forced to apologize at the bar of the House for their breach of parliamentary privilege.

These events showed that Parliament could be of some help to trade unionists, although they did not make the railway companies any friendlier towards unionism. The A.S.R.S. accordingly took the lead among the trade unions which wished to see more effective representation of the interests of labour in Parliament. In addition, the last three years of the nineteenth century saw a succession of civil cases in the law courts whose cumulative effect seemed to be an erosion of the statutory protection for trade unions which had been thought to exist in Acts passed between 1871 and 1875. Again, thoughtful trade unionists saw that the need for a powerful group of M.P.s to protect union interests in the Commons was becoming more urgent.

However, for three years the torpor of the post-1895 T.U.C. was not disturbed. The Congress was dominated by Coal and Cotton, and the miners and cotton workers were amongst the last union leaders to abandon their opposition to independent labour representation. However, the miners had a radicalizing experience similar to the engineers' lock-out of 1897. This was the South Wales coal strike, which lasted for five months in 1898. The miners rebelled against their ultra-moderate leaders, and fought a prolonged battle whose immediate rewards were scanty. But it had two long-term effects of importance: it recruited South Wales miners in large numbers to the Miners' Federation of Great Britain, and it introduced Keir Hardie to South Wales.

The I.L.P. thought the strike was an excellent opportunity for propaganda in what had, up till then, been a very weak area. The *Labour Leader* opened a strike fund for miners' wives and children; an I.L.P. organizer was sent to South Wales to set up new branches; and Hardie himself spent several weeks there recruiting for the I.L.P. The Scots puritan ex-miner and the Welsh nonconformist miners got on very well together. As the organizer reported of one of Hardie's meetings, 'Sunday afternoon we had a good meeting on Penydarren "Tips" between Merthyr and Dowlais. The meeting was of a religious character, opened by Hymn, Lesson and Prayer, and Keir preached the sermon to a large and attentive audience.' Much of the gain was only temporary. The I.L.P. recruited hundreds of members, many of whom dropped out again after the excitement of the strike was over. Between 1898 and 1899 I.L.P. membership at Merthyr dropped from 278 to 24 and at near-by Pen-y-daren from 110 to 45; and it was difficult for head office to keep in touch with local enthusiasts. (One problem was revealed in a letter from the treasurer of the South Wales

I.L.P. Federation to head office. It began, 'Excuse my bad grammar comrade. I am a welshman and my English is rather limited.' Nevertheless the seed had been sown; the harvest was to be reaped within two years.

The first stirrings of a new attitude to the I.L.P. among trade unionists came from Scotland. The Scottish Trades Union Congress was set up in 1897, expressly in reaction to the 1895 standing orders row which excluded trades councils from the national T.U.C.; it was therefore a more radical body. Hardie visited its 1899 congress, and although worried by a certain 'lack of business capacity', was nevertheless pleased to report that 60 per cent of the delegates were I.L.P. supporters. At the I.L.P.'s suggestion, the S.T.U.C. passed a resolution on behalf of 'united working-class action at the next General Election', and a special conference held on 6 January 1900 set up the 'Scottish Workers' Parliamentary Elections Committee'. Bob Smillie, Hardie's friend from Lanarkshire Miners days, was in the chair. Like the I.L.P. foundation conference seven years earlier, this conference steered a careful line between Lib-Labbery and overdogmatism. On the one hand, a motion to drop the word 'independent' from the description of the candidates the committee was to sponsor was heavily defeated; on the other, a motion to add 'nationalization of the means of production, distribution, and exchange' to the list of the committee's objectives was also defeated, with Hardie's approval. At first sight this might seem odd, since nationalization of the means of production, distribution and exchange was precisely what the I.L.P. was supposed to favour. But Hardie, the party tactician, saw that it would be counter-productive to force this policy on the new committee. If the I.L.P. delegates had supported the motion, he explained, it would have appeared to non-socialist delegates from the trade unions and the co-operative societies to be a 'carefully prepared trap'.

Matters in England followed a generally similar course, though one littered with more obstacles. The I.L.P. wrote to the other socialist organizations and the T.U.C. in August 1898, suggesting joint arrangements to promote united labour candidatures. The T.U.C. was favourably disposed, but its Parliamentary Committee, a somewhat torpid body, took no immediate action. The crucial event was a resolution from the Railway Servants at the Congress of 1899. This instructed the Parliamentary Committee 'to invite the cooperation of all the cooperative, socialistic, trade unions and other working organizations to jointly cooperate . . . in convening a special congress . . . to devise ways and means for securing an increased number of labour representatives to the next Parliament'. Philip Snowden thought that

Hardie had drafted this resolution. If so, it hardly rises to the level of
Hardie's usually competent grammar and syntax. It is much more
likely that it was an autonomous production from within the A.S.R.S.
which, as we have seen, had every reason to favour the objectives of
the resolution. It was carried by 546,000 to 434,000 votes, a majority
much more convincing than the figures suggest. The bulk of the votes
against independent labour representation came from Coal and
Cotton, which commanded 350,000 between them. Thus almost all
the other important unions must have voted with the Railway
Servants – and the I.L.P.

Nevertheless, the passing of the resolution was no guarantee that
anything would happen. It is significant that Hardie and the *Labour
Leader* took hardly any notice of the T.U.C.'s decision. The new
organization might, after all, go the way of the Labour Electoral
Association and other T.U.C.-sponsored bodies for labour representation. The I.L.P.'s chance would come when the conference mentioned in the resolution was summoned; and it would have to play a
very careful hand, to avoid antagonizing Lib-Lab opinion on the
T.U.C. A hint of Hardie's approach can be got from the I.L.P.
National Council's discussion, on 8 January 1900, of the forthcoming
conference, when it found that the recommendations on the preliminary agenda were not what had been expected. The Council decided to try to get a trade union to send in amendments to the proposed
agenda. Only if this failed would the party itself submit one. The
I.L.P. had to keep a low profile. It must remain in the background as
far as practicable, or it could not possibly get its way.

The Conference finally met on 27 and 28 February 1900. Held at
a high point of the Boer War, it attracted much less press attention
than the founding conference of the I.L.P. seven years earlier, and we
would know very little of its proceedings had not a report of them been
prepared after the meeting by Ramsay MacDonald and circulated
around the trade unions. The meeting, in the rather gloomy surroundings of the Memorial Hall, Farringdon Street, London, was a
resounding success for Hardie and the I.L.P. Once again, a course had
to be steered between Scylla and Charybdis. James Macdonald of the
S.D.F. moved that the Committee should sponsor a parliamentary
party 'based upon a recognition of the class war, and having for its
ultimate object the socialization of the means of production, distribution, and exchange'. Alex Wilkie of the Shipwrights wanted
Labour members to support a 'labour platform ... of, say, four or five
planks, embracing questions upon which the vast majority of the
workers in the country are in agreement', but wished to see these

members 'left entirely free on all purely political questions'. For a
Lib-Lab like Wilkie, 'political questions' meant the real stuff of
politics like Welsh Disestablishment and Home Rule; 'labour questions' were a separate small category which had nothing to do with
party politics. Hardie proposed a middle course. It went closer to
Wilkie's ideas than to Macdonald's – not surprisingly, because the
Lib-Labs controlled bigger battalions than the extreme socialists –
but it did insist on 'a distinct Labour Group in Parliament, who shall
have their own Whips, and agree upon their policy'. This amendment
was accepted, and the I.L.P. had scored its first success.

Hardie and his friends scored two other important successes. In the
first place, the I.L.P. got a representation on the executive of the new
body, which was called the Labour Representation Committee, far
out of proportion to its size. The agreed committee was to consist of
seven trade union representatives, two each from the I.L.P. and the
S.D.F., and one from the Fabian Society. The toleration of Lib-Labs
like Wilkie was pushed to the limit by this proposal, but they eventually swallowed it. In the second place, Ramsay MacDonald was
appointed unanimously as secretary of the new organization. (It is
often said that many delegates thought they were voting for the
militant S.D.F.er James Macdonald of the London Trades Council.
The story has no foundation; its popularity is largely due to attempts
to belittle the role of Ramsay MacDonald in the early Labour Party
after the events of 1931 had turned him from hero to villain in the eyes
of many socialists.) MacDonald's work as secretary to this body, the
L.R.C., was to be perhaps the best service he ever did for the British
labour movement; and his election secured a crucial office for a member of the I.L.P.

The L.R.C. had barely got off the ground when a General Election
was upon it. By the late summer of 1900, British success in the Boer
War, after early reverses, seemed secure; so the Conservative Government decided that the time was ripe to hold a General Election. Such
a procedure was then regarded as opportunist but has since become
extremely familiar. The constituencies polled during October 1900.

Keir Hardie's position was complicated. In 1896 he had reaffirmed
his intention to run again in West Ham South, but moves to oust him
were already under way. In 1899, much to the chagrin of the I.L.P.,
he resigned his candidature in favour of Will Thorne, of the Gasworkers and the S.D.F. Hardie had no real choice. His introduction to
the constituency had been largely due to Thorne, one of his leading
helpers in 1892 and 1895; now that Thorne wanted the seat for himself, Hardie was in no position to gainsay him. So he had to look

around for a seat. When the General Election was announced, two possibilities were in the offing: Preston and Merthyr Tydfil. Both represented the kind of constituency where, for purely mechanical reasons, an independent Labour candidate could be expected to do best. That is to say, both were double-member seats where the opposition party could be expected to put up, at most, only one candidate. Preston was a safe Conservative seat; Merthyr a safe Liberal one – although there was no properly organized Liberal Association in the division, a fact which brought Hardie nothing but good.

Hardie was very uncertain which seat to fight, and exchanged several letters with Glasier about the problem. Temperamentally he felt much more drawn to Nonconformist mining Merthyr than to Preston, although both he and Glasier thought he was more likely to do well in Preston. Organization was a problem in both places. The I.L.P. Council recognized in May that it would have to 'force the pace' if it wished Preston to be fought. In Merthyr, despite the I.L.P. campaign of 1898, there was no organization to speak of. The Secretary of the Merthyr Trades Council wrote to MacDonald, as Secretary of the L.R.C., in June asking for 'some information concerning the National Labour Party of which you are Secretary of. I may Say that we are moveing through our Council in bring[ing] out a labour candidate at the next parliamentary election in the Merthyr Boroughs.' In Preston there was no difficulty in getting agreement on Hardie as a candidate. In Merthyr things were very different, as the Trades Council was split between I.L.P.ers and Lib-Lab. 'Nearly the whole of the miners leaders are very strong in their liberalism and we shall have all our work cut out to keep them out of the selected candidate [;] however myself and others are going to make a Stand of I.L.P.ism.' So wrote Dai Davies, the secretary of the Merthyr Trades Council, and it proved an accurate prophecy of events. A selection conference was held on 22 September 1900, attended by about eighty delegates. Nearly half of these were miners, who wanted the nomination for William Brace, the leading South Wales figure in the Miners' Federation of Great Britain. Brace, although a leader of the 1898 strike, was no I.L.P.er and would have sat as a Lib-Lab. His supporters sensed that they were a minority at the meeting and walked out – apparently prematurely, because the rest of the delegates were by no means united behind Hardie. When he had narrowly beaten the other candidates in a vote and his name was put to the meeting for formal endorsement, seven delegates still voted against it. It seems likely that, had Brace's friends been more patient, they would have got him the nomination.

Meanwhile, Hardie was over two hundred miles away, in Preston. It seems clear that he and his advisers had decided to concentrate on the bird in hand. The previous day he had written to one of the Merthyr I.L.P.ers, 'I have decided to accept Preston. It is not likely now that Merthyr will succeed in putting forward a Labour candidate.' When, therefore, the news reached Hardie that he had indeed been nominated at Merthyr, he was placed in an embarrassing position. He decided on the bold decision: to fight both seats. This was not unprecedented: some Irish members, and Mr Gladstone, had on occasion actually won in more than one seat. Preston polled on 1 October, and Merthyr not until the next day, so that it was just possible for Hardie to make an appearance in both places. (He spent two days in Merthyr and the rest of his time at Preston). But it was a very risky decision. Hardie laid himself open to the jibes of his Conservative opponents in Preston ('This gay Lothario is apparently desirous of becoming a political bigamist') while being unable to present himself in person to the voters of Merthyr. He probably still thought he had no real chance of election.

The Preston result was declared on 1 October. Hardie had polled respectably, with 4,834 votes, but was nowhere near his Conservative opponents, who both got over 8,000. Immediately he rushed down to Merthyr, where polling was in progress by the time he arrived. There was no time to do anything except to go round the polling stations in a motor car. It was the first time Hardie had been in one, but it had to be abandoned when it refused to go up the steep hills which hem in and define the Merthyr and Aberdare valleys. When the votes were counted that evening, Hardie was in. The full figures were:

D. A. Thomas (Lib.)	8,508
J. K. Hardie (Ind. Lab.)	5,745
W. P. Morgan (Lib.)	4,004

After the result was announced, Hardie recalled, 'I witnessed a sight I had never hoped to see this side of the pearly gate. My wife was making a speech to the delighted crowd.' It was certainly the only political speech Mrs Hardie ever made.

Hardie thought there were three reasons for his success at Merthyr. One was 'the genuine desire which the great strike left for direct Independent Labour representation'; the second, 'the healthy anti-war sentiment which animated all the better-class Liberals,' and the third, hostility to Pritchard Morgan, the sitting M.P. whom Hardie had ousted. Of these, undoubtedly the most solid reason was the last. D. A. Thomas and W. Pritchard Morgan belonged to the same party, but they were no friends. Far from fighting on a common platform, they attacked each other during the campaign. Thomas was a prominent local man, head of a colliery company; Morgan was a former Conservative from Cardiff, first elected as a Liberal after a free-lance campaign in 1888. Since 1895 his relations with Thomas had been very bad. Morgan spent little time in the Commons and none in the constituency, but a great deal in China, where he had extensive business interests. These did not endear him to the Merthyr electorate when Thomas claimed to have unearthed a boast by Morgan to shareholders that he could mine Chinese coal at a shilling a ton. Since South Wales coal was largely mined for export, this was a very damaging accusation. The published list of votes makes it clear what happened in the election:

Votes for Thomas alone:	2,070
Votes for Morgan alone:	1,472
Votes for Hardie alone:	867
Votes for Thomas and Hardie:	4,437
Votes for Thomas and Morgan:	2,091
Votes for Hardie and Morgan:	441

Clearly it was not the demand for socialism that ensured Hardie's election. As at West Ham, socialism hardly appeared in his election address, which concluded grandly, 'My cause is the cause of Labour – the cause of Humanity – the cause of God.' Hardie won because twice as many electors saw Thomas plus Hardie as the Liberal 'ticket' as supported Thomas and Morgan together. Thomas unambiguously asked the voters to support himself and Hardie.

Hardie, then, had two great strokes of luck: first, the withdrawal of the miners from the selection conference on 22 September, which left him unexpectedly in possession of the field; secondly, the disharmony between the two Liberal members. A third, minor, asset was the absence of a Conservative candidate. Then, as now, the valleys of South Wales were about the most inhospitable places in Britain for Conservatives, so they always had difficulty in finding candidates. After much searching the Conservative Whips in 1900 found Arnott Reid, *The Times* correspondent in Singapore, who was willing to stand in Merthyr. The Chief Whip told the local Conservatives that he was 'a good speaker and fighter, and a man well suited to a mining constituency'. What happened then must be told in Hardie's words, from his account in the *Labour Leader*.

He [Reid] had set out from the Carlton Club on his journey, but . . . ere he reached the station he had forgotten the name of the constituency for which he was bound. He knew it to be a colliery district, and concluded it must be in the neighbourhood of Newcastle, to which place he accordingly took a ticket. Finding himself stranded there, and that all the constituencies already had candidates, he wired the Carlton for information, and was advised that Merthyr was in Wales, somewhere near Cardiff.

Reid thereupon went to Cardiff, and went to the *Western Mail* office to issue his manifesto. The *Merthyr Express* takes up the tale.

> He was still in Cardiff at eleven o'clock, and when someone asked if he wasn't going up to Merthyr to get nominated, he asked, in surprise, 'Merthyr? Isn't this Merthyr?'

Sadly, he did not get to Merthyr until after the close of nominations. The only relic of his campaign was the manifesto, which the *Merthyr Express*, with amused tolerance, thought 'would rank for all time amongst the curiosities of electoral literature'. It was an amazingly tactless and inappropriate document, which extolled Reid's life, loves, and commercial dealings on two continents, and assured the electorate that they were 'ignorant, knowing only Wales. I know the world.' It was a tragi-comedy: Reid died not long afterwards, from the effects of sunstroke contracted on the voyage from Singapore.

While Hardie was fighting Preston and Merthyr, a number of other Labour candidatures were under way. After Barnsley, the I.L.P. was determined to avoid any more fights in inappropriate seats. In 1899 the N.A.C. recommended that the party should contest not more than 25 seats at the next General Election, a proposal which the next I.L.P. conference accepted. But during 1900 the war and the party's poverty – it was virtually bankrupt – delayed the process of nomination. In the event, the I.L.P. fought only eight seats, including both Preston and Merthyr, and one seat was fought by a joint I.L.P. and S.D.F. candidate. The drastic reduction in the number of seats fought from 1895 did the I.L.P. no real harm, as it concentrated on its best seats, and had no results as bad as its 'tail' of hopeless fights in 1895. In most of the seats it was fighting for the second time, the I.L.P. improved on its previous position (and in Halifax, it did better than in 1897, though not so well as in 1895 or 1893). In four seats – Preston, Merthyr, Manchester South-West, and Blackburn, fought by Philip Snowden, the I.L.P. produced good results at its first attempt.

The reduced number of I.L.P. contests was partly counterbalanced by six other independent labour contests under the umbrella of the Labour Representation Committee – one sponsored by the S.D.E., one by a trades council, and four by trade unions. It was these four which showed most promise. Trade unions, being cautious with their members' money, were not going to waste their funds and their efforts.

But if the number of contests was depressingly small, the figures were excellent. Three of the union-sponsored candidates came close to winning; John Hodge of the Steel Smelters (helped by Hardie after the Merthyr fight was over) in a straight fight with a Liberal in Gower, Will Thorne against a Conservative in South West Ham, and Wilkie of the Shipwrights in alliance with a Liberal against two Conservatives in the two-member seat of Sunderland. The fourth union candidate did win. Richard Bell, secretary of the A.S.R.S., won Derby, the headquarters of the Midland Railway, in dual harness with a Liberal.

Now that the I.L.P. no longer bore the sole burden of promoting Labour candidatures, the strain on its finances and organization was much reduced. The problems had not vanished, however; they had merely shifted. The I.L.P. had managed, by clever manipulation, to gain an influence greatly disproportionate to its size on the L.R.C. But could it keep any control over the larger body? Could it hope to convert it to socialist ideas? What sort of control could be exercised over trade-union M.P.s, elected under the L.R.C. banner? Was the parliamentary party to be able to implement the policy which Hardie had persuaded the first L.R.C. conference to accept – namely a 'distinct Labour Group in Parliament, who shall have their own Whips'? The vital years from 1900 to 1906 were to see the first hints of answers to these questions.

5

THE YEARS OF
THE L.R.C.
1900–1906

Hardie always saw himself as a propagandist in
Parliament, not a party leader. In 1892 he had been the sole independent labour member, and it would have been impossible for him to
have used his membership in any other way than he did – making
propagandist speeches about working-class grievances, nagging the
Local Government Board, and so on. In 1900 things were not very
different. There was no question of forming a Parliamentary Labour
Party out of the two Labour M.P.s – Hardie and Bell. Hardie regarded
the Labour Party essentially as a single-issue pressure group. As the
Irish Party was a minority group which effectively pressed the claims
of Ireland, so Hardie envisaged a minority Labour Party to bring the

grievances of the working class before Parliament. As late as 1905 his vision of the future Labour Party was still modest: he hoped labour would become an 'influence second in importance only to that of the Irish Nationalist Party'. At one point he even saw the advent of labour as part of the break-up of party politics as such, in favour of a 'group system in the House of Commons'. Hardie had in mind what some modern reformers have called a system of 'functional representation', where M.P.s represented interests such as Labour and the Irish, rather than constituencies. On this, Hardie's views were not so very different from those of the Lib-Labs, who also saw the role of labour in Parliament as being a working-class pressure-group. Neither they nor Hardie saw the implications of electoral arithmetic. Already in 1900 the majority of the voters were working-class, and any franchise reform would increase this proportion. There were far more workers than there were Irishmen in the British Isles, so the party representing the workers ought to be, potentially, a party of government. But Hardie never saw the Labour Party in this light.

Hardie's view of himself as a lobbyist rather than a politician in a broader sense may help to explain his curious attitude to the question of parliamentary leadership. Outside the House of Commons, Hardie was the unchallenged leader of the fiercely independent I.L.P. In the parliamentary context, he could be astonishingly deferential to two unlikely men: John Morley and John Burns.

Hardie's last brush with Morley had been his attack on him in 1892 on account of Morley's refusal to support the Miners' Eight-Hours Bill. But by 1900 the political scene had changed. The Eight-Hours Bill, though still a hardy annual, was no longer Hardie's leading political passion; and Morley stood out as the most uncompromisingly pro-Boer of the Liberal leaders. Perhaps it was this which prompted Hardie, in June 1900, to make a quite uncharacteristic appeal to Morley to be leader of the Labour Party. In an 'open letter', published in the *Labour Leader*, Hardie wrote to Morley:

You are now, Sir, at the banks of your Rubicon. Will you cross? . . . There is no other man in politics to whom the democracy can look for a lead . . . A section of very earnest Radicals are thoroughly ashamed of modern Liberalism, and anxious to put themselves right with their own conscience; working-class movements are coming together . . . Already 212,000 Trade Unionists have paid the affiliation fee to the Labour Representation Committee. What is wanted to fuse these elements is a man with the brain to dare, the hand to do, and the heart to inspire. Will you be that man?
> I am,
> Yours respectfully,
> J. Keir Hardie.

Morley did not reply. But Hardie's deferential approach was not a mere aberration arising out of his and Morley's common position as pro-Boers. This may be seen from Hardie's extensive attempts to enlist John Burns as the leader of independent labour.

Hardie's relations with Burns had previously been stormy, and had reached their nadir at the T.U.C. standing orders row in 1894 and 1895, when Burns's hatred for Hardie made him willing to sacrifice his own position in order to keep Hardie out. Hardie felt no friendlier towards Burns at this time. But it was not long before he started to cultivate Burns. In 1897 he wrote to David Lowe, reporting a long conversation with Burns: 'He is very 'Umble, and sorry he is not in the I.L.P. . . . I think he will come over. It would be excellent business at this juncture'. The forecast was not borne out; Burns remained aloof. He did attend the foundation conference of the L.R.C., and there made a sardonic speech saying that he had had enough of working-class trains, working-class margarine, and now a working-class party; a contribution which might be taken as a criticism of either Hardie or the Lib-Labs, according to taste.

After the 1900 General Election, Hardie renewed his efforts, sometimes working through Liberal intermediaries, to get Burns to come out into the open as leader of the Labour Party. Again Hardie's deference seems out of character with his behaviour as leader of the I.L.P. In December 1900, writing of his failure to receive notification of a December session of Parliament, he went on: 'Leaders of Parties . . . send out notices to their followers announcing when Parliament is to meet, and the fact that John Burns has not yet taken to fulfilling this part of his duties accounts for my having been unsummoned.' Reporting to the 1901 Conference of the I.L.P., Hardie stressed that he thought it was up to Burns to take the initiative in forming a Labour group in the House of Commons, since 'his ability, experience, and position in the Labour movement mark him out as the political head of such a movement'. This was uncharacteristically modest. Hardie was the same age as Burns and had been no later in starting his political career – Hardie had first come to public notice in 1888, and Burns in 1889. Only failing any initiative by Burns, Hardie argued, should he and Bell take any action.

The whole episode seems out of character for Hardie. Perhaps he was already worried that Bell would be an unreliable colleague; perhaps he was diffident about his own ability to act as a party leader, seeing himself as a pressure-group leader rather than a parliamentarian in a broader sense. Whatever the reason, Hardie took no effective action to form a parliamentary Labour group until after three

D

Labour by-election victories in 1902 and 1903. On his own initiative he was not prepared to take action in support of the proposal he had so deftly steered through the founding conference of the L.R.C. – for a 'distinct Labour Group with their own Whips'. Bernard Shaw, in his supercilious way, made a shrewd point when he described a Fabian meeting where Hardie 'had attacked the Fabians as being leaders with no followers, whereupon I had deplored the predicament of a movement hung up between two Societies, one of which consisted of leaders with no followers, and the other of followers with no leaders'.

Hardie's work in Parliament in the first two or three years after 1900 closely resembled his activities in the Parliament of 1892. As before, there was a steady stream of parliamentary questions, mostly about workmen's grievances, although Hardie's catholic taste for protest also led him to complain about the alleged ill-treatment of albatrosses on ships bound for Australia, and the lack of accommodation for cyclists in the trains of a proposed electric railway under the Tyne between North and South Shields. The Miners' Eight-Hours Bill made its annual appearance, always getting a second reading and rarely getting any further. In February 1901 Hardie spoke more in sorrow than in anger of the opposition of Charles Fenwick to the bill: 'If the angels of heaven do weep, it must be when a representative of working men . . . draws forth the enthusiastic cheers of employers of labour in opposing a measure which is introduced for the benefit of working men.' But the attack had lost its old verve. Hardie was fully resigned to the fact that the Northumberland miners' leaders would continue, as long as they were able, to obstruct the Miners' Eight-Hours Bill.

Also in character, and widely reported, was Hardie's speech on Queen Victoria's funeral in 1901. Hardie again made himself the spokesman of British radicalism against the grain of conventional opinion. He complained about the 'sickening sycophancy' of the press: 'the columns of graphic lying about London's tears and the nation's mourning are simply the products of a diseased imagination.' He went on to deplore the fact that the funeral of the Queen, a lover of 'domestic simplicity', was taken to be an occasion for military pomp. It was reminiscent of the Royal Baby speech of 1894, but it was less effective and had less impact. Few people believed Hardie's contention that the Queen would have disapproved of military pomp and (by implication) the Boer War itself; and Hardie, being honest with himself, knew very well that the British working class in no way shared his anti-war republicanism.

Another occasion of some note was Hardie's motion on behalf of a

Socialist Commonwealth on 23 April 1901. Having secured a lowly place on the ballot for private members' bills, Hardie had half an hour before a midnight adjournment to present his blueprint. His speech was received with tolerant curiosity. It was by no means a call to the barricades. After presenting some (slightly dubious) statistics about the unchanging poverty of the poor and the growth of monopolistic trusts, Hardie went on to say that though his motion had no prospect of immediate success, still 'the last has not been heard of the socialist movement either in the country or on the floor of this House'. The reactionary Conservative Sir Frederick Banbury had only to speak for two or three minutes before the motion was talked out without a vote.

Hardie was uneasily conscious that his impact in Parliament was lessening. As he said to Glasier, 'Somehow none of us seem to have the grit and go of former years. Would to God the Liberals were again in office. Then we could make things hum once more'. For two reasons it was harder to make an impression under a Tory than a Liberal Government. There was little to differentiate Hardie's attacks on the Government from those of the orthodox Liberals sitting around him, whereas his position in 1892, as an independent member attacking a Liberal Government, had been much more distinctive. And there was less reason for the Government, on its side, to pay any attention to Hardie's attacks. Hardie and independent labour represented a potential electoral threat to a Liberal Government, but were of no consequence to a Conservative one.

During the years 1900 to 1902 Hardie was again plagued with worries about finance and accommodation. From 1892 to 1895 he had stayed with Frank Smith, who would accept no money from him. After 1900 this was no longer possible, and Hardie, with no regular source of income, found himself close to bankruptcy. He had not only to feed and clothe himself in London, but also to provide such items as tea on the terrace of the House of Commons for constituents and guests, which was a small hospitality to them but a major item of expenditure to Hardie, costing him up to £2 a week. Further, like every Welsh M.P., Hardie was constantly being cajoled to give subscriptions to numerous chapels in his constituency. Matters only started to improve when a fund was started in 1901, within the I.L.P., to pay Hardie a parliamentary salary. Originally a semi-private arrangement started at the initiative of H. Russell Smart, the fund was taken over officially by the I.L.P. when Smart's organization of it proved unsatisfactory. After this Hardie always had a regular, though scarcely generous, income. He took an attic flat in Nevill's Court, off Fleet Street, which became his London home for the rest of his life and was a favourite port of call for visiting I.L.P.ers and foreign socialists – as was the slightly more salubrious London home of Ramsay MacDonald, a few blocks away in Lincoln's Inn Fields.

The most important events of these years, however, were taking place outside Parliament. Although Hardie had a constituency connection with the Taff Vale affair, he took no active part in it. However, it must be sketched in here, as it is essential to understanding the growth of the Labour Party after 1900. In August 1900 there was a strike of signalmen on the Taff Vale Railway, a small line which waxed rich by carrying coal from pits in Merthyr Vale and adjoining valleys down to Cardiff for export. The strike spread to other grades of railwaymen on the line. The company's general manager, an aggressive opponent of trade unionism, introduced a large number of 'free labourers' or blacklegs to try to get the trains moving. The A.S.R.S. distributed a leaflet inviting these men to call at union headquarters for 'information and assistance'. This strategy was successful in the short run, but disastrous in the long term. In September 1900 the company obtained an injunction against the A.S.R.S. on account of the damage done to its interests by the union's leaflet.

If previous cases had threatened to breach the unions' immunity to civil action arising out of industrial disputes, this opened the floodgates. Counsel to the T.U.C., which was in session at the time, described the judgment as 'one of the most dangerous things ever done against Trade Unions'. Trade unionists were therefore relieved when Mr Justice Farwell's decision against the union was overturned by the Court of Appeal in November 1900; but the company announced its intention of appealing to the House of Lords, and the legal machinery ground slowly but inexorably on. To the surprise and dismay of the world of labour, the judgment of the five Law Lords, delivered in July 1901, was unanimously hostile to the A.S.R.S. The Appeal Court ruling was overturned, and the original decision of Mr Justice Farwell upheld. The highest legal authority in the land was given to the view that the A.S.R.S.'s very mild leaflet was 'most improper . . . a distinct threat', in Farwell's words. If such a leaflet was sufficient authority for an employer to sue a union, then virtually any industrial action could put a union in the same position. Having been given the authority to sue the union for damages, the Taff Vale company proceeded to do so, and in December 1902 it obtained judgement for a sum of £23,000, including its own costs; it was estimated that the A.S.R.S.'s costs amounted to almost as much again.

The Taff Vale case sounded the death-knell of Lib-Labbery. Had it not been for Taff Vale, the L.R.C. might have gone the way of the

Labour Electoral Association and earlier bodies of the same sort, and
become an ineffective appendage of the Liberal Party. But Taff Vale
convinced trade unionists that the need for labour representation was
more urgent than ever before. Hardie did not omit to rub the message
in. He said to an audience of A.S.R.S. members in 1902, 'Do you suppose for one moment that if these decisions had been given, not against
the respectable, easy-going trade-union movement of Great Britain,
but against the United Irish League, we would not have heard of the
matter in the House of Commons?' For all the success of Hardie and
Bell at the 1900 election, the L.R.C. had started life as a sickly child.
Only forty-one unions, affiliating on a membership of just over
350,000, supported the Committee in early 1901; this represented 29
per cent of the membership of the T.U.C. A year later, after the House
of Lords decision on Taff Vale, the affiliated membership had risen to
over 450,000, which was 32 per cent of T.U.C. membership. And by
January 1903, after the A.S.R.S. had actually paid over its cheque,
affiliation had nearly doubled: it stood at nearly 850,000, representing
56 per cent of the membership of the T.U.C. Thus by 1903 the L.R.C.
stood in roughly the same relationship to the T.U.C. as does the
modern Labour Party: today, the membership of the T.U.C. is about
$8\frac{1}{2}$ million, and the number of trade unionists affiliated through their
union to the Labour Party is about $5\frac{1}{2}$ million. This was a transfor-
mation of great importance. The trade unions were taking a decisive
step down the road to independent labour representation. It is ironic
to reflect that Ammon Beasley, the union-hating general manager of
the Taff Vale Railway Company, played an essential part in the foundation of the Labour Party.

The new, invigorated L.R.C. had its first opportunity to show its
teeth when, in the summer of 1902, a parliamentary vacancy arose in a
seat dominated by the cotton industry – the Clitheroe division of
Lancashire. Much of Lancashire was Conservative, but Clitheroe was a
strong Liberal outpost. This helped the L.R.C., as did the fact that a
local version of the Taff Vale case had recently been fought and lost by
the local weavers' union in Blackburn. The I.L.P. wanted to put up
Philip Snowden for Clitheroe. But the local weavers had other ideas:
they favoured David Shackleton, a union official, local councillor, and
magistrate. Special committees of both the I.L.P. Executive and the
L.R.C. discussed the position, and Hardie attended both. The I.L.P.
persuaded Snowden to withdraw in favour of Shackleton, whom the
L.R.C. endorsed. The favoured Liberal candidate, who was a pro-Boer
radical, then said he was not prepared to fight Shackleton, and, after
several days of trying, the Liberals were unable to find a substitute.

The Conservatives were also without a champion; and thus, on 1 August 1902, David Shackleton was elected unopposed as Labour M.P. for Clitheroe.

Despite any appearances to the contrary, this was a result of enormous significance. Shackleton was no socialist; temperamentally he was poles apart from Hardie. Lancashire weavers, like North-Eastern miners, were opposed to limitations on children's hours of labour, because the parents of young 'half-timers' working at the mills could add the children's wages to their own. Shackleton therefore spoke against any attempt, on humanitarian grounds, to abolish the 'half-timer' system. He would genially point to his own ample proportions to show that being a half-timer did not necessarily do a child any harm when he grew up. He seemed an inappropriate parliamentary colleague for Keir Hardie. But Hardie joined in and approved of the I.L.P. move to withdraw Snowden in favour of Shackleton. Hardie appreciated the value of the trade-union connection in the L.R.C., and did not want to alienate unionists by forcing socialism on them, Clitheroe was a trade-union seat, because trade unions were going to pay the candidate's costs. Shackleton differed from the Lib-Labs in only one respect: he was elected as L.R.C. candidate and he would not describe himself in public as a Liberal. It might seem, therefore, that he was very much closer to the Lib-Labs than to Hardie. But Hardie knew (at least sometimes) when to forgo socialist principles in favour of parliamentary advantage, and he knew that the accession of Shackleton would greatly strengthen his own position. This was especially true in that Bell was showing signs of an absorption into the Liberal ranks that would be complete by 1904. For the moment the cohesion and credibility of the L.R.C. were more important than socialism. This was, perhaps, signified by the decision of the L.R.C., in September 1902, that any future Labour candidate should be required to sign the Committee's constitution before being officially endorsed. The constitution committed candidates to independence, but not to socialism.

Two months after Clitheroe there came another opportunity to put an L.R.C. nominee into Parliament, in which Hardie was again involved, but this time the attempt went badly wrong. The Cleveland division of North Yorkshire looked in some ways to be a promising Labour prospect. It contained a large number of ironstone miners – perhaps as many as 8,000 – and their union was affiliated to the L.R.C. It surrounded the most spectacular boom-town of nineteenth-century Britain, namely Middlesbrough, which had been created from nothing at the mouth of the Tees by the coming of the railways and the growth

of the iron industry. Middlesbrough had returned Havelock Wilson
as an independent Labour M.P. (of a sort) in 1892. Cleveland was
traditionally Liberal; it was also traditionally in the hands of the
Pease family of Quaker industrialists, who had founded the Stockton
and Darlington Railway. Sir A. E. Pease retired as member for Cleveland in 1902; Hardie and the L.R.C. set about trying to find a Labour
candidate. The obvious contender was Joseph Toyn, the miners'
secretary, who was in a similar position in Cleveland to Shackleton's
in Clitheroe. But Toyn lacked Shackleton's force of personality, and
declined to stand as an independent Labour candidate. A succession of
misfortunes dogged Hardie's attempts to get one. The office arrangements were bungled by a stand-in secretary at the L.R.C. (Ramsay
MacDonald being away in South Africa) and Hardie him. elf was in
poor health. This may have been why he and his L.R.C. colleagues
singularly failed to influence a meeting of trade-union delegates at
Guisborough, which was called to select a Labour candidate. Con-
fusion was caused after the name of Herbert Samuel was suggested
from the floor and accepted by a majority of those present. This led
Hardie to deliver a brusque lecture on political principles, according
to one newspaper report:

> 'The motion is out of order', declared Mr Hardie. 'A good deal of educ-
> ation is still required in Cleveland', he proceeded, 'and the best thing is to
> agree to a resolution closing the meeting. It is quite evident that there is a
> section in the constituency who has made up its mind [*sic*] to support the
> rich man (cries of "No, No") at the expense of its fellows.'

Samuel was a radical, but he was certainly not a labour candidate. He
was endorsed by the Liberals and won the seat in the by-election.

This was a time when the L.R.C. could ill afford tactical defeats like
Cleveland, and Hardie looked as if had been outmanoeuvred by the
'old guard'. The L.R.C. was internally split between a Lib-Lab faction led by Alex Wilkie and an I.L.P. faction led by Pete Curran.
Wilkie and Curran both laid claim to the Labour nomination at
Jarrow, where the imminent death of the sitting Liberal member was
confidently (but wrongly) expected. In addition, the T.U.C., although
it had sponsored the L.R.C., was showing some disturbing signs of
turning its back on it – even in spite of Taff Vale. The leadership of
Congress was looking to Sir Charles Dilke, the prominent radical, and
to Burns to be its parliamentary lobbyists; Hardie frequently complained in the *Labour Leader* that the T.U.C. was ignoring its own
parliamentary representatives, the L.R.C. members. Furthermore, a
number of labour politicians, united by little beyond a common dis-
taste for Keir Hardie, were promoting a body called the National

Democratic League, which, it was hoped, would quietly supplant the L.R.C. as the political arm of trade-unionism. Richard Bell was drifting farther and farther away from Hardie and into the arms of the Liberal Party.

In the early months of 1903 the tide turned sharply. At the end of 1902 the very future of the L.R.C. looked in doubt – it might just have quietly withered away, like the Labour Electoral Association before it. By the end of 1903 it possessed four M.P.s, united as a parliamentary group with a Whip and a secretary; it also possessed the priceless asset of a secret electoral pact with the Liberals carving up working-class seats in England and Wales between the two parties. The National Democratic League had vanished into the shadows, and the T.U.C. was working closely with the L.R.C. in drafting a parliamentary bill to reverse the effects of Taff Vale on the legal position of trade unions. Hardie was not solely responsible for this turn of events – indeed he was not even the leading actor in them. But, as they were so vital for the future success of the Labour Party, some account of them must be given.

An important first step was the clarification of the aims and methods of the L.R.C. at its Annual Conference, held in Newcastle in February. Almost the whole conference was devoted to constitutional matters, and it concluded with agreement on a revised constitution which considerably tightened up the terms and conditions of independence from other parties. Candidates must 'strictly abstain' from supporting any Liberal or Conservative, and must sign a pledge of their consent to this constitution. The composition of the executive was also changed, and the marked over-representation which the I.L.P. had secured in 1900 was annulled. This was no longer as serious a blow to the I.L.P. as it might have been, because the L.R.C. had already been successfully pushed in the direction the I.L.P. wanted it to go. The tightening up of the constitution was itself an achievement of the I.L.P.ers, which outweighed the effects of the drop in their representation in the executive.

While the conference was in session, it was announced that a by-election was to be held at Woolwich. Here there was no chance of a repetition of the Cleveland fiasco, because a local Labour Representation Committee had already selected Will Crooks, a popular local figure who was a Progressive member of the London County Council, to be their candidate. Like Shackleton, Crooks was no socialist; but he stood as a Labour candidate, and was not opposed by the Liberals. In fact, Liberalism was notoriously weak in London; like a surprisingly large number of other working-class seats in and around London,

Woolwich was a Conservative stronghold. The Liberals had fought neither at the General Election of 1900 nor at a previous by-election in 1902. The home of Woolwich Arsenal was not perhaps a good place in which to raise the pro-Boer standard. But Crooks convincingly broke the Conservative grip on the constituency; a Conservative majority of nearly 3,000 the last time the seat had been contested was turned into a Labour majority of over 3,000. Woolwich had a special moral, which was not lost on Hardie. It was an example of a place where an independent Labour candidate who could capture the votes of Tory working men was at an electoral advantage compared to a Liberal who could not. This could be of strategic importance in areas of the country where a substantial proportion of working-class voters voted Conservative – especially in Lancashire and London.

Will Crooks was extremely popular in the labour movement, and later carved out a reputation as the licensed jester of the House of Commons. But he was no serious parliamentarian, and this was speedily demonstrated by a disastrous maiden speech. Hardie and Burns, who were sitting quite amicably together, listening in their roles of elder statesmen of the labour movement, clucked mournfully over Crooks' 'positively painful' speech and assured each other that they would not have done so badly. However, within a further two months a much more significant figure was to appear among the ranks of Labour parliamentarians.

The sprawling Durham constituency of Barnard Castle shared two characteristics with Cleveland – mineral workings and Peases. Indeed, a Pease had been member for the area ever since 1832, with a gap of only sixteen years – a truly remarkable record. For the General Election of 1900, Sir Joseph Pease, the Liberal member, had as his election agent an active Methodist called Arthur Henderson, who was secretary of the ironfounders' union and had been a Newcastle city councillor. It was an open secret that Henderson had political ambitions of his own. Like Shackleton and Crooks, he was essentially a Lib-Lab by temperament, and there was no love lost between him and the I.L.P. Bruce Glasier, for instance, wrote to Hardie to report on a local L.R.C. meeting in Durham which Henderson had addressed. 'Arthur Henderson . . . declared that nothing but Independence would do: concluding with an appeal to *us* to let bygones be bygones with the Old Trade Unionists (i.e. such as himself) for this was a new movement. He is, I fear, a sleek backboneless customer.' It was to be several years before it became clear that Glasier's judgement as to the strength of Henderson's backbone was badly wrong. But as even this sour appraisal indicates, Henderson now backed the L.R.C. for tactical reasons, if not for ideological ones. As he was still Sir Joseph Pease's election agent, any inclination on his part to desert the Liberals could be politically very embarrassing.

The first hints of a by-election came early in 1903, when gossip columnists whispered of financial difficulties which had led to Pease's abrupt retirement as Chairman of the North-Eastern Railway. Whether or not the rumours were true, Pease did announce that he intended to resign from Parliament, although he took no immediate steps to carry out his intention. In April, Henderson – still Pease's agent – was selected as prospective Labour candidate. The local Liberals were stung into action. The leaders of the Liberal Party in the North-East of England were more hostile to independent labour representation than their counterparts anywhere else. Outside the mining seats, local Liberal associations were flatly opposed to accepting working-class candidates, and Arthur Henderson himself had been rejected as a potential Liberal candidate in Newcastle in 1895. Samuel Storey, in 1903 a leading North-East Liberal (though later a recruit to Chamberlainite Unionism), warned his colleagues against 'coquetting' with Socialism, on the grounds that the Liberals would eventually be swallowed up by the socialists. It is not surprising, therefore, that immediately Henderson announced that he would be fighting Barnard Castle, the Liberals nominated a rival candidate. Their candidate, a protégé of Storey, shared (unfortunately as it turned out) his enthusiasm for Joseph Chamberlain's campaign for Protection, which was at the time wreaking havoc in the Conservative Party. While all this was going on, Henderson was drafted across the Pennines to act as Labour agent in a by-election at Preston, where the Labour candidate came much closer than Hardie in 1900 to defeating the Conservatives. Nevertheless, the I.L.P. thought the result was disappointing, and tended to blame what was regarded as Henderson's incompetence.

In public, however, all was amity in the Labour camp when the question of Barnard Castle was brought to a head by the sudden death of Pease in June 1903. The by-election was a three-cornered one, but much local Liberal opinion, including the Press, was backing Henderson all but openly, on account of the Protectionist views of the official Liberal. This may have helped Henderson to win by the narrow margin of 47, from the Conservative, with the official Liberal some way behind.

Thus by July 1903 the L.R.C. could be publicly seen to be much strengthened by its by-election victories, two of which had introduced potential parliamentary heavyweights into the Commons.

What was not publicly known was that the L.R.C.'s position had been still further strengthened by a secret deal, to which only Hardie and Ramsay MacDonald among the Labour leaders were parties.

Hardie's attitude to pacts and deals was still tantalizingly elusive. Indeed, he sometimes gave the impression of having different opinions for the benefit of different audiences. He was unflinching in his opposition to any coalition between the Independent Labour and the Lib-Lab M.P.s, and denounced proposals along these lines made by, for example, Robert Blatchford. Yet, perhaps surprisingly, he made overtures to radical Liberals in a series of open letters which he wrote in the *Labour Leader*, the most striking of which was addressed to Lloyd George. Hardie appealed to Lloyd George to spurn the temptations of Cabinet office in a future Liberal government in favour of the leadership of a radical coalition which would break away from the 'Whiggish' liberalism of Lord Rosebery and his Liberal-Imperialist friends. Hardie apparently envisaged a radical coalition of the eighty-five or so Irish members, fifty Labour M.P.s and twenty-five radical Liberals under the overall leadership of Lloyd George. This, he thought, would have the effect of forcing Whigs and Tories to come together against this new threat, thus re-drawing the lines of party politics. Again we may note Hardie's diffident tendency to regard himself as a labour leader rather than a political leader. Lloyd George, not Keir Hardie, was to be the parliamentary leader of the new radical coalition. Returning to more everyday politics, Hardie endorsed the nomination of a Labour candidate for the two-member seat of York (despite a complaint from Glasier that the man chosen was an unknown and undistinguished trade unionist), and called on the Liberals to nominate only one. When the next election came round, the Liberals did precisely this. Their reasons, however, were not connected with any published appeals by Hardie in the *Labour Leader*. Their actions were determined by the much more important secret negotiations which were going on at the same time.

At the beginning of 1903 the Liberal Party had still not fully recovered from the defeats of 1895 and 1900. The Boer War had exacerbated an already serious split between the two main factions. On one side stood Rosebery, Sir Edward Grey, and Asquith – the 'Liberal Imperialists' who favoured the war; on the other Lloyd George and Morley, leading a pro-Boer faction. Campbell-Bannerman, the party leader, was much closer in sympathy to the pro-Boers than to the Liberal Imperialists. In 1903 the serious splits in the Conservative Party arising out of Chamberlain's tariff campaign were beginning to become evident; accordingly Liberal Party managers decided that it was high time they improved their own party's fitness to fight elections. They could not do anything about the main division in the party. But they could attempt to settle the nagging side-issue of labour representation in a way that would be of advantage to both parties. Therefore the Liberal Chief Whip, Herbert Gladstone (the youngest son of W.E.Gladstone) began cautious negotiations with the secretary of the L.R.C., Ramsay MacDonald. Gladstone asked MacDonald to supply him with a list of constituencies the L.R.C. intended to fight at the next election, and engaged in preliminary discussions about a pact. Hardie was kept fully informed, but so far as is known no Liberal other than Herbert Gladstone was involved in drawing up the pact, although once drawn up it had to be sanctioned by Campbell-Bannerman. After a more formal meeting with Mac-Donald, in March 1903, Gladstone submitted to Campbell-Bannerman a list, divided into four categories, of seats in which agreements might be made between the Liberal Party and the L.R.C. In twenty-three seats, Gladstone thought, there was 'no difficulty'. Nine of these were double-member boroughs (including York) where Liberals and Labour could put up one candidate each; a number of the rest were Conservative-held. A further five constituencies Gladstone regarded as 'adjustable'; four of these were double-member seats. Five seats were 'claimed by the L.R.C. and difficult'; however, Gladstone listed six 'available alternatives' to them.

This was the MacDonald-Gladstone pact: after the Taff Vale decision perhaps the most momentous event in the early history of the Labour Party. But as things stood in 1903 it was by no means certain that it would come to anything. First, there was the problem of secrecy. If the pact should leak out – if the single-minded enthusiasts of either party should even guess that it existed – then it was doomed. It would almost certainly have to be disavowed by the L.R.C. under pressure from its I.L.P. wing. For this reason MacDonald went to elaborate and conspiratorial lengths, in his correspondence with Herbert Gladstone's secretary, to vet meeting-places for himself and Gladstone so that no journalist might get even the least hint that they were talking to each other. But this cloak-and-dagger behaviour would be in vain if members of the Liberal Party or L.R.C. supporters came to suspect the existence of a pact because they found pressure being put on them not to put up candidates in seats which had been assigned to the other party.

The Liberal side was worried about Keir Hardie. Ramsay Mac-Donald they could trust. He spoke their language, he understood their

problems; he had once – after all – been secretary to a Liberal M.P.
He kept up a political correspondence with Liberal politicians, and
from one of them – Herbert Samuel – he got a confidential letter suggesting that a pact between Labour and the Liberals would be de-
sirable. (In his reply MacDonald gave subtle hints that a pact already
existed.) But Hardie was different. He did not keep up a friendly
correspondence with such as Herbert Samuel. He was much more
abrasive, not averse to biting the hand that fed him. Had not his response to being given a free hand by the Liberals in 1892 been to go
and launch a bitter attack on John Morley? In a word, he was un-
trustworthy. 'I doubt Keir Hardie's good faith', wrote Herbert
Gladstone's secretary. Hardie had only to reveal the existence of the
pact, and all would be lost.

But he did not. It is a tribute to a not often recognized side of
Hardie's character that he was prepared to swallow a deal of which he
almost certainly did disapprove. Even if he did not disapprove of the
pact itself, he must have found it very painful and a considerable
psychological burden to have to tell reassuring lies to every member
of the I.L.P. who suspected that something was afoot with the
Liberals. In later years Hardie was often to be criticized for his failure
to cooperate with his parliamentary colleagues. The criticisms were
no doubt often well deserved. But his cooperation with MacDonald in
enforcing the electoral pact with the Liberals shows that, when it
really mattered, Keir Hardie was perfectly well able to follow his head
rather than his heart.

The hard political problem for both sides was this: how were they
to persuade local enthusiasts not to run candidates in seats assigned
to the other party – without admitting to these (probably somewhat
suspicious) persons that a pact existed? The Liberals reserved the
right to support Liberal candidates in seats assigned to the L.R.C.
under the pact if all efforts to withdraw them failed. Hardie and
MacDonald, likewise, had no real way of stopping a determined local
L.R.C. – let alone a body like the S.D.F. – from fighting seats allocated
to the Liberals. Their usual method was blithely to deny that a pact
existed, and then to point out that, nevertheless, both parties would
benefit greatly if one of them stood down. In one constituency, for
example, Hardie exhorted Labour supporters in 1904:

You can take it for granted that there will be no Liberal candidate in
the field. Although there has been no definite arrangement made at the
Liberal headquarters, and no compact entered into, I think that in the
future the Liberals will try to do away with all three-cornered fights . . .
The Liberals will receive no encouragement from headquarters . . . but

still ... the local Liberals may take the bit between their teeth and bring one out themselves.*

Ramsay MacDonald played a greater part than Hardie in these negotiations; not only was it part of his job as secretary of the L.R.C., but he was temperamentally more suited than Hardie to this sort of negotiation. Hardie, for his part, had once again to concentrate on the changed parliamentary circumstances brought about by the arrival of Crooks, Shackleton, and Henderson in the Commons.

Simple arithmetic might suggest that the Independent Labour strength in the Commons was now five. In fact it was four. Richard Bell had never been a close colleague of Hardie's. He would happily have stood as a Liberal had not his union, the A.S.R.S., insisted that he run under the auspices of the L.R.C. His whole attitude was much less rebellious than Hardie's – much more inclined to work within the system and on good terms with its custodians. Even making Bell chairman of the L.R.C. in 1902 did not halt his drift towards the Liberals. For the first two years of their association Hardie was conciliatory. He knew that he had always to win the confidence of non-socialist trade unionists as well as the socialists of the I.L.P. This may have been why Hardie never pressed the proposal to form a Parliamentary Labour group consisting of himself and Bell. But Hardie was adamant that any bridge-building had to be done by himself, not by Richard Bell. His tolerance ran out in the face of a proposal by Bell, in March 1903, to call a meeting of the 'advanced Radical Section and Labour Members' to consider their parliamentary strategy. This, Hardie acidly informed Bell, was contrary to the constitution of the L.R.C. 'I will not be present and ask you not to again take the unwarrantable liberty of inviting me to any future meetings of the kind.' Bell may have wondered why his action should get such a devastating response, in the light of Hardie's predilection for making grandiose offers to Liberal leaders through the columns of the *Labour Leader*. Bell was apparently only putting into practice what Hardie had advocated in his open letter to Lloyd George. At any rate, the incident marked what was virtually the final break between Hardie and Bell. A rather ghostly 'Labour Group' had been formed at Westminster from Hardie, Bell, and Shackleton, but it could not work effectively because of Bell's flirtation with the Liberals. However, after the Barnard Castle by-election, the Labour group was reconstituted with Hardie, Shackleton, Crooks and Henderson; Bell

---

* Unfortunately we do not know exactly where Hardie said this. The quotation is from a cutting taken from an unidentified newspaper dated 8 December 1904 in the Hardie papers in the National Library of Scotland.

was invited to the first meeting but did not turn up. MacDonald, although not yet an M.P., was secretary of the group.

The existence of a Labour group added a little, but not very much, to Hardie's parliamentary effectiveness. Being a formal group entitled the Labour members to be officially recognized as a party by the Speaker. None the less, the Labour members relatively rarely got a hearing on the burning issues of the day, such as Free Trade *versus* Protection; and even when they did, their contribution was by no means distinctive. They merely shared the conventional Liberal view that Protection was something which produced dear food because of tariffs and other nations' retaliation – the 'little loaf' in place of the 'big loaf'. One measure in which Hardie took a more active part, however, was the Aliens Bill of 1905. This measure, aimed at keeping 'foreign paupers' out of the country, was the product of anti-Jewish agitation, notably in the East End of London. Hardie, like other Labour leaders, was by no means free of anti-semitism himself. Like many on the left, he believed that the South African War had largely been caused by the manipulations of Jewish capitalists on the Rand. But in 1905 there had been no such thing as Nazism; nobody therefore thought there was anything particularly deplorable in anti-semitism. The Jewish plutocrat was an automatic stereotype – a bogeyman for the left, in the same way as, for instance, the U.S. imperialist in the 1960s. None the less, on the Aliens Bill, Hardie's humanitarianism overrode any anti-Jewish sentiments he may have felt. He claimed (somewhat optimistically) that the Bill had no working-class support, and condemned the Government for trying to keep out Jewish refugees from Tsarist autocracy in Poland, which was under Russian rule at the time. These men, said Hardie, were 'to be condemned by the Bill to remain in a country that does not know how to treat them'.

Hardie's oldest parliamentary concern – unemployment – did get some consideration from the Balfour Government. It promised to introduce an Unemployed Workmen Act in 1904, and eventually did so, after much prevarication, in August 1905. It was a rather feeble measure, not surprisingly, since Balfour's considered view was that it would be an 'absolutely fatal admission' that it was 'the duty of the State to find remunerative work for everyone desiring it'. But the Act no doubt owed something to the ceaseless pressure from the labour lobby, ranging from Hardie's parliamentary questions to mass demonstrations of the unemployed in the streets, which were, after a lull, again making themselves felt. Hardie's attitude to these demonstrations was curiously ambivalent. Most of the demonstrations were organized by the S.D.F., and Hardie was an outspoken opponent of that party's class-war ideas. He had a rooted aversion to violence of any sort. But in the Commons he asked Balfour whether the marches by the unemployed should not hasten the Government in introducing their Bill, to receive the stern and righteous rebuke that the arrangements of the House of Commons were not to be interfered with at the behest of a group of demonstrators. Interestingly, it was Crooks who intervened to reiterate Hardie's question in a more mollifying way. Later, Hardie caused a considerable stir when he sent a highly belligerent telegram to a group of demonstrators in Manchester who had been dispersed by the police on 1 August 1905. The telegram ran:

> Hearty congratulations. The spirit of the Peterloo massacre* is again upon the authorities. So, too is the spirit of revolt which then wrenched the Reform Bill from a reactionary Government, a spirit which is strong in the working classes and neither bludgeons nor prisons can destroy it. As our fathers won then we shall win now if only we have their pluck. Fight on – Hardie.

Commentators were struck not so much by the expensive leisurely style of the telegram as by its alarmingly seditious tone. To the scandalized Press of the day Hardie seemed to be inciting the demonstrators to armed revolt against the authorities. It is certainly very different in tone from Hardie's more usual mollifying view of Socialism: that talk of a 'class war' or 'revolutionary struggle' was grievously misplaced. Perhaps the truth is simply this: that Hardie could not control his tongue when passionately moved. We have already seen examples of this in relation to the engineers' lock-out in 1897 and the Overtoun affair in 1899. Hardie's apparently violent reaction to the unemployment agitation of 1905 may have been in the same category.

An important legislative aim of the Labour members at this time was a Bill to reverse the effects of the Taff Vale judgment. Here Hardie did not play a leading role; the main negotiator among the Labour M.P.s was Shackleton. A Trades Disputes Bill received a second reading in 1904 and another in 1905. On both occasions there were signs of a split between the labour lobby, which wanted unconditional immunity for trade unions from actions for damages arising out of strikes, and a number of Liberals who saw legal obstacles, not to say objections of principle, to this proposal. Under a Conservative Government the question was at any rate only academic. Reversal of Taff Vale would have to wait.

---

* In 1819 the Manchester Yeomanry dispersed a crowd at a peaceful reform meeting at St Peter's Fields, in Manchester. Eleven demonstrators were killed. The incident became known as 'Peterloo' in ironic evocation of Waterloo.

It may be thought from this account that Hardie's activity in Parliament was less vigorous during the years 1903–5 than it had been in 1892–5 or even 1900–1903. This was true, but it was not Hardie's fault. During these years he was twice struck down by severe illness, and he had generally become much less robust than before. Indeed, Hardie's personal life between 1900 and 1906 was much less happy or successful than his political life.

Hardie's friends had been warning him for many years before 1900 that his constitution could not stand indefinitely the demands he made upon it: incessant travelling, long hours of waiting for trains, irregular meals, hundreds of meetings – many of them out of doors in all weathers, working up to sixteen hours a day. In July 1901 Hardie felt unwell. His friends diagnosed the effects of overwork, but could not keep him away from the platform or out of the offices of the *Labour Leader*. Nothing serious seemed to come of this particular incident. But 1902 was a year of family unhappiness, as well as overwork for Hardie himself. At the beginning of the year his daughter Agnes fell gravely ill with appendicitis, aggravated by peritonitis and pleurisy. In the medical circumstances of the day it seemed very unlikely that she would recover, and she lay desperately ill for two months before eventually recovering. Within a further month Hardie's mother and stepfather both died within a few hours of each other. Although he had rarely referred to them in adult life, his comments in the *Labour Leader* make it clear that he was very much shocked by his bereavement, inevitable though it was. Towards the end of the year he was again ill with what he tried initially to brush off as 'a chill, which finally settled in the appendix'. He would not be dissuaded from going to the abortive Cleveland selection conference; perhaps his illness contributed to his failure to control it more effectively. But his condition continued to get worse until, after a month of trying, his friends persuaded him to take a break from speaking and writing. But Hardie was incapable of using his holidays in a medically sensible fashion. He used this break to go and meet European socialists in Brussels, where, no doubt because he entered the Belgian Parliament building in his ordinary clothes, he was promptly arrested on suspicion of being an anarchist. The affair was soon cleared up, but it could scarcely have benefited his health.

In January 1903 Hardie was back in the editorial chair of the *Labour Leader*, heedless of all warnings of trouble in store. It is tempting to say that his illness in the autumn of 1903 was inevitable. In late July he collapsed after an open-air meeting in West Ham, rested briefly in Cumnock, returned indefatigably to the fray – and collapsed again in mid-October. He was diagnosed as having appendicitis – a dangerous illness at the time, and one which attracted much popular interest because of Edward VII's near-fatal attack of it just before his coronation had been due to take place in 1902. Hardie was taken to a London clinic, where he received goodwill messages from all manner of people, including Major Banes, his Conservative antagonist in West Ham. He was successfully operated on, on 22 October 1903. It soon became known that the patient had been visited by King Edward's own doctor, who read Hardie a letter from the King to the effect that 'having undergone an operation for appendicitis, he had a fellow-feeling for all who had to endure similar suffering . . . The King . . . hoped the patient was progressing favourably.' Needless to say, this message caused a great flutter in all the gossip columns, where Hardie's attacks on Edward VII when he was Prince of Wales had not been forgotten. Hardie, staunch republican though he was, admitted that the King's letter was 'really a very human document'.

Hardie's recovery was slow and long drawn out. But by the beginning of 1904 he was again being inundated with requests to give speeches all over the country. A columnist in the *Labour Leader* said, with justice, 'Anyone who is aiding and abetting this sort of lunacy might be more eligibly employed in stopping rat-holes.' But Hardie's colleagues in the upper reaches of the I.L.P. were far from blameless, for with extraordinarily thoughtless timing they chose this opportunity to wrest control of the *Labour Leader* out of Hardie's hands.

There had been complaints about the *Labour Leader* almost since its first issue. It was a vehicle for Hardie's personal views, and he used its columns for attacks on other labour politicians who did not get fair opportunities to reply. (There was some truth in this.) It did not give full or accurate coverage of I.L.P. activities. But above all, it was dull: earnest in a Calvinistic fashion, and woefully dull. MacDonald complained to Glasier, Glasier complained to Hardie, but to no real effect. The tone remained heavy and puritanical, and the only occasions on which it brightened up were themselves connected with Hardie's puritan morality, such as the Glasgow prostitutes affair in 1896. There was no doubt that Blatchford's *Clarion*, whose circulation was up to five times as great as that of the *Labour Leader*, was a much brighter paper, though the political waywardness of its proprietor meant that it was much less of an asset to the I.L.P. It could recruit readers for socialism, but it could not sustain their enthusiasm for the everyday requirements of Labour politics. Therefore, from 1902 onwards, Hardie was under heavy pressure from the I.L.P. to give up the

editorship and control of the *Labour Leader*. There were several
stumbling blocks. Hardie undoubtedly did want an uncensored voice
for his opinions; he wanted financial terms for the surrender of the
paper which made some recognition of the amount of money he had
put into it over the years; and he found it difficult to endure the
psychological pain of giving up something which was virtually his
single-handed creation.

In 1903 Hardie agreed in principle to give up the editorship and
control of the *Labour Leader*, but he failed to take any practical steps
to effect its transfer to the I.L.P. The party therefore took advantage
of Hardie's illness to complete the takeover. Hardie lost control of the
paper as from 1 January 1904. Hardie's published comments, in the
last number of the personal column he had written every week for
twelve years, made it clear to anyone reading between the lines how
unhappy he was at the transfer. He said that he had always intended
that the paper should eventually come under I.L.P. control, but hoped
he could keep it for his lifetime; he added that he still harboured
thoughts of starting 'a little monthly sheet of my own, just to find an
outlet for my own views and opinions on men and events' (though
this was something he had just specifically promised the I.L.P. not to
do.) In private, he was more forthright. He let out a cry of anguish in a
letter to Glasier (himself, whether or not Hardie knew it, one of the
prime movers in the transfer).

> Nothing that I can recall has ever depressed me so much . . . I have
> struggled and sacrificed and paid everyone connected with the paper the
> full 20/- in the pound, and now when it comes to my turn to be paid I am
> asked to accept 17/-. Nothing, I repeat, which I have ever experienced has
> raised the same feeling of heart-breaking resentment as this.

This unseemly affair was probably in the best interests of the I.L.P.,
but it did nothing to aid Hardie's recovery. He did not return to
London, but spent the early months of 1904 in Scotland, mostly at
Cumnock. From there he went on a continental holiday, in the early
stages of which he was accompanied by Ramsay MacDonald. Although
Hardie noted ruefully, 'Mac is not an ideal travelling companion', it
was probably the most restful of his foreign tours. He visited France,
Switzerland, and northern Italy – and kept entirely clear of politics.
He returned to Britain in July 1904 feeling better, although still not
entirely recovered.

But Hardie returned to his work as leader of the parliamentary
Labour party for only two months (during which he exchanged
letters with Glasier deploring the ineffectiveness of the Labour group)
before going off again to another International Socialist Congress, this

time in Amsterdam. This Congress was at least more constructive than the fiasco of 1896. Hardie observed how the socialist movement was split between those whom he regarded as the sterile dogmatists of the class war and the more moderate pragmatists concerned with the real world of politics. In a perceptive comment on the Congress, Hardie noted how almost all the representatives of nations that had some sort of constitutional government fell into the latter camp:

Wherever free Parliamentary institutions exist, and where Socialism has attained the status of being recognized as a Party, dogmatic absolutism is giving way before the advent of a more practical set of working principles. The schoolman is being displaced by the statesman.

The Amsterdam Congress was the happy conclusion of a generally unhappy period of Hardie's personal life. He had been further aged by his recurrent bouts of illness, and from time to time spoke as if he wished to give up his parliamentary career altogether. In May 1902, for instance, he had written in his column in the *Labour Leader*, 'The day, I hope, is not far distant when I will be free to roam the country at large as a free lance; but, being in Parliament, it is due to the movement, no less than to the constituency which returned me, that I do the work of that assembly.' And in 1903 he told a disbelieving audience in Merthyr that he thought 'his work in the Labour movement was drawing towards its close'. 'As a pioneer in the work,' Hardie said, 'I have had my day and done my share. It is now for younger and abler men to take up the work . . . But I should like to – and, God helping me, I will – fight the next election at least.' These statements might have sounded incongruous, coming as they did from a man who was not yet fifty years old. But already Hardie looked old far beyond his years – he looked more like sixty-five than fifty. Contemporaries or near-contemporaries, like MacDonald or Snowden, had thirty years of political life still stretching ahead of them, but Hardie felt his day was done. It was partly the effect of his failing health; partly, also, a feeling he shared with many of his critics, that he was better suited to the life of the solitary pioneer than to that of the head of an established movement in national politics. At all events, none of his colleagues would hear of the idea of his retiring, and he went forward to fight his next General Election.

The maximum permitted time between one General Election and the next was seven years, but during 1905 it became clear that the Balfour Government would be unable to survive its first full term. The Conservative Party was hopelessly split over Chamberlain's Protection campaign. Neither Chamberlain nor the free-traders in the

party were satisfied by Balfour's unhappy efforts to equivocate between them, and representatives of both wings resigned from the
Government. The Conservatives suffered a series of disastrous by-
election defeats, in apparently impregnable seats such as Whitby and
Brighton. It was obvious to everybody that the Government had lost
control of its fate; obvious to everyone except the Protectionists that
Protection was a massive electoral liability. The 'dear loaf' seemed
infallibly destined to lose the Government the next election. Eventually, in December 1905, Balfour decided that he could go on no
longer. He resigned, hoping that the Liberals, split as they were between Imperialists and Little Englanders, would be unable to form a
caretaker Ministry. He was disappointed; a minority Liberal Government was formed under Campbell-Bannerman, who called a General
Election for January 1906.

On balance, Hardie looked more secure at Merthyr than he had done
at West Ham. At West Ham he had had no real organization to help
him at all, except at election times; at Merthyr he had a small band of
devoted enthusiasts well versed in the devious ways of trade-union
politics. Dai Davies, the secretary of the Merthyr Trades Council, and
Llewellyn Francis, of Pen-y-daren on the outskirts of Merthyr, were
Hardie's leading supporters, and they kept a close eye on constituency
affairs and their Member's interests.

Merthyr Boroughs in Hardie's day was a peculiar constituency.
Twenty miles north of Cardiff, the Afon Cynon met the river Taff;
upstream from here mining villages clung on to the hillsides of both
valleys, the Taff going north and Cynon or Aberdare valley going
north-west. The valleys were separated by the 1,500-foot-high ridge
of Mynydd Merthyr, and connected only by footpaths, or a desolate
road at the head of the valleys, or by the occasional train through the
long tunnel that pierced the mountain. In each valley, geography and
the intense community feeling of South Wales bound men together,
politically as well as socially. The eastern valley, the Taff Vale with
Merthyr at its head, was Hardie's stronghold. In Troedyrhiw and
Aberfan, Merthyr and Pen-y-daren, and in the lunar landscape of
Dowlais, perched around its steelworks 1,200 feet above sea level,
Hardie was a popular favourite. In the western valley he was less well
known and less admired. The two communities might have been
scores of miles apart for all they knew of each other; even the local
paper produced an entirely different edition for each valley. In
Aberdare and Mountain Ash, the main communities of the western
valley, the miners were much more attached to their traditional
Lib-Lab leaders and paid little attention to the goings-on across the

mountain. Try as they might, Hardie's constituency workers never established the hold over the Aberdare valley which they had over Merthyr proper.

In general, the relationship between Hardie and his supporters like Dai Davies was one of wary amiability. Hardie criticized his constituency helpers for being inefficient at office work. This may well have been true, but Hardie undoubtedly owed much to the talents of Davies, not least for fending off, in 1905, the threat of a Miners' candidate in the constituency (which would have breached the MacDonald –Gladstone agreement and endangered the delicate relationship between Hardie and D.A. Thomas.) For his part, Davies did his best to restrain Hardie's taste for unnecessary and damaging polemics. He wrote to MacDonald enclosing cuttings of a vituperative argument between Hardie and Richard Bell which was going on in the columns of the *Merthyr Express*, and saying, 'I am afraid it will do Hardie a certain amount of harm unless we take him in hand ourselves.' He apparently tried to stop Hardie from seeing copies of the newspaper, in order to force him to break off the argument.

When the 1906 General Election was announced, all seemed set for an unopposed return for Hardie and Thomas; accordingly, Hardie departed to stump the country on behalf of L.R.C. and I.L.P. candidates elsewhere. But he had left his flank exposed through his inattention to traditional Welsh Nonconformist concerns. Hardie had refused to respond to the frequent appeals for donations to chapels in his constituency which every Welsh M.P. received – even if he had wished to give money, he would not have had it to give. And he had been somewhat unresponsive to two of the issues which had stirred traditional opinion in the valleys far more than Protection or the Taff Vale case, namely the Education Act of 1902 and the Welsh Revival of 1904.

Balfour's Act to consolidate and extend the provision of free education was generally admirable; but Nonconformist opinion was enraged by the proposal to give aid from the rates for voluntary schools – which effectively meant Anglican schools. Nonconformist ministers all over Wales led campaigns of civil disobedience and refusal to pay their rates. They received the powerful backing of Lloyd George. But Hardie's opposition to the Education Act was relatively perfunctory. He was reported in the local Press as saying that 'he approached the subject purely as a workmen's representative . . . On the religious aspect he had not much to say, except that he strongly objected to being taxed to pay for the teaching of a dogma he neither approved nor believed in.' But he did not take his 'strong objections' to the length of taking any part in the debates in Parliament over the Education Bill.

In the autumn of 1904 came the latest (and as it turned out the last) of the evangelical revivals, led by earnest fundamentalist missionaries, which had swept Wales from time to time since the Industrial Revolution. Scores of thousands of miners and steelworkers forswore drink and strong language in favour of a renewed devotion to the chapels of their youth. It was the last great era for the building of the stark, stern chapels which still dominate every Welsh village with their somehow forbidding Biblical titles. But again, Hardie was not as impressed as he should have been. Of one of the leading missionaries, who was campaigning in his constituency, Hardie said, 'I can only hope that the results of his labours will be permanent, but I confess that in this respect I am not over-sanguine, for waves of emotionalism sweep over people periodically.'

Even in the Edwardian era the allegiance of the Welsh working class to the chapel was fading, but religious affairs still bulked large in men's lives. So, when the 1906 election came round, Hardie was suddenly vulnerable to the challenge of Henry Radcliffe, a Cardiff shipowner, who appeared as a last-minute Liberal candidate. (The absence of any properly constituted Liberal Association in the division made it only too easy for candidates like Radcliffe and Pritchard Morgan to assume the label of 'Liberal' without being challenged.) Radcliffe ran his campaign on traditional issues: disestablishment of the Anglican Church in Wales, opposition to the Balfour Education Act. He carefully avoided issues such as Taff Vale or even Protection, but (according to the *Labour Leader*) busily spread rumours up and down the valleys that Keir Hardie was an atheist. Overall, however, Radcliffe's was a quiet campaign – but so was Hardie's, since he hardly showed his face in the constituency. When the results were announced, it became clear that Radcliffe had come far too close for comfort. He got 7,776 votes to Hardie's 10,189 and 13,971 for D. A. Thomas.

Hardie was saved by one thing only: loyal and unstinted support from D. A. Thomas and his friends. Thomas publicly warned Radcliffe not to intervene, and announced that the Liberal Association (meaning himself) would not support a second Liberal candidate – a declaration which no doubt caused Herbert Gladstone to draw a secret sigh of relief. In his speech after the result was announced, Hardie described Thomas as 'his friend and colleague' – as well he might. The coal-owner had saved the ex-miner from losing his seat. The analysis of the voting published in the local Press showed that 7,409 votes had been cast for Thomas and Hardie jointly, and 5,878 for Thomas and

Radcliffe. If Thomas had encouraged his fellow-Liberal rather than Hardie, these figures would, at the very least, have been reversed, and Hardie would have lost. In later years D. A. Thomas and labour were to be bitterly opposed to one another; but in 1906 he did the labour movement a service of the first importance.

But Merthyr was typical only of itself. Overall, the election of 1906 was a triumphant vindication of Hardie and the principle of independent labour representation. The L.R.C. put up fifty candidates. Twenty-nine of these won, and the effective strength of independent labour in 1906 is usually counted as thirty, because the successful Miners' candidate in Chester-le-Street, in County Durham, was an avowed I.L.P.er. And yet, in one sense, this triumphant result for Labour was only a sideshow. At the centre of things was the great Liberal victory – the party's greatest ever electoral triumph. The Liberals took 400 seats, and the Conservatives were reduced to their lowest-ever total of 157. Arthur Balfour lost his own seat in Manchester.

The 1906 election brought to office a famous reforming Government, and it set the infant Labour Party firmly on its feet. But it is curious that it was fought more on issues of the past than of the future. Only the Labour candidates were very much interested in the reversal of Taff Vale or the possibility of Old Age Pensions. For most candidates the election was about the Big Loaf and the Little Loaf (which was the Liberal way of contrasting free trade with Protection); the 1902 Education Act; the level of government expenditure; and – to an extent which is now difficult to fathom – Chinese labour. A scandal had arisen out of the discovery that Chinese indentured labourers were being brought in on very unfavourable terms to work in mines owned by British proprietors in South Africa. Liberal spokesmen opposed the system on humanitarian grounds; working-class audiences agreed with them because it appeared to restrict the opportunities for British emigrants to South Africa, emigration being seen as the one sure way to escape poverty and unemployment at home.

The crucial factor in the election result, however, was almost certainly a deeply ingrained fear among many voters that a Conservative Government would lead to Protection, and Protection would lead to dear food. In converting the Conservative Party, the Protectionists had not given nearly enough attention to the much more important task of converting public opinion. The young journalist Leo Amery was one of the few who saw the importance of this, but by his own admission the Tariff Reform League he set up was a failure as a propaganda organization.

The swing to the Liberals should not be exaggerated. The Conservatives did much better than during the by-elections of 1905. The Liberals' share of the votes cast was only 49 per cent, and the Conservative share was as high as 43·6 per cent. This was translated into a Liberal landslide in terms of seats only because of the nature of the statistical distribution of seats. At the dissolution of Parliament, there were a large number of Conservative marginal seats which were vulnerable to only a small swing against the Conservatives. What was important, however, was not the voters' behaviour so much as the politicians' perception of how the voters had behaved. In the midst of a welter of comment about the overwhelming Liberal victory, the President of the Royal Statistical Society pointed out that the result was largely the consequence of the fall of so many Conservative marginals, and an equally dramatic reversal was likely if there was a swing of no more than three or four per cent against the Liberals. In the prevailing atmosphere this still small voice commanded little attention.

The Labour Representation Committee, then, was the more-or-less accidental beneficiary of the Liberal triumph, but it had benefited enormously from the MacDonald–Gladstone pact. Almost all the successful Labour M.P.s had been given a free run against the Conservatives, with no Liberal intervening. Hardie was one of the few who had had to fight a Liberal. Several important figures now entered Parliament for the first time. Ramsay MacDonald became M.P. for Leicester, in improbable double harness with Henry Broadhurst; Philip Snowden was elected for Blackburn in company with a Conservative. Henderson was returned with an increased majority, and Shackleton, opposed only by an Independent, produced Labour's largest majority. For the first time it became possible to envisage an effective parliamentary party, with the full apparatus of Whips and departmental spokesmen. What sort of party this would be, and what role in it there would be for Keir Hardie, were questions which remained to be answered.

6

THE LIBERALS
IN OFFICE
1906-10

Commentators saw what they wanted to see in
the Labour successes of 1906. To Balfour the thirty Labour M.P.s were
harbingers of a European revolution which Campbell-Bannerman
would be powerless to prevent (although Balfour languidly refused to
display any immediate alarm at the prospect). 'CB is a mere cork', he
wrote, 'dancing on a torrent which he cannot control, and what is
going on here is a faint echo of the same movement which has produced
massacres in St Petersburg, riots in Vienna, and Socialist processions
in Berlin.' On the other hand, Herbert Gladstone's secretary wrote to
him exultantly to claim the Labour successes as a personal triumph
for Herbert Gladstone.

The results of the policy you adopted towards Labour are seen to be outstandingly good . . . the friendliness of the Labour leaders were [*sic*] reflected in the confidence and enthusiasm of the Labour people in the country . . .

No avowed Socialist won . . . Was there ever such a justification of policy by results ?

Moreover the attitude of the Labour representatives has been greatly influenced by our own past relations. They are strongly favourable to the Government. There are not more than seven irreconcilable. Even they are very friendly with me. There is no reason to anticipate any change if the same policy be continued. But will it be ?

Both of these views were very much exaggerated. The Labour Party (as the Labour Representation Committee's thirty M.P.s decided to call themselves at their first meeting after the election) was not a band of professional revolutionaries, nor was it merely a group of personal friends of Herbert Gladstone, willing to do anything to oblige the Liberal Party. But these views, caricatures though they were, demonstrated the extremes between which the party must steer. Keir Hardie had still to fight off revolutionary socialist purists on his left, at the same time as he had to try to evade the clutches of Liberal trade unionists on his right. At the Labour M.P.s' meeting on 19 February 1906 the first thing that had to be settled was the party's name. The L.R.C. passed into history* and the name 'Labour Party' was adopted for use both inside and outside Parliament. The next was the leadership. Here the conflict between the 'irreconcilables' and the rest was bound to reappear. Two candidates were put up: Keir Hardie and David Shackleton. Hardie had still not been forgiven by some of the staider trade unionists for his attacks on the T.U.C. leadership in the 1890s and many of the Labour M.P.s were in any case not at all committed to socialism. Furthermore, although Shackleton had only been an M.P. for just over three years to Hardie's nine, he was clearly a better Parliamentarian in some ways. Although no orator, he had a detailed grasp of procedure which Hardie lacked. Trade unionists had been impressed by his handling of the T.U.C.'s Bill to reverse Taff Vale in 1904 and 1905.

Some of Hardie's friends realized that it might be best if he did not run for the post. Glasier, for instance, was very much aware of the

---

* Except for the purposes of the General Post Office. On 1 January 1906 the Assistant Secretary of the L.R.C. reported to the Committee that he had negotiated with the G.P.O. for the telegraphic address 'Labrepcom London'. 'The code word is composed of the first three letters of each word forming the title of the Committee.' In 1974 the telegraphic address of the Labour Party, according to its current letterhead, is still 'Labrepcom London'.

prickly relationships between leading members of the party. He tried
to put Hardie off in a long, flattering letter:

> You should not accept nomination for the chairmanship unless it un-
> expectedly happens that the feeling in favour of your doing so is *unani-
> mous* and *enthusiastic* – and hardly even were it so. It is much more im-
> portant . . . that you should be *free to lead the Socialist policy*, than that
> you should be stuck in the official chairmanship where you would be
> bound . . . to adopt a personal attitude acceptable to the moderates . . .
>
> If you and our men can lead the Socialist line then in a few years the
> Party will be a Socialist party.

Nevertheless, Hardie persisted with his candidature. On the first vote
he tied with Shackleton, on a show of hands. MacDonald did not vote.
A ballot vote was then called for, and the result was again a tie, with
MacDonald abstaining. Finally, after MacDonald's colleagues insisted that he must vote, another ballot resulted in a majority of one
for Hardie.* The other offices in the party all went to 'organization
men'. Shackleton became vice-chairman, MacDonald secretary and
Henderson chief Whip.

In his capacity as secretary of the party, Ramsay MacDonald had
drawn up a memorandum listing matters for decision by the party.
Apart from the party's title and the election of officers there were two
points to decide:

1. Upon which side of the House should our Party sit?
2. Attitude of our Party to the other Labour members.

The second of these could scarcely be settled on the spot. There were
still some seventeen Lib-Labs outside the self-styled 'Labour Party'.
Relations between the two groups were much better than they had
been in Hardie's earlier years, because there was very little except
accidental local circumstances dividing Lib-Labs in the Labour
Party, like Shackleton and Henderson, from Lib-Labs outside it, like
the majority of the miners' members. But for the moment there were
no attempts to bring them into the fold. On MacDonald's first point it
was only too easy to decide. There was no room for the Labour Party
on the Government benches, which were overflowing with 400 Liberals.
The Labour Party had perforce to sit on the opposition side of the

---

* There is a well-known story to the effect that MacDonald actually voted
for Shackleton, and that the final result came about because another member
switched from Shackleton to Hardie on the last ballot. The story is false in
fact, but true in spirit. MacDonald later wrote to Glasier to admit that he
had voted for Hardie, but extremely reluctantly, because he did not believe
that Hardie would make a good leader for the party.

House below the gangway, with the Irish behind them and the Tories on their right. Whether this position truly reflected their attitude to the Liberal administration remained to be seen.

The Government announced by Campbell-Bannerman after Balfour's resignation in November 1905 had been generally welcomed. It was recognized that the Liberal front bench was unusually talented, with such members as Asquith at the Exchequer, Sir Edward Grey at the Foreign Office, and Morley at the India Office. The up-and-coming radical Lloyd George was made President of the Board of Trade, but Campbell-Bannerman's most striking appointment was to make John Burns the President of the Local Government Board. He was the first working man ever to become a Cabinet Minister. His response to his appointment was characteristic in its unashamed conceit. Campbell-Bannerman later recalled:

> Naturally, I expected him to be somewhat overpowered by the announcement. But, to my surprise, he seemed to think that the obligation was on my side. 'Bravo, Sir Henry!', he said, slapping me on the back. 'Bravo! That is the most popular thing you have yet done!'

Hardie was often criticized for his vanity; but he never reached the sublime heights touched by John Burns.

Campbell-Bannerman's Government seemed to face only one major problem, of unknown dimensions. In the Commons it had a clear majority, even in the unlikely event of Labour, the Irish, and the Conservatives all combining against it. This meant that, for the time being, the whole controversial business of Home Rule could be left to slumber. By no means all the Liberal Party was enthusiastic for Home Rule; but whatever it did, the Irish Party could do the Government no harm – so why not let the sleeping dog of Home Rule lie? By contrast, the House of Lords was as Conservative as ever. Nobody knew how it was going to treat the Government's programme of legislation.

One of the first tests ended in an outstanding triumph for the Labour members. As we have seen, all Labour politicians – socialist and trade-unionist alike – wanted legislation to protect trade unions from the consequences of the Taff Vale judgement. When the T.U.C. saw the size of the A.S.R.S.'s bill in 1903, it became enthusiastic for a measure to make trade unions immune from liability to damages arising out of strikes or picketing. A Bill to this effect had been unsuccessfully presented by Shackleton in 1904 and 1905. During the election campaign a large number of Liberal candidates, including Campbell-Bannerman himself, had promised that a Liberal Government would bring in legislation on the lines demanded by the T.U.C.

This was a hostage to fortune, because many Liberal lawyers, including Asquith, strongly disliked the immunity proposal. After much argument in Cabinet, therefore, the Government introduced a Bill which did not give the unions immunity. The Attorney-General complained that immunity would 'create a privilege for the proletariat and give a sort of benefit of clergy to trade unions'. The Labour M.P.s and the T.U.C. were furious, and immediately decided to press ahead with their own Bill which did give immunity. They revelled in reminding Liberal M.P.s of what they had said on the hustings. Hardie made a decisive intervention when he was able to produce a photograph showing that the Attorney-General had issued election posters in his own constituency approving of the T.U.C.'s Bill. When the Labour Party Bill came up for discussion, rumours were already flying about that the Government would abandon its own Bill and accept the Labour one, immunity clause and all. The young Unionist F.E.Smith sarcastically congratulated Hardie on the 'captures he had made on the Front Bench'. Hardie made a powerful speech in which he met the Liberal objections to immunity squarely. Of course the Bill was class legislation, said Hardie. 'What was the Workmen's Compensation Act but class legislation? That act took the workman outside the operation of the common law of the land because the circumstances of the case justified that's being done.' On behalf of the Labour Party, Hardie concluded that they would refuse to accept the Government Bill as a settlement of the question. Immediately after this, a remarkable thing happened. Campbell-Bannerman rose, and to the surprise of many of his own supporters and the astonished scorn of the Unionists he announced that he would support the Labour Bill, making the extraordinary claim that the differences between it and the Government Bill were minor and technical, and could be adjusted in Committee. Subsequent stages of the Bill dragged on through 1906, although Hardie took no further part beyond making some technical points at the committee stage. But the Bill as presented to the House of Lords was much closer to the Labour Party's proposals than to the Government's.

It is perhaps surprising that the Lords let it through unmolested. The Government and the Lords were already set on a collision course, the Lords having rejected an important Education Bill because they did not think it gave enough protection to Anglican interests. However, the advice of the Conservative leader in the Lords, Lord Lansdowne, was that the peers should let the Trade Disputes Bill through. Even though the Bill was 'fraught with danger to the community', Lansdowne thought that 'it is useless for us, situated as we are, to oppose this measure'. Unionist peers, said Lansdowne with remarkable candour, should obstruct the Commons only on ground 'as favourable as possible to ourselves'. We must assume, therefore, that Lansdowne thought that, if the peers rejected the Trade Disputes Bill, there would be such a clamour that the Lords' own position would be at risk. It is not obvious that this would have been the case.

The Trade Disputes Act was the outstanding achievement of the Labour Party during the entire term of the Liberal Government. The detailed supervision of the passage of the Bill, and the negotiations with Campbell-Bannerman, had been entrusted to Shackleton, and he was given a well-deserved banquet by the Labour Party and the T.U.C. after the Act was passed, in recognition of his achievement. It is customary to decry Hardie's abilities as leader of the Parliamentary Labour Party, but it is worth bearing in mind that there was never a legislative success remotely comparable to the Trade Disputes Act under the leadership of any of his successors up to 1915.

For it must be appreciated that the 1906 Act marked a sharp break with traditional Liberalism. In previous chapters we have noted some of the issues on which the old individualistic radicalism was in conflict with the new, collectivist radicalism. The Miners' Eight-Hours Bill is a good example. Hardie himself was only one of many politicians of the period who warmed to collectivist ideas as he shook off the Gladstonian individualist views of his youth. The 1906 Act, as finally passed, had two main features which made it unacceptable to Liberal individualists. It gave trade unions immunity from actions for damages arising out of the activities of their officers, which angered those who thought that individual union officials should be held responsible for the consequences of their actions; and it stipulated that it was not an offence for trade unionists to encourage other workers to break their contracts of employment. Even Sidney Webb, the leading Fabian expert on trade unionism, did not favour these proposals. Nevertheless, the Act went through, ultimately, without even a division. The philosophy behind the Trade Disputes Act was very different to that underlying the more traditional legislative proposals of the Government – licensing reform, the abolition of plural voting, Welsh disestablishment and so on. These belonged to the old individualistic Liberalism; the Trade Disputes Act was the first herald of a new, collectivist Liberalism of which more was to be seen before long. And its passing, against the grain of traditional Liberal ideology, reflects great credit on Shackleton, Hardie, and the Labour lobby. For they had no real sanctions. They could not threaten to bring down the Government. It was inconceivable that the thirty

Labour members could have found enough rebels in the other parties to force a Bill incorporating legal immunity through the Commons if both front benches had set their faces against it. Furthermore, as far as we can tell, there was no real surge of public opinion behind the Labour proposals. True, both the Labour candidates and some Liberals had campaigned for a reversal of the Taff Vale judgement, and trade-union leaders were demanding it. But there is no evidence at all that the Edwardian electorate as a whole was particularly concerned. It is very hard to see what the Labour Party could have done if the Government had simply turned down their requests. If the Irish could have got Home Rule, or women the vote, as easily as the Labour Party got legal immunity for trade unions, Edwardian history might have been very different.

But it is in the nature of politics that politicians get faint praise for their successes, but strident condemnation for their failures. The I.L.P. admitted that the Trade Disputes Act was quite an impressive concession to have come from a capitalist administration. But this did not stop a rising tide of discontent in the party, in part directed at Hardie which was manifested on two questions: women's suffrage and the Grayson affair.

Looking back on the Edwardian era, we may well wonder how so obvious a reform as women's suffrage could cause such a fuss. Women could already vote in local elections, and stand for election to such bodies as Poor Law Guardians: who could possibly oppose their being granted the vote in parliamentary elections? Remarkable though it may seem, every Government contained bitter opponents of women's suffrage, and the great reform administration of 1906 was no exception. Asquith in particular was totally opposed to any reform. So no Government initiative could be expected. To understand why the movement made no progess before 1914 we must also appreciate that the supporters of reform were deeply divided between two organizations and between two parliamentary strategies.

The National Union of Women's Suffrage Societies traced its origins back to 1867; one of its founders was the great liberal writer and philosopher John Stuart Mill, who had written a book called *The Subjection of Women*. It was respectable, constitutional, and rather boring. In 1903 it was joined by the Women's Social and Political Union, founded by Mrs Pankhurst — whom we last met at Boggart Hole Clough in 1896 – and her daughters Christabel and Sylvia. From the outset the W.S.P.U. concentrated on headline-hitting demonstrations, and it was not long before the term 'suffragette' was coined to denote its supporters.

E

The two wings of the movement were split on strategy as well as tactics. Should suffragists press for a complete enfranchisement of women, or for the enfranchisement of women on the same terms as men? The latter proposal was legislatively easy – it could be brought about by a one-clause Act of Parliament – but would be limited in its effect, since the existing suffrage for men was based on household franchise. In other words, the basic qualification for being eligible to vote was to be a householder. But the small number of women householders would be middle- and upper-class; the proposal would be of no benefit to working-class housewives. It was also unlikely to help the Liberal and Labour parties electorally. For this reason most of the Labour Party supported the proposal for wider enfranchisement, and in this they had the support of most of the 'constitutional' suffragists. (From an electoral point of view even this was altruistic; as far as is known, women voters have, from their first enfranchisement in 1918 to the present day, been quite consistently more pro-Conservative than men.) The 'universal female suffrage' proposal also had the unwelcome support of many politicians who did not really want women's suffrage at all, but were happy to pay lip-service to it at the same time as seeing it banished to the probably distant day when the Government could get round to reforming the franchise for men.* The 'limited suffrage' proposal's supporters were more unexpected. They included the W.S.P.U., and they included Keir Hardie. The W.S.P.U. was predominantly an organization of middle-class women with time on their hands. Their attitude to politics was very different from that of, say, somebody attempting to form a trade union among women workers, because they were apparently more concerned with gestures than with achievements. The Pankhursts were not interested in politics in the everyday sense of bargaining and negotiation; it was no concern of theirs that enfranchising middle-class spinsters would not help the cause of progressive reform.

Hardie's position is at first more difficult to grasp. His public justification of it was this:

If the women have a Bill of their own, short, simple, and easily understood, and they concentrate upon that, even though it should never be discussed in Parliament until the general Adult Suffrage Bill is reached, they would, by their agitation, have created the necessary volume of public opinion to make it impossible for politicians to overlook their claims.

* For such people, of course, the argument against the 'limited suffrage' proposal was that 'the present measure would block the way for a far more sweeping reform'. See F. M. Cornford, *Microcosmographia Academica*, (Cambridge 1908), ch. 8: compulsory reading for all conservative obstructionists.

In other words, the 'limited suffrage' proposal was valuable for propaganda reasons. But Hardie also had a tactical and an emotional attachment to it. The tactical point was that, by the rules of parliamentary procedure, any women's suffrage resolution could be 'blocked' by the presence of other resolutions on similar subjects. Realizing that some of the pretended friends of universal adult suffrage merely wished to block any discussion of suffrage by procedural tricks, Hardie strongly advised the Labour Party to back the 'limited suffrage' proposal. In addition, Hardie had a strong emotional attachment to the militant suffragettes – and, as we have seen, it was the militants, not the constitutionalists, who wanted limited female suffrage. Other leading I.L.P.ers complained about Hardie's continued attachment to Mrs Pankhurst at a time when she had taken to denouncing the Labour Party and all its works. Hardie also employed a suffragette, Mary Travers-Symons, as his personal secretary, and was later involved in long acrimonious correspondence with the Speaker in an unsuccessful attempt to have her permitted to re-enter the Houses of Parliament after she took part in a demonstration there.

The Labour Party Conference of 1907 met in Belfast in January, and women's suffrage was the most contentious question discussed. A resolution appeared on the agenda supporting 'limited suffrage'. Its friends were not helped by the W.S.P.U., who, with a fine sense of political timing, issued a manifesto a few days earlier claiming that the Labour Party was no better than the Tories. Hardie, speaking in support of 'limited suffrage', said patiently, 'We have to learn to distinguish between a great principle and its advocates'; but none the less, an amendment describing the 'limited suffrage' idea as a 'retrograde step' was carried by 605,000 votes to 268,000. Later the same day, in a speech at the winding-up of the conference, Hardie made a statement which must have astonished and dismayed his audience.

> The intimation I wish to make to the Conference and friends is that, if the motion they carried this morning was intended to limit the action of the Party in the House of Commons, I shall have to seriously consider whether I shall remain a member of the Parliamentary Party. I say this with great respect and feeling. The party is largely my own child, and I could not sever myself lightly from what has been my life-work. But I cannot be untrue to my principles.

Arthur Henderson saved the day by drafting a formula whereby individual members of the Parliamentary Party were to be free to support, or not as they wished, a 'limited franchise' Bill being moved that session. Hardie did not carry out his threat to resign. But there was another suffrage row to come only three months later, this time at the I.L.P. Conference. The Conference carried a resolution asking for the vote to be 'immediately extended to women on the same conditions as men', Hardie making an emotional speech in its favour. This was, of course, the W.S.P.U. policy; and it obviously riled a number of delegates who were becoming somewhat exasperated by that body's tactics. (The N.A.C. had reported mildly that the W.S.P.U. had 'caused some irritation' by refusing to support Labour candidates at by-elections.) Some leading members of the W.S.P.U. had recently been imprisoned after violent demonstrations, and a row suddenly blew up when the Standing Orders Committee of the conference proposed to send a telegram to the 'women imprisoned for their fidelity to the cause of sex equality'. Glasier and Margaret MacDonald* objected to this on the grounds that it favoured 'a special kind of martyrdom' at the expense of other suffragists who were loyal to the Labour Party. Hardie spoke up for sending the telegram – 'it would be a graceful act' – but a resolution to refer the matter back to the Standing Orders Committee was very nearly carried. Hardie, for the first time ever, was isolated from the other I.L.P. leaders and out of tune with the mood of the conference.

Hardie's abrupt reactions on these two occasions can, in part, be ascribed to his emotional over-involvement with the W.S.P.U. But in the case of the row at the Labour Party Conference, a more important and more serious dispute lay behind this. For two or three years a number of delegates led by Ben Tillett had been pressing for an acknowledgement that the Parliamentary Labour Party was the agent of Conference, and was bound to do what Conference instructed it to. From one point of view this was an eminently reasonable request. The party had started life as an extra-parliamentary body – a committee, as its first title indicated, to secure the representation of labour in Parliament. Candidates' election expenses and parliamentary allowances were paid for by affiliated organizations: what more natural than that he who paid the piper should call the tune? It was not long, however, before Labour M.P.s started to press an opposite view. They were Members of Parliament, with a responsibility for their decisions which no outside body could have. It was not only impracticable, given the requirements of day-to-day parliamentary tactics, but undesirable that Labour M.P.s should consider themselves the delegates of the L.R.C., bound to do precisely what Conference told them to.

One cannot say that there was a right and a wrong side to this dispute. The views of the opposing sides arose out of two incompatible

* The wife of J. Ramsay MacDonald. She died comparatively young, in 1911.

theories of representation, both entirely justifiable. On one theory, the representative is simply the mouthpiece of those he represents, and can have no authority to do anything beyond what they permit him to do. On the other, representation entails responsibility for decisions which those who send the representatives cannot take, because they lack the necessary information or are not in a position to balance competing claims. The first impulse of the Labour Party's National Executive in 1907 was to lean right over to the second of these views. They recommended to Conference 'That resolutions on the Agenda, which seek to instruct the Parliamentary Party as to their action in the House of Commons, be so amended by the Standing Orders Committee as to register the opinions of Conference without prejudice to any future course of action that may be considered advisable by the Party in Parliament.' This drew angry protests. Tillett complained that it 'challenges and repudiates the Sovereignty of the Conference' – as indeed it did. The final version, agreed by the 1907 Conference, committed the National Executive and the Parliamentary Labour Party to joint discussions on how Conference decisions were to be implemented in Parliament. Hardie made the singularly unconvincing claim that 'having read the original recommendation and the amended form, except in the matter of wording he could see no difference whatever. Both expressed the same thing.' This was the background to Hardie's outburst at the end of the Conference. He took Conference's opposition to his version of tactics on the suffrage question to be a breach of the newly established agreement as to the respective roles of Conference and the Parliamentary Party.

The position of Conference vis-à-vis the parliamentary leadership of the Labour Party is a perennial problem. Each successive Leader of the Labour Party, whatever he may have said before attaining that position, has in practice endorsed Hardie's view: that Conference cannot dictate policy to the Parliamentary Labour Party (P.L.P.). As early as 1910 Hardie put this view concisely, although in a way which suggested that he had an unusually short memory: 'In the House of Commons, the members of the Party decide their own policy without interference from the Executive or any outside authority. This is the right which the Parliamentary Party has always claimed, and which has never been seriously challenged.' The question has always come to life at times when relations between Conference and the P.L.P. have been most strained. Thus, in 1960, Hugh Gaitskell launched an impassioned attack on a Conference decision asking the party to support unilateral nuclear disarmament. He asked if Labour M.P.s were to be expected to act 'like well-behaved sheep' and change their minds on the question at Conference's behest. Thus again in the early 1970s the question arose continually, as Conference became more determinedly left-wing and suspected that the Parliamentary Party was not with it. But no move to persuade the Parliamentary Party to change its view has yet succeeded. Thus the principles laid down by Hardie and the National Executive in 1907 have been of fundamental importance to the whole subsequent development of the Labour Party.

Needless to say, Hardie's stance was widely resented. Tillett (who detested Hardie as much as Hardie detested him) launched a savage attack called *Is the Parliamentary Labour Party a Failure?* And it was not long before the malcontents had a figure round whom to rally in a young man called Victor Grayson, who had recently abandoned his studies for the ministry of the Unitarian church. Grayson was only twenty-five in 1907, but was coming to prominence as a leading I.L.P. orator in Manchester. He attracted the attention of socialists in the Colne Valley division of the West Riding (near Huddersfield), where a Liberal M.P. had been returned unopposed in 1906. The Colne Valley Labour League wrote to MacDonald, as Secretary of the Labour Party, inviting the party to endorse Grayson as Labour candidate for the constituency. MacDonald advised the League that it must first affiliate to the party, and summon a joint selection conference with local trade unions. However, it did neither of these things, but put Grayson forward on its own initiative without consulting the unions. The awkward position the Labour Party was thus put in was highlighted by the elevation of the sitting member to the House of Lords in 1907, which meant that a by-election must be fought. Hardie and Snowden favoured Grayson's candidature, but the rest of the Labour leadership was against. Seeing that he was not going to get official endorsement, Grayson decided to make a virtue of necessity. He wrote to MacDonald, 'This cleavage has to come some time, and nothing will be lost by precipitating it,' and accordingly stood as a 'clean Socialist', denouncing the I.L.P. for its alleged compromising and its association with the trade unions. In this he was warmly supported by Blatchford. In July 1907 Grayson was elected, by a majority of 153, Socialist M.P. for Colne Valley. The election heralded a period of considerable internal strife in the Labour Party, during which Hardie's earlier enthusiasm for Grayson was soon to cool down.

However, before the Colne Valley by-election actually took place, Hardie was thousands of miles away. The life he was leading was making impossible demands on him, and he had not regained his full strength after the illnesses of 1903 and 1904. Yet, Hardie being the sort of man he was, he still undertook meetings like one in Cambridge in February 1907, when he was howled down by a crowd of drunken public-school hooligans. In March the inevitable happened. Hardie fell ill with what was successively described as 'a chill', 'a severe chill', and 'acute inflammation of the bowels'. He was suffering from a chronic condition of inflammation of the intestinal tract, nowadays known as 'Crohn's disease'. It also appears, though this was not publicly mentioned at the time, that Hardie suffered a mild stroke; in a letter to Glasier he complained of 'a strange numbness all down the left side'. In late April he underwent a minor operation to remove his bowel obstruction, and he was ordered to take a complete rest. At first he went to Wemyss Bay Hydropathic, on the Clyde coast. But a rest home full of the convalescent Scots bourgeoisie was not the place for Keir Hardie, and he became restless – while (for once) agreeing with his doctors that he could not return to parliamentary work for a long time. And so the idea of a world cruise emerged. It was a recommended form of convalescence (when doctors could not think of anything else); but it was only likely to work if the patient kept out of situations which could lead to stress. This Hardie was quite unable to do. He decided that he wanted to visit Canada, India, the Antipodes, and South Africa, and wrote to Glasier that he intended to try to cover his costs by journalistic work. Glasier must have dissuaded him, because he fell back on finance from philanthropic sources. His main backer was Joseph Fels, a very rich Jewish-American for whose 'Fels-Naphtha Soap' the most astounding medical claims were made in every newspaper. Fels scattered money around liberally in socialist and radical causes, from Keir Hardie to Lenin.

With his financial support secured, Hardie sailed from Liverpool on 12 July 1907, having first had to endure a number of farewell demonstrations from I.L.P. supporters in various towns. His first visit was to Canada, which he crossed from Atlantic to Pacific. At one point he was taken ill again, and had to have hospital treatment in Calgary. Otherwise this part of the journey passed without incident, although Hardie took the opportunity to write home to the *Labour Leader* that unemployment was as high in Canada as at home: the working class should not be duped into believing that emigration would solve all their problems.

From the Pacific coast of Canada Hardie sailed to Asia, first stopping off very briefly in Japan, and then going to India. This was where the trouble started. Before this journey, Hardie had taken relatively little interest in the British Empire (except for South Africa); his only contribution to discussion in Parliament had been a demand for greater accountability of the Indian Secretary of State to the Commons. He admitted that 'India was an afterthought' to his world tour. But it was an afterthought with explosive consequences.

India in 1907 was in turmoil for two reasons – the partition of Bengal and the *swadeshi* movement. In 1905, the unbending and auto-cratic Viceroy, Lord Curzon, had decided that the province of Bengal should be divided into two. This provoked uproar because the new province of East Bengal (the area which became East Pakistan in 1947, and is now Bangladesh) was predominantly Muslim, and the Hindu majority in Bengal as a whole resented their loss of control over part of the area. At the same time, opposition to British rule was being encouraged by the Congress movement (entirely Hindu in its in-spiration). A new recruit to the movement was a lawyer named Mohandas Karamchand Gandhi who had recently returned to India from South Africa, and was encouraging his compatriots to civil disobedience and non-violent boycotts of British goods. This was what was known as *swadeshi*. Others shared Gandhi's objectives but were less scrupulous about means, and there were some violent demonstrations involving destruction of British property. The Hindu leaders were protesting both against British rule and against the Muslim domination of East Bengal. Keir Hardie found himself in the middle of this confused situation when he stepped ashore in Calcutta. He toured the area with Hindu guides, and it was not long before a howl of rage at his conduct was going up from some of the English-language papers, to be re-echoed and magnified in Britain.

Reuter's correspondent in Calcutta cabled that Hardie had said, 'The condition of East Bengal is worse than that of Russia', and that 'atrocities by officials were worse than the behaviour of the Turks in Armenia'. This sparked off a chorus of protest in Britain, led and orchestrated by *The Times* under headlines like

THE UNREST IN INDIA
Inflammatory Speeches by Mr Keir Hardie

Column after column was filled with Hardie's alleged seditious speeches, with speculation that he had been duped by 'native agitators', with snippets of purported news such as the following:

Sydney: The Australian Labour party do not look forward with pleasure to his [Hardie's] coming visit, as they fear that a similar display of blatant ignorance by this self-styled 'comrade' will discredit their cause here.

Punch published a much-lauded cartoon showing a stern Britannia removing a protesting Hardie, complete with a torch marked *Sedition*, from what appeared to be the precincts of the Taj Mahal. Even Hardie's colleagues in the Labour Party were a little alarmed. Shackleton thought MacDonald should obtain copies of the Indian Press to find out what Hardie had actually said.

What he had actually said was so mild that the whole fuss was utterly preposterous – an alarmingly hypersensitive reaction to the spectacle of a Briton criticizing the British Raj. His comments had been wilfully distorted to make them seem more extreme. This was shown by Sir Henry Cotton, a Liberal M.P. with impeccable credentials as a mainstay of the British Raj as he had spent thirty years in the Indian Civil Service. But *The Times*, which emerges extremely badly from this affair, continued to print the distorted reports regardless. Hardie had protested against bureaucratic misrule in Bengal, and said that the solution was for India to be given Dominion self-rule on the same lines as Canada. He had not even demanded immediate independence for India: 'It may be that the people of India are not yet fit for the colonial form of self-government, but . . . sooner or later a beginning must be made towards enfranchising the masses and opening the way for the educated native to fill the higher and better paid positions.' This was what had set off the explosive accusations of 'sedition', although other aspects of Hardie's views might equally have alarmed conventional Anglo-Indian opinion. Hardie recalled, for instance, how he refused to keep an appointment with a magistrate who had insulted a group of educated Hindus accompanying him: 'It took me about twenty-five seconds', Hardie wrote later, 'to express my opinion of him and his conduct, at the end of which time I left him standing where he was and joined my friends.' Small wonder that the English community in India were furious: here was a man who ventured to talk with natives on (almost) equal terms!

One of the complaints against Hardie was that he had been taken in by anti-Muslim propaganda. This is the only charge that has a shred of truth. Hindu unrest in Bengal was mostly directed against Curzon's partition, and hence against the Muslim majority in East Bengal. But it was conducted by the same Congress leaders who were opposing British rule, so Hardie naturally sympathized with them. Hardie's guide in Calcutta, described by *The Times* as 'a prominent agitator', was one of these, and he no doubt offered Hardie a rather partial view of the situation in Bengal. When Hardie explained that the 'outrages' he was alleged to have complained of were actually 'outrages by Mahomedans on Hindu widows', it is perhaps just as well that his rebuttals did not get such prominence as the original stories of his 'sedition'. However, Hardie was aware of communal problems. In the diary he kept in India, and in his book, *India: Impressions and Suggestions*, he noted how in most areas all the officials were Hindus, even in communities containing both Hindus and Muslims.

The uproar over Hardie's views on India is as difficult to understand today as the obstacles to female suffrage. What Hardie actually said in India may seem so commonplace that there is a danger of underestimating his contribution. The idea that India might eventually become a self-governing dominion was revolutionary in 1907. *The Times* called it 'one of the childish generalizations which are characteristic of arrogance coupled with half-education'. Even advanced Liberals shared the view that 'natives' were inferior, unreliable people. John Morley was 'amazed' that his Viceroy should have proposed 'a *Native* member of Council'. Hardie was the first Labour politician to express concern at the status of non-white citizens of the British Empire. He raised the question frequently in Commons debates during the remainder of his life; he bequeathed to the Labour Party an interest in decolonization which culminated in the granting of Indian independence by Attlee's Government in 1947.

From India, Hardie moved on to Australia and New Zealand, where he was warmly welcomed – the suggestions to the contrary in *The Times* being mere prejudice unsupported by a shred of evidence. The Australian visit was mainly social, and Hardie was pleased at meeting again some figures from his past, notably Andrew Fisher, the leader of the Australian Labour Party who was soon to become Prime Minister of Australia. Hardie was very proud of his feat of scoring eight runs in a cricket match in Adelaide in which he played for the Australian Parliament against the Press. The trip to New Zealand had an unfortunate start. Near Wellington, Hardie was pitched out of a motor car which overturned while he was in it. He was shaken, but not seriously hurt. It was just another instance of Hardie's uncanny ability to do himself harm on what was supposed to be a rest cure. Although he enjoyed the visit 'down under', he had written to Glasier in November that he would rather have gone straight home from India than endure the cold weather and 'dreadfully stuck-up' company of his voyage to Australia.

Hardie was next due to visit South Africa, where his notoriety had preceded him. A man who favoured equal treatment for coloured men was not destined to be popular, and he did not mince his words when he got to South Africa. He told the Press that the trade unions, which were refusing to admit non-whites to membership, should admit them

and demand equal wages for them. 'This produced as much sen-
sation', Hardie noted, 'as though I had proposed to cut the throat of
every white man in South Africa.' The outcome was that, wherever
Hardie went, he was accompanied by violent demonstrations. The
last time Hardie had faced such receptions was during the Boer War –
for defending the very people who, in many cases, were now leading
the attacks on him. The largest meeting, and the stormiest scene, was
at Johannesburg. For the rest of his life Hardie treasured a Union
Jack which was rescued from the mob on this occasion. It was hung
on the wall at Nevill's Court as a battle souvenir.

Hardie's commitment to radical equality was by no means absolute.
As we have seen, he did not think India yet ready for independence;
and, in a curious speech in Australia, he said, 'The experiment of
keeping Australia white is a great one.' The threat to White Australia
came from the Chinese and Japanese who, not being citizens of the
British Empire, did not get much sympathy from Hardie. None the
less, Hardie was a long way ahead of his time, and for the rest of his
parliamentary career he was a stern defender of the rights of Indians
and non-white South Africans.

Hardie returned home in May 1908, to a tumultuous reception in
'welcome home' demonstrations in London and Manchester. But the
I.L.P.'s adulation of him was not echoed by his parliamentary
colleagues, some of whom had been criticizing his leadership of the
P.L.P. almost from the outset. In July 1906 MacDonald penned a
long complaint to Glasier, one of whose functions in life was to act as a
clearing-house for complaints by the Labour leadership about one
another. MacDonald complained that Hardie neglected the business
of the House and did things without consulting his colleagues, and
concluded, 'The result is we are getting into the objectionable habit
of coming to decisions without consulting him.' In spite of rumblings
like these Hardie was re-elected leader in 1907, so that the party had
rather mixed feelings on hearing of his world-cruise plan. Shackleton,
as acting leader, went as an envoy to Cumnock with the official view
that the party was a little reluctant to let him go; but Hardie was
determined. However, few members of the P.L.P. can have been
seriously distressed by his absence, which allowed a change in the
leadership to be made without embarrassment.

The obvious successor was Shackleton. Not only was he one of the
ablest members of the party in Parliament, but also Hardie and
MacDonald agreed that a trade unionist ought to be given a spell at
the helm in the interests of party unity. Hardie wanted out of the
leadership to allow the socialists to 'gang oor ain gait' (as he wrote to

Snowden), but he saw the strategic importance of maintaining the alliance with the trade unionists. Unfortunately Shackleton refused to stand for the leadership, allegedly because he was upset by criticism of him in the *Labour Leader*. MacDonald wrote a long, reflective letter to Glasier in which he pondered the options open to himself, and decided that he ought not to put up for the leadership, so that he could make a bid for it when it came round again to the socialists' 'turn'. The upshot was that Arthur Henderson (who was still regarded as an unimaginative Lib-Lab trade unionist) was nominated unopposed for the parliamentary leadership.

Hardie's first activity in Parliament after his return to the back benches was a re-assertion of his old republicanism – with a new twist. He led Labour protests against a visit by Edward VII to the Tsar of Russia – and was involved in a scene when the chairman refused to let him use the word 'atrocities' in relation to the Tsar's regime, on the grounds that Russia was a friendly power. On refusing to withdraw the word he was required to leave the Chamber, in spite of a mollifying intervention by Asquith. Shortly after this the King held a reception at Windsor for all M.P.s – or rather, for all except three. Hardie wrote to Glasier:

> I have just learnt (authoritatively) that my name was struck off the list of invites to Windsor on Saturday last by express order of the King owing to my speech re his visit to Russia. Now I have never been to one of the parties nor do I ever intend to, but I am not going to stand that . . . Ponsonby M.P. (C.B.'s successor)* who voted with us was treated in like manner, and I regret to say so was Grayson. I don't want to be mixed up with him in a matter of this kind.
>
> . . . I regard the thing as unconstitutional in the highest degree and if nothing else can be done shall bring an impeachment.

The decision was reversed after the Labour Party threatened to boycott the garden party altogether, so that Hardie's dire threats were never carried out. His stance is a little curious. It seems rather illogical to demand an invitation from a person whose position one thinks should not exist to a party one does not propose to attend. Republicanism, vanity, and the constitutional position of M.P.s seem to have pulled Hardie in conflicting directions.

The reference to Grayson in the above letter shows that the honeymoon was over. The malcontents, headed by Tillett and Grayson, were vigorously attacking the P.L.P. for its failure to do anything

---

* Arthur Ponsonby, a radical Liberal who became M.P. for Stirling after Campbell-Bannerman died in 1908. An opponent of the First World War, he later joined the Labour Party.

about unemployment. For the working class the Edwardian years were by no means the golden age of post-war memories. Throughout the reign, wages lagged behind prices, and unemployment rose to a peak in 1905 and another in 1908. The Labour Party's difficulty was that it had no real solution to offer short of socialism, and it was distinctly short of ideas for palliatives to unemployment while capitalism lasted. Hardie pressed the Government to extend the scope of Balfour's Unemployed Workman Act of 1905, but the Local Government Board under John Burns pursued a policy of masterly inaction. Complaints grew that the P.L.P. was not doing enough for the unemployed, and they were redoubled after two demonstrations by Grayson in the Commons in October 1908. On the 15th he demanded an adjournment debate on unemployment. On being told that he could not have it, because it was not in the timetable, he said, 'I must personally refuse to be bound by such rules . . . Oh yes, you well-fed human beings can say "Order", but the unemployed have been goaded into disorder.' As he left the House, escorted by the Sergeant-at-Arms, he turned round to the Labour members to shout 'You are traitors to your class'. The following day he interrupted a debate to shout, 'There are thousands of people dying in the streets while you are trifling with the Bill . . . I shall not keep order. I am alone in this House, but I am going to fight . . . I shall obstruct the proceedings so long as the House refuses to consider this Question.' On Asquith's motion, Grayson was suspended from attendance and ordered out; on the way he turned round to shout, 'This House is a House of murderers.'

These tactics placed Hardie in a very awkward position. He knew that Grayson's scenes were entirely stage-managed, and that Grayson had, up till then, done nothing at all in the campaign to get the Government to do something about unemployment. But he also knew that Grayson's actions would be very popular with the rank and file of the I.L.P., who would see no reason why the parliamentary timetable should get in the way of an assault on employment. In any case, Hardie felt so strongly on unemployment that he used language almost as violent as Grayson's. Shortly after Grayson's 'scenes', he spoke in the Commons in a style reminiscent of his 'Peterloo' telegram of 1905.

> If these people [the unemployed] were to be placed outside the law they had no right to expect them to obey the law, and if the worst came to the worst, he would . . . go amongst his own people who were suffering from hunger and cold, and he would take the responsibility, and the consequences, for the advice he would give them.

A speech like this pointed to the rift between Hardie and MacDonald, for whom the parliamentary timetable was sacred and who was contemptuous of expressive emotional gestures, whether genuine or feigned. Hardie shared neither view and had no objections in principle to scenes such as Grayson had engineered. He was only saved from an awkward conflict of loyalties by the folly of Grayson and his supporters.

In November 1908 Grayson, Hardie, and H. M. Hyndman were due to speak at a meeting in Holborn Town Hall – but Grayson and Hyndman refused to speak on the same platform as Hardie, and the meeting was cancelled. This was a fatal error. Even the most passionate of Grayson's supporters were not against Hardie, and a calculated insult to the founder of the Labour Party was too much for most of them to stomach. Grayson's complaints against the leadership were widely expected to be aired at the Labour Party Conference in 1909, but not a word from him was heard. It was said that he had been thoroughly wined and dined, then taken for a drive in the country – and left there, so as to ensure that he would miss the relevant debate.

The climax to these manoeuvres came at the I.L.P. Conference, later in 1909. The N.A.C. report to Conference contained a paragraph explaining that Grayson had refused to be put on the I.L.P. speakers' panel, and that after the Holborn incident that party ceased negotiating with him. By a narrow majority the Conference decided to refer back this paragraph. Hardie, Snowden, Glasier, and MacDonald thereupon announced that they were all resigning from the N.A.C., to which they had just been re-elected. This was a bombshell to the Conference, which immediately recanted in obsequious terms; but the 'Big Four' were adamant. Hardie complained that Grayson was being 'used' by others (meaning Hyndman) who wanted to destroy what Hardie called the 'Labour Alliance' – the link between the I.L.P. and the trade unions; it was up to the I.L.P. as a whole to decide what they thought of this.

For various reasons, all four were probably glad to be out of office. MacDonald had complained to Glasier not long before that 'there is as much fraternity in the I.L.P. as there is nutriment in a cabbage'. After the conference Glasier said sententiously to Hardie, 'I felt the hand of God is in our resignation.' Hardie wanted out in order to be ·free to play the lone wolf, as he preferred to do. It is possible, also, that the strain was telling in other ways. For instance, the I.L.P. leadership were constantly having to deny to Conference that there had ever been any electoral pact with the Liberal Party. Diplomatic lying on such points was second nature to Ramsay MacDonald, but very hard for Keir Hardie. In resigning from his positions of responsibility, first in the Parliamentary Party and then in the I.L.P., he may have been trying to get away from such distasteful situations.

The difficulties and dramas of the I.L.P. were played out in a very obscure corner of the political stage of 1909. The Liberal Government was obviously moving closer to a confrontation with the House of Lords, which had thrown out a succession of Bills on topics dear to Liberal hearts: education, licensing reform, plural voting. On the other hand, they had not thrown out Old Age Pensions. These were introduced by Lloyd George, who became Chancellor of the Exchequer in the reshuffle of 1908, after Asquith succeeded Campbell-Bannerman as Prime Minister. The Lords were letting through another measure – like the Trade Disputes Act – associated with the new, collectivist Liberalism, while feeling it safe to block the programme of the old, individualist Liberalism. These events helped to enhance the reputation of Lloyd George and embarrass the Labour Party. Lloyd George's fame as the leading reformer spread to all corners of the land. (Readers of Flora Thompson will recall how 'that Lord George' was blessed as the man who had brought Old Age Pensions to Lark Rise.) He also sponsored other notable measures of reform in the same year, such as the setting up of Labour Exchanges and the establishment of Trade Boards to regulate wages in badly paid occupations. These measures put the Labour Party in a dilemma. They did not want to oppose them; but in supporting them, how could they avoid seeming indistinguishable from the Liberals? There was some danger that Lloyd George's reforms would eclipse the Labour Party altogether.

Old Age Pensions had to be paid for. So did a greatly accelerated naval programme, which arose out of a scare sweeping the country in 1909 that German battleship construction was threatening British naval supremacy. Accordingly, Lloyd George produced a Budget which proposed a number of innovations: petrol tax, an increased spirits duty, higher income tax (with 'supertax' of 6d. in the pound on incomes over £5,000 a year), death duties ranging from 4 per cent to 15 per cent, and taxes on land – on unearned increment, undeveloped land, and mineral rights. After a slow start, these latter provisions gradually led to a crescendo of protest as Conservative and landowning interests began to take them in. The Duke of Buccleuch announced that he would no longer be able to pay subscriptions to his local football club because of the swingeing impact of Lloyd George's Budget. Lloyd George retorted in style: 'A fully equipped duke costs

as much to keep up as two Dreadnoughts;* and they are just as great
a terror, and they last longer.' Before long, an awesome possibility
began to loom: that the House of Lords would reject the Budget.
Since the seventeenth century it had been universally accepted that
money matters were the province of the Commons alone; were the
Lords going to break this convention? Should 'five hundred men,
ordinary men chosen accidentally from among the unemployed', in
Lloyd George's memorable phrase, override the wishes of the Commons? In the summer and autumn of 1909 the Budget struggle
eclipsed all else; nothing Hardie or the Labour Party had ever said or
done was as spectacular as Lloyd George's campaign. Unionist peers,
urged on by the party leadership, eventually decided on the exciting
and reckless course. On 30 November 1909 Lloyd George's Budget
was rejected by the House of Lords by 350 votes to 75. There was no
alternative but to call a General Election: the Lords had refused the
money to pay for the Government's current programme. They had
also made the Liberals a gift of the finest slogan for decades: The Peers
against the People. It provided an excellent opportunity for the
Liberals to revive their fortunes, which had been sagging badly at by-
elections.

On the whole, the position of the Labour Party as it shaped up to the
election of January 1910 was not very happy. On the credit side, the
strength of the P.L.P. had soared to forty-five because the miners'
unions had affiliated to the Labour Party in 1909. All the miners'
M.P.s, except three veterans including Burt and Fenwick, fought the
January 1910 election as Labour candidates. But this was not all gain
from the socialists' point of view: for Hardie it meant that the Labour
Party would be 'controlled by Coal and Cotton, and . . . that means
more reaction'. And on other fronts the Labour Party was not doing
well. Its by-election record had been poor. Not only had it made no
gains, but it had never even come a good second. In Croydon, Frank
Smith had managed to reduce the Labour vote from 20·2 to 4·2 per
cent of the votes cast in a by-election in 1909, and this was merely the
worst of a run of bad results, which only highlighted the embarrassing
success of Victor Grayson. And the party stood to lose heavily from
the 'Osborne judgement'. W.V.Osborne was a Lib-Lab branch
secretary in the railwaymen's union, who challenged the union's legal
right to give funds to the Labour Party. The Law Lords eventually
ruled in Osborne's favour: a ruling, which, it has been said, owed more
to lawyers' dislike of trade union 'privileges' under the 1906 Act than
to any dispassionate consideration of rights and wrongs. In January

* The improved battleships being built because of the 'naval scare'.

1910 the effects of the Osborne judgement on Labour Party finance were not yet severe, but the outlook for the future was grave. The party acquired one distinctive plank to its platform: reversal of the Osborne judgement was a Labour slogan alone.

Early in January 1910 Hardie went down to Merthyr. He was determined not to repeat the mistake of 1906 by neglecting his own constituency. D.A.Thomas was no longer his running mate, for he had exchanged his Merthyr seat for Cardiff. Since Cardiff was much less safe, this seems an odd move: the likeliest reason is that Thomas, as a coal-owner, was acutely aware that there was likely to be serious trouble in the pits before long, and he wanted to move out of the constituency many of his collieries were in before his position became embarrassing. He was replaced by a young Liberal called Edgar Jones, whose relations with Hardie were, at least to begin with, quite cordial. It was a four-cornered fight; there was a Unionist candidate, and Pritchard Morgan, the defeated eccentric Liberal of 1900, re-emerged to challenge Hardie. Morgan's supporters busily attacked Hardie's alleged atheism and claimed that he owned large estates in Scotland. The local newspaper, which had previously been benevolently neutral towards Hardie, was this time hostile. It pointed out that Hardie owed most of his votes to supporters of labour representation, not to socialists as such, and urged electors to cast their two votes for Jones and Pritchard Morgan. Mindful of the lessons of 1906, Hardie fought on Welsh issues. Many of his constituency speeches were about Welsh disestablishment, a subject in which he had not shown the slightest interest in the Commons. Merthyr polled on 20 January; when the results were in, Hardie had won handsomely, although Jones beat him to the top of the poll. This was the only one of Hardie's elections in Merthyr for which a complete breakdown of votes was not published in the *Merthyr Express*. But informed guesses gave the following figures:

	Plumpers*	Splits	Total
Jones (Liberal)	375	15,073	15,448
Hardie (Labour)	1,872	11,969	13,841
Fox-Davies (Unionist)	3,186	1,570	4,756
Morgan (Liberal)	75	3,564	3,639

For the third time Hardie had got in because the voters regarded him, rather than the nominal second Liberal, as the official Liberal's running mate.

Nationally the election of January 1910 resulted in a slight setback

* 'Plumpers': those who cast only one vote; 'Splits': those who cast two.

for Labour. There were four losses and no gains, and in addition Victor Grayson came bottom of the poll in Colne Valley, a result which caused little grief in the P.L.P. The Liberals lost their overall majority, and were reduced to the same number of seats as the Conservatives. They were going to have to depend on the Irish and Labour for support in the next Parliament. Home Rule was bound to return to the political agenda, and the Labour members pressed for a reversal of the Osborne judgement as their price for supporting the Liberals. But the constitutional crisis remained the principal issue of domestic politics, as the country awaited developments in the spring of 1910.

7

LAST YEARS

The Labour Party was very confused and un-
certain what to do when the new House of Commons met to discuss
the Lords' rejection of Lloyd George's Budget. The Liberals were
divided between two alternatives: a Bill to replace the Lords' right to
reject Government legislation by a 'suspensory veto',* and a scheme
to modify the whole composition of the House of Lords so as to make
it more democratic. Hardie wanted to see the Lords abolished altogether. He was impatient with the majority of the P.L.P., which

---

* I.e., the principle eventually adopted in the 1911 Parliament Act, that if a
measure is passed by the Commons in three consecutive sessions it must become
law even if rejected by the Lords.

was in favour of the 'suspensory veto'. The Labour Party had also to consider a tactical point, namely that it could not afford to provoke a Government defeat. Such a defeat followed by a dissolution would be disastrous for Labour; with the Osborne judgment just beginning to bite, the Labour Party would be bankrupted by another election. George Barnes, who had succeeded Henderson as leader, had to ask for an adjournment while Labour sorted out its views. The next day Hardie made a fierce speech.

> We want to apply the remedy [to the House of Lords] which was used by a Scotch farmer to a mad dog. He was told the way to cure its madness was to cut off part of its tail. He carried out that advice, and when subsequently asked about what he had done, he explained that he had cut off the tail from behind the ears. That is our plan for dealing with the House of Lords.

Though Hardie stressed that he was putting a personal view, he found himself in trouble with the P.L.P. for going beyond party policy. Increasingly, 'ganging oor ain gait' was leading to friction between Hardie and his staider successors as party leader.

Hardie's position was unenviable. The Labour Party had had difficulty in remaining distinctive in the previous Parliament, when the Liberals had a huge majority – although it had scored one legislative triumph in the Trade Disputes Act. In the new Parliament the Liberals depended on the Labour Party for their majority, but it still seemed to be unable to take a distinctive position. The party ought to have been using its bargaining position in the Commons to force concessions – so long as it could avoid having its bluff called by the threat of a dissolution – but under the inexperienced and unadventurous leadership of George Barnes the party was behaving simply as an appendage to the Liberals. It was in this frame of mind that Hardie said bitterly to the 1910 Conference of the I.L.P., 'At the present time the Labour Party has almost ceased to count.' It was becoming harder to defend the 'Labour alliance' against the purist extremists. It was evident that the parliamentary alliance of socialists and trade unionists was achieving very little, and thus the arguments of Hardie's left-wing opponents in the I.L.P. were becoming more plausible. Four members of the N.A.C. produced a pamphlet called *Let Us Reform the Labour Party*. Known as the 'Green Manifesto', it was a document similar to Tillett's earlier effort. It called for a reassertion of socialism and a break with the compromising politics of the P.L.P. Hardie's position – 'My Confession of Faith in the Labour Alliance', as he called it in one of his pamphlets – was saved only because none of his opponents was a serious politician. The authors of the Green Mani-

festo neither had nor tried to secure much support in the I.L.P. Tillett
was a loner, too vituperative to make stable political alliances.
Grayson was becoming an alcoholic and dropping out of politics.
Blatchford had cut himself off from the rest of the Left by his noisy
support for the jingoistic campaigns of the 'naval scare' – 'We want
eight [Dreadnoughts] and we won't wait.' A few of the malcontents in
the I.L.P. left, and joined forces with Hyndman's S.D.F. to form the
British Socialist Party in 1912; but it never looked like having any
substantial working-class support, a position which was little changed
when it joined with some other fringe groups to form the Communist
Party of Great Britain in 1920. While Hardie stayed with the I.L.P.,
the I.L.P. was bound to remain Britain's only important socialist
party. It kept up the 'Labour alliance' through all the difficulties of
the years 1911 to 1914, and this was largely due to Hardie's steadfast-
ness.

In April 1910 the Lords passed the 1909 Budget, knowing that the
only alternative must be the swamping of the Upper House by up to
500 Liberal peers* to push it through. The Government then started
to think out its ideas on House of Lords reform, but the process was
rudely interrupted by the sudden death of Edward VII on 6 May.
Amid a chorus of (largely genuine) grief, it was left to Hardie to make
some of the acerbic comments for which he was well known. The
King's funeral, he complained, was an occasion of military pomp –
just like Queen Victoria's in 1901, when Hardie had made the same
complaint. 'The King who was being buried, and who was lauded and
glorified, with some reason, as Edward the Peacemaker, had not a
single representative of peace at his funeral.' Edward was succeeded
by his eldest surviving son, who became George V, and Hardie
promptly moved the deletion of allowances for the new King's sons
and daughters from the Civil List. The Royal Family, said Hardie with
echoes of Lloyd George, should not be 'recipients of outdoor relief'.
'What this proposes', he went on, 'is that we should provide for
Members of the Royal Family an income to enable them to live a life
of luxury, ease, and idleness [Several Hon. Members: "Withdraw!"].'
But the Labour amendments to reduce the Civil List got only about
twenty votes each, five or six of which came from radical Liberals.
Since the Labour Party was forty strong, this was not very impressive.
Keir Hardie's republicanism was not shared by a large number of his
colleagues.

* If this had ever come about, the House of Lords might have become a much
more interesting place. The Liberal Chief Whip's list of possible Liberal peers
included Bertrand Russell, Baden-Powell, Thomas Hardy and J.M.Barrie.

Another colliery disaster at this time brought back echoes of 1894. After an explosion at the Wellington Pit, Whitehaven, rescue attempts had to be abandoned and a shaft bricked up to stop the spread of fire and poisonous fumes while 136 miners were still unaccounted for. The new Home Secretary, Winston Churchill, launched a furious assault on Hardie on the strength of a Press report of a speech Hardie had made in Wales:

Here 136 miners were behind a fire from which there was no escape, and, speaking as a collier, let them mark his opinion – these men were still alive when the wall was built to put out the fire. While there was such a lot of mummery shown at the one man [i.e. Edward VII], those men in the North of England were uncared for.

Churchill called Hardie's comments 'cruel and disgraceful'. The two men cordially detested each other, as was to become amply clear before the year 1910 was out.

In September, Hardie travelled to Copenhagen for another meeting of the Socialist International. The International had matured considerably, now that its leading members were important politicians in their respective countries. Furthermore, the ridiculous disproportion between the size of the Labour Party delegation and the troops of Hyndman's stage army was modified: this time the I.L.P., Fabians and Labour Party had sixty-one delegates to twenty-four from the S.D.F. So there was no prospect of a repetition of the ridiculous farce of 1896. Nevertheless, Hardie found himself in a rather lonely position. The 'naval scare' in Britain and Germany had awakened delegates to the dangers of militarism, and Hardie proposed that the International should call a general strike, 'especially in industries that supply war material', if war in Europe seemed imminent. This was unpopular for various reasons. A number of the German delegates, for instance, wanted to ensure that the German workers were protected against any possible Russian invasion, and did not relish the idea of a general strike against war. The main objection to Hardie's resolution, however, was simply that it was hopelessly unrealistic. Nobody had the courage to say this in so many words, though Glasier muttered in private, 'The idea of the workers ceasing work in the event of war is really a very doubtful one.' If Hardie really thought that there was any chance that the workers would down tools in the event of a European war, he was simply blind to public opinion, not least working-class public opinion – and this in spite of having lived through the Boer War. This blindness was to have tragic enough effects before long.

Hardie's attention was abruptly recalled to home affairs by an up-surge of industrial unrest in his constituency. This was the 'Cambrian Combine' strike of 1910 and 1911. Before the strike of 1898 the South Wales coalfield had been very placid; by 1910 the miners were among the most militant, and the coal-owners the most obdurate, in the country. For such a transition there were many reasons, some social and some economic. The chapels were rapidly losing their grip: the 1904 revival had indeed been the last fling of Welsh Nonconformity. The decline of the chapels meant the decline of social attitudes in-hibiting industrial militancy. Men no longer believed that the evils of this world must be borne in patience till they reached a better one, nor that conflict between master and man was sinful. In any case, a large influx of English immigrants to the valleys was making them less Welsh and breaking down the old Welsh-speaking, Nonconformist culture. And the South Wales mining industry was falling on hard times. Most South Wales coal is steam coal: useless in domestic grates, which cannot provide enough air for it to ignite properly, but excellent for steam-raising in marine and factory boilers. Seams are sometimes thin and often geologically faulted. Most South Wales coal went for export and into ships' bunkers. The market for it was therefore much more uncertain than that for household coal. The amount of household coal burnt does not vary much from winter to winter, but the demand for South Wales coal could fluctuate wildly according to whether trade and industry were prospering or in the doldrums; and, unlike household coal, it had to be sold at a price which was competitive with coal from overseas. In fact, prices for South Wales coal were steadily deteriorating during the later Edwardian years. New methods of cost-accounting were making owners conscious – too conscious – of their labour bills, and piece-rates remained low in South Wales. Miners worked long hours to keep their earnings up – until the Eight-Hours Act, the campaign for which had launched Hardie into politics twenty years earlier, was finally passed in 1909. The ironic conse-quence was severe trouble in South Wales. With his chance of big wages through long hours lost, the South Wales miner became very worried about his piece-rate. And the geological faulting of the coal-field meant an alarming proportion of the 'bad places' which we last met in Ayrshire away back in 1881. A hewer paid so much per ton was bound to suffer badly if the seam he was mining suddenly came to a halt.

These conditions encouraged a growing revolt of South Wales miners away from their Lib-Lab leaders, and an informed observer could have seen that trouble was bound to break out before long.

Perhaps, as we have said, this was why D.A.Thomas abandoned Merthyr Boroughs for Cardiff in January 1910. The serious trouble started with a strike, or rather a lock-out, at Ely colliery, near Cardiff, in September 1910, when hewers refused to accept a piece-rate of 1s 9d. per ton. The dispute spread when miners in all the other pits in a group called the Cambrian Combine (of which D.A.Thomas was the chairman) struck in sympathy; they were joined by employees of the Powell Duffryn Collieries in the Aberdare Valley, in Hardie's constituency.

The strike was unofficial and against the advice of the leaders of the union, who attacked the 'sudden and unconstitutional methods' of their members. Perhaps as a result, most of the miners involved went back to work, but in the Aberdare and Rhondda valleys they stayed on strike. There can be little doubt that this was mainly a spontaneous burst of frustration at their worsening conditions of employment. But some observers were alarmed, and others delighted, at the emergence of militant left-wing groups of miners who put forward doctrines of 'syndicalism'. The syndicalists argued that socialism should be achieved, not by parliamentary means, but through a succession of strikes lasting until the capitalists were unable to carry on, whereupon the workers would take over the means of production. One of the many novel features of syndicalism was that it outflanked Keir Hardie on the left. His reaction to the coal strike of 1910–11 was, perhaps because of this, highly emotional.

The strike hit the national headlines on 7 November, when there was an outburst of looting after a riot in Tonypandy, one of the mining communities in the Rhondda valley. In a state of great agitation the local magistrates (not a totally separate body of men from the local coal-owners) telephoned Winston Churchill, the Home Secretary, with a demand for troops to be sent in to quell the rioters. Fortunately Churchill was not wholly convinced that the revolution was about to start; and, with a General Election approaching, he took great care to avoid any action which could be construed as strike-breaking by troops at the Government's request. At very short notice, Churchill picked General C.F.N.Macready to command the troops in South Wales. It was an inspired choice. Macready was a first-rate politician and diplomat, who remained cool while all about him were frantically crying ruin and revolution. The Chief Constable of Glamorgan had been locked into mine buildings near Tonypandy by strikers, and, as Macready drily recorded, he 'was naturally influenced by his immediate surroundings, and at the moment of no assistance towards helping to a general view of the situation'.

Macready made it plain that the troops would do what he thought right, not what the coal-owners wanted; he arranged a meeting with the strike leaders, over tea and ginger beer, at which he had some success in persuading them that he was not the agent of the coal-owners. Thanks to this diplomacy the troops were never used, except in one small affray. Contrary to the version of the incident which has become part of the folk tradition of the British labour movement, most of the troops never went near Tonypandy, but remained at Pontypridd, at the foot of the Rhondda valley. With the soldiers kept in the background, so as not to provoke trouble, the police remained in control.

On 15 November, the disturbances at Tonypandy and Aberdare were discussed in a stormy debate in the Commons. Hardie opened by complaining that at Tonypandy the police had dispersed pickets which were perfectly legal under the 1906 Act. He went on to say that the trouble at Tonypandy was no more than a little window-smashing (a minority interpretation), and added that at Aberaman (near Aberdare) the colliery owners had tried to keep their striking employees out by putting up an electric fence: 'the first time ... that Mr Andrew Carnegie's "Homestead"* methods have been adopted by British employers'. Hardie was supported by his fellow member for Merthyr, Edgar Jones, who complained with justice that most commentators were failing to distinguish Aberdare from Rhondda, two quite different places – 'That is the misfortune of governing Wales from London.'

Hardie's speech, moderate until almost the end, had been marked by a violent peroration. Many of the miners fought in the Boer War, he observed, and went on, 'These men are now at war with the colliery owners; and they can see no great harm in applying the principles they learnt in South Africa to the present enemy.' Churchill took the opportunity to seize on this statement and make a fierce attack on Hardie for his extremism, in the course of which he was able to ignore the substantive points that had been made.

Hardie scored a minor victory in that Churchill ordered the coal-owners to remove the electric fence, which was illegal. But on various charges of police brutality by Hardie, who said 'The colliers of South Wales have no intention of being bludgeoned in order to make a Liberal holiday', Churchill was unyielding. Hardie persevered, but he got little support. In an adjournment debate in March 1911 he let his tongue run away with him again when he called the Liberal member

* A strike at Carnegie's steelworks at Homestead had been violently broken up by hired thugs in 1892.

for East Glamorgan a 'reptile of the viper order'. This was no way to win parliamentary friends, and Hardie's motion criticizing the police got only twenty-three votes. Nobody except the Labour members supported him, and by no means all of those.

The affair of the Cambrian Combine strike does not show Hardie at his best. His speeches in Parliament were poor performances for several reasons. He tried to maintain that the serious rioting in Tonypandy was much less of a threat to public order than it was; the violence of his language alienated potential supporters; and he never effectively put across the strongest part of his argument, namely that Tonypandy and Aberaman were separated by two mountain ranges but the Government spoke of them as if they were the same place. It seems likely that Hardie was disoriented by the upsurge of violence and the emergence of syndicalism. Not knowing what to make of it, he did not know how to react to the incidents of the strike.

While the Cambrian Combine strike was still in progress, a second General Election loomed. An attempt to agree on a plan for House of Lords reform between the Government and the Unionists had failed. The Government therefore announced another dissolution of Parliament, having got from a very reluctant George V a secret promise that, if the Liberals were returned, he would be prepared to create enough peers to allow the Government proposals for a suspensory veto to be passed through the House of Lords. Polling was to take place in December, and Hardie went back to his constituency to conduct his campaign.

The *Merthyr Express* thought that there should be no contest in the constituency because of the 'disturbed condition of the Aberdare valley'. However, the local Liberals seriously discussed putting up a second candidate to oppose Hardie. Liberal–Labour relations in the valleys had worsened. The miners' leaders had abandoned their Lib-Labbery and were putting up Labour candidates against sitting Liberal members in several seats in the South Wales mining valleys. There was an obvious risk of retaliation in the shape of Liberal opposition to Labour incumbents, and it is clear that the Merthyr Liberal Association discussed long and hard the possibility of putting up a second Liberal candidate. The eventual decision not to was obviously unpopular with a substantial section of the party; a flood of letters of complaint in the local Press appeared after the decision had been announced. At the last moment the ubiquitous Pritchard Morgan popped up to fill the gap; there was also a Unionist candidate. Morgan then had second thoughts and withdrew again, so that the overall result was in little doubt. Hardie and Jones were returned again, with Hardie still just failing to come top of the poll. The detailed analysis of the votes, once again published in the *Merthyr Express*, is of interest.

	Hardie (Lab.)	Jones (Lib.)	Watts (Unionist)
Plumpers	2,634	2,188	3,506
Hardie and Jones	8,586	8,586	—
Hardie and Watts	287	—	287
Jones and Watts	—	1,484	1,484
Totals	11,507	12,258	5,277

It is noteworthy that Hardie's 'plumpers' were still not very numerous – there were still more Unionist plumpers than Independent Labour ones. (As a matter of fact, Hardie still had many fewer plumpers in Merthyr in 1910 than he had had in Preston in 1900.) This rather tends to show that the new mood of syndicalism had not affected ordinary miners' voting habits. In a number of the valley constituencies, it is clear that Liberals must have received more miners' votes than the Labour candidates who stood against them. This was notably true in East Glamorgan, where the unsuccessful miners' candidate was C. B. Stanton, an outspoken rebel against the old leadership of Brace and Mabon. In every case except one where there were fights between Liberal and Labour candidates in the valleys, the Liberal won. The days when South Wales was to be the strongest Labour-voting area in Britain were yet to come.

The overall result of the December 1910 election was stalemate. The number of Labour candidates was cut from seventy-eight to fifty-six because of the financial effects of the Osborne judgement. The number of Labour wins rose slightly, however. Four gains and two losses raised Labour strength to forty-two. The total strength of the Liberal and Unionist parties remained exactly the same; although quite a number of seats changed hands, in the end conflicting movements cancelled each other out. Everybody except the most diehard members of the House of Lords now realized that the Liberals, in office for the third consecutive time, must be allowed to press on with their suspensory veto plans, threatening the diehards with the creation of peers if they resisted. The Parliament Act, finally passed in August 1911, allowed the Lords to reject measures presented by the Commons twice, but required them to let them through when presented for the third time. At a stroke, the parliamentary timetable for 1912, 1913, and 1914 was filled. It was obvious that all the old Liberal measures – Welsh disestablishment, plural voting, and Home Rule – were going to be revived for a triple passage through the Commons. It did not look as though there would be much opportunity for the distinctive Labour presence to make itself felt. In any case, the Labour demands being pressed by MacDonald – payment of M.P.s and reversal of the Osborne judgement – were what might be called procedural rather than substantive. They were designed to make it easier for the Labour Party to be effective in Parliament, not to improve the conditions of the working class.

The first substantive measure that was discussed went badly awry from Labour's point of view. An epoch-making Royal Commission on the Poor Law reported in 1909. All its members agreed that reform was badly needed in the interests of the sick and unemployed, who up till then had only the very dubious assistance of the harsh 'New Poor Law' of 1834. A minority report, drafted by Beatrice Webb, argued that providing insurance against sickness and unemployment ought to be entirely the responsibility of the state. This was too strong for the majority of the commission, and it was too strong for Lloyd George, who introduced his proposals for National Insurance in May 1911. The National Insurance Bill had two sections, the first dealing with sickness and the second with unemployment. Both were to be financed on a contributory basis: for sickness insurance, for instance, payment was to be 4d. a week by the insured employee, 3d. by his employer, and 2d. by the state.

The Labour Party was deeply divided on National Insurance. For one thing, here was another example of the Liberals stealing the thunder. The Liberal Party – or at least Lloyd George – was again seeming more radical than the Labour Party, and members like Hardie bitterly resented their party's failure to make an impact. But the split went much deeper. Many Labour members were fully in favour of Lloyd George's proposal, and in particular most trade-union sponsored M.P.s strongly supported it. Lloyd George had provided that both halves of the scheme should be run through existing friendly societies. This could be a tremendous boost to the prestige of trade unions; and status as a recognized friendly society under the National Insurance Act would be of immense value to a trade union recruiting new members. On the other hand a small but intense minority of the Labour members wanted a non-contributory scheme. With Snowden in the lead, and Hardie a little distance behind, this group demanded that the principles of the Poor Law Minority Report should be observed, and that workers should not have to contribute to the fund. Even if the Bill had not been highly favourable to trade unions, these views would not have appealed to all Labour M.P.s.

Ex-Liberals brought up to revere the Victorian virtues of thrift and temperance (as Hardie himself had been before he turned to socialism) thought a contributory scheme was right and proper.

Not surprisingly, the Labour performance in the National Insurance debates was a mess. A few Labour members busily attacked the Bill in committee. Hardie said that sickness insurance was merely 'a porous plaster to cover the disease that poverty causes', which may have been true, but was not a very helpful guide to action. Lloyd George found it very hard to pin down exactly what the Labour Party wanted, although one member who did know what he wanted was Ramsay MacDonald. MacDonald's objective was to deliver Labour support for National Insurance to Lloyd George in return for a promise of payment of members and reversal of the Osborne judgment. The credibility of this offer was damaged by the Third Reading debate on the Bill, which resulted in an enormous majority for it and a hopelessly split Labour Party. Five Labour members, including Snowden and George Lansbury, voted against; Hardie abstained; the great majority of Labour members voted in support. Small wonder that W. J. Braithwaite, one of Lloyd George's principal Civil Service advisors on the Bill, recorded something as near as it was proper to go to annoyance at the attitude of the Labour Party negotiators: 'The worst of it is that they don't speak for their men, don't know what their men want, and can't bind their men to obey – rather difficult people to deal with.'

Hardie was by now a habitual rebel in the Labour Party, and was drifting further and further away from MacDonald, who succeeded Barnes as leader in 1911. Hardie's relations with MacDonald had been distant since an acrimonious exchange of letters in 1910, when Hardie had indicated that he did not want MacDonald to go for the leadership of the party. They worsened steadily during the years 1911 to 1913, as MacDonald became more and more the parliamentarian and Hardie more and more the rebel. Hardie's awkward position in the Parliamentary Party was shown most clearly on two issues: industrial relations and women's suffrage.

The eventual failure of the Cambrian Combine strike did not mark the end of the new wave of industrial unrest: it was barely the beginning. The highlights of 1911 were a seamen's strike, and soon after it a national railway strike. The railway strike was settled by Lloyd George, the Government's favourite trouble-shooter, after Asquith had made a bad situation worse by walking out on the railwaymen's leaders after failing to get an agreement, saying as he went, 'Then your blood be on your own head.' It was unfortunate language. A

badly rattled Government allowed troops to be sent to the main
trouble spots to 'reinforce the civil power'. Two men were killed during
a riot in Liverpool; two more when strikers tried to stop a train
manned by blacklegs in Llanelli, in South Wales. This was another
and worse version of Tonypandy, and Hardie's reaction was similar.
Again he was involved in furious parliamentary exchanges. In
Hardie's view, Asquith's brusque statement to the railwaymen was a
promise that troops would be brought in to shoot down strikers – a
promise fulfilled at Llanelli. Hardie wrote a pamphlet in his most
devastating Overtoun style, called *Killing No Murder: the Government
and the Railway Strike*, to put across this point of view. To Lloyd
George this was disgraceful misrepresentation; in any case the
Llanelli crowd had been one of dangerous rioters. The main lesson of
the incidents was that the British Army needed more officers like
Macready, who did not lose their heads in the face of crowds of angry
strikers.

The unrest continued. There was no bloodshed in 1912, but the
number of days lost through strikes soared to more than three times
the 1911 level. The biggest strike was a national stoppage in the coal
industry, the product of unprecedented unity among the miners. The
age-old problem of 'abnormal places' had come to a head. To protect
its members, the Miners' Federation was demanding a minimum
wage of 5s. a shift for men and 2s. for boys regardless of conditions.
Hardie pointed proudly to the miners' unity. For the first time ever,
miners in prosperous districts were prepared to strike in the interests
of their less fortunate fellows in Scotland and South Wales. 'There
never was a more unselfish dispute in the whole history of the working-
class movement,' Hardie said, and as he said so, he no doubt thought
back to his own early days. If the temperament of 1912 had existed
among the Scots miners between 1879 and 1886, Hardie's early career
might have been very much more successful than it was.

The Government rushed through a Coal Mines (Minimum Wages)
Bill which set up machinery to determine minimum wages. But it
could not bring itself to write the sums of 5s and 2s. into the Bill; it
was too great a step away from the old, *laissez-faire* liberalism for the
Government to tolerate, even in this crisis. The miners stated that the
Bill would not do; Hardie and MacDonald announced that the Labour
Party would vote against the third reading. The Bill was enacted, but
it was irrelevant to the strike, which eventually ended in April because
of failing support among the miners.

There was a brief resurgence of violence in 1913, this time in Dublin.
In Britain, the Government had learned the lesson of Liverpool and

Llanelli, and kept troops well clear of industrial disturbances; but in
Ireland there were violent riots during a strike of Dublin tramwaymen
orgnanized by the charismatic but erratic James Larkin. Hardie
went to Dublin to make a fiery speech at the graveside of two men
killed in the rioting; in the lofty opinion of *The Times*, 'the intervention of Mr Keir Hardie . . . is regarded as something worse than an
impertinence'. Hardie defended Larkin against Snowden, who wrote,
'The old Trade Unionism looked facts in the face, and acted with regard to commonsense. The new Trade Unionism, call it what you will
– Syndicalism, Carsonism, Larkinism, does neither.' Hardie's attitude
to syndicalism thus left him in a rather lonely position in the Labour
Party in Parliament. He said pugnaciously in the Commons: 'Syndicalism is the direct outcome of the apathy and the indifference of this
House towards working-class questions, and I rejoice at the growth
of Syndicalism.' Here he parted company even with his I.L.P. associates such as Snowden and Glasier. Glasier commented acidly,
'Syndicalism is now on the lips of all politicians – the majority of
whom do not know what it means . . . It is a gratifying addition to the
locution of the average politician and editor.' There was a good deal
of truth in this. Syndicalism was used as a passionate rallying-cry by
some strike leaders, and it was used in the Press and on the platform to
strike a chill down the spines of the comfortable bourgeoisie. But it is
ridiculous to suppose that the strike wave of 1911–13 was due to the
influence of syndicalism on the workers. It is also wrong to assume that
Hardie actually agreed with the programme of syndicalism. The
clearest statement of it was in *The Miners' Next Step*, a pamphlet
published at Tonypandy in 1912. The workers must strike and strike
and strike again, its authors argued, until the capitalists could no
longer carry on; then the workers would take over their industries,
and send delegates, mandated to obey their instructions, to Westminster. Given Hardie's view of the proper relations between M.P.s
and the party outside Parliament, it is difficult to envisage his accepting this programme. In any case, the strikes of 1911–13 owed little to
ideology. They were either spontaneous protests by the unskilled and
unorganized, or, as with the coal strikes, explosions of anger over long-
standing grievances which got more burdensome as real wages declined.

There was a widespread feeling that syndicalism was pushing the
Parliamentary Labour Party into the shade, and it was no doubt this
that led Hardie to give syndicalism his outspoken support. But we
should not be deluded by appearances. For all his violence of language,
Hardie was not a violent man, and outside Parliament he criticized
syndicalism for ignoring the machinery of constitutional action.

Hardie was no real friend of the notions of 'direct action' being proposed by such men as Tom Mann, Ben Tillett, and the authors of *The Miners' Next Step*. Nevertheless, he was, in public, much more sympathetic to syndicalism than most Labour M.P.s.

He was also out of step on women's franchise. Hardie and George Lansbury, the newly elected member for Bow and Bromley, were the only supporters of the W.S.P.U. in the Labour Party. This was quixotic on Hardie's part, since the W.S.P.U. in their wisdom had now chosen to make him one of the chief beneficiaries of their disruption. Lansbury's action was more quixotic still. He resigned his seat in order to re-fight it as a Labour and Women's Suffrage candidate after the P.L.P. refused to accept his policy of subordinating all else to women's suffrage. Hardie was his only supporter, and when he found himself in a minority of one on the National Executive of the Labour Party he resigned from it in order to be able to speak for Lansbury. Having more or less sacrificed his seat on behalf of the W.S.P.U., Lansbury got no help from them whatever, and lost the ensuing by-election to a Unionist.

This left Hardie even more isolated, as Lansbury had been his most consistent supporter ever since December 1910. However, Hardie did manage to carry the Parliamentary Party with him on the vexed question of the force-feeding of suffragettes. From about 1909 onwards some of the militant suffragettes had gone on hunger-strike on being imprisoned, and had been forcibly fed to prevent them from dying of starvation. Hardie frequently complained about this in Parliament and in the country: 'If one of these women should happen to die under this treatment no justification whatever will satisfy the people of England.' The Government, at a loss to know what to do, eventually introduced a Prisoners (Ill-Health) Discharge Bill, which allowed hunger-strikers to be discharged, on condition that they were re-arrested when fit to serve the rest of their sentences. This was a pointless measure, as suffragettes merely hunger-struck, were released, and hunger-struck again as soon as they were re-admitted, gaining a maximum of publicity for their cause in the meantime. Opposition to the Bill was led by an incongruous pair: Keir Hardie and Lord Robert Cecil, a right-wing Tory who dubbed the measure the 'Cat-and-Mouse' Bill, as it has ever since been known. 'Can anything more inhuman and more barbarous be conceived?' Hardie asked. Initially Hardie was in a small minority, but eventually he got the whole Labour Party to oppose the third reading of the Bill.

Hardie's position was more emotional than logical. Glasier remarked in private that he could not see what right the suffragettes had to complain. 'They claim the right to break the law and then . . . complain of the iniquity of being treated as law-breakers.' This was irrefutable, and Hardie's complaints that forced feeding was barbarous were beside the point as he had no alternative to propose except letting the suffragettes go. Of course, the Cat-and-Mouse Bill was a mistake. But nobody pointed out that the only way for the Home Secretary to avoid anything of the sort was to abandon forced feeding and let hunger-strikers commit slow suicide. However, until 1974 no Home Secretary had the courage to take this view.

In Parliament, then, Hardie was in a minority, sometimes a minority of one. But we must not forget that the founder of the I.L.P. had many other things to worry about: not least the I.L.P. In the party, Hardie's reputation had risen, not fallen, as a result of the incidents of 1909 and 1910. In 1912 the I.L.P. Conference was held in Merthyr as a tribute to Hardie; and in 1913 Hardie was asked to rejoin the N.A.C. so as to be able to preside over the party's twenty-first birthday conference the following year. As he returned to the chair, he said, 'Nature never intended me to be a leader. I find myself far happier among the rank and file.'

The 1914 conference, with Hardie in the chair, was an emotional occasion. It was held at Bradford, as the first conference had been, and was opened by a rendition of 'The Song of Liberty', specially written by Granville Bantock, a leading composer of the day. Hardie's main speech was devoted to showing how the climate of public opinion had changed since 1893.

In these days, and for many years thereafter, it was tenaciously upheld by the public authorities, here and elsewhere, that it was an offence against the laws of nature and ruinous to the State for public authorities to provide food for starving children, or independent aid for the aged poor. Even safety regulations in mines and factories were taboo. They interfered with the 'freedom of the individual'. As for such proposals as an eight-hour day, a minimum wage, the right to work, and municipal houses, any serious mention of such classed a man as a fool . . .
And if today there is a kindlier social atmosphere it is mainly because of the twenty-one years' work of the I.L.P.

There was much truth in Hardie's claim. Liberalism in 1893 was old Liberalism, individualist Liberalism, dedicated to *laisser-faire* and Welsh disestablishment. From 1906 the new, collectivist Liberalism came increasingly to the fore. Many of the actions of the Governments of 1906 to 1914 were light-years away from the ideology of nineteenth-century Liberalism. Some, like the Trade Disputes Act, the Miners' Eight-Hours Act, and the Minimum Wage Act, were the direct result of Labour pressure. Others, like Old Age Pensions and National

F

Insurance, did not originate on the Labour side. But the Liberal Government would not have pressed them if it had not been worried about the possibility of losing working-class votes to the new Labour Party. And what are we to make of the dog that did not bark: the House of Lords which let these measures pass? We must conclude that Lord Lansdowne was just as frightened of what Labour might do as was Lloyd George. And organized labour would not have been what it was without Hardie and the I.L.P.

At the end of the conference Hardie made an emotional speech declining re-election to the chair. Again he said, 'Nature never intended me to occupy an official position.' He added that he had no wish, as he got older, to obstruct the up-and-coming members of the party, and concluded: 'While I have anything to give, it shall be given ungrudgingly to the child of my life – the I.L.P.'

Meanwhile national politics went on its disturbing way. The early summer of 1914 was an alarming time for politicians. The militant suffragettes were demonstrating that they were fit to be given the vote by burning down medieval churches; several trade unions were threatening united strike action; Ulster seemed on the brink of civil war as armed Protestants prepared to defy Home Rule. The assassination of Archduke Franz Ferdinand of Austria in Sarajevo on 28 June did not attract much attention in Britain. A month later, however, Austria had declared war on Serbia. Germany was threatening to support Austria, and a meeting of the International Socialist Bureau was hurriedly summoned at Brussels to decide what to do. Hardie attended and spoke to massive anti-war demonstrations. A manifesto was issued over the signature of Hardie and Arthur Henderson.* Headed, 'An Appeal to the British Working Class', it ran, in part:

You have never been consulted about the war. Whatever may be the rights and wrongs of the sudden crushing attack made by the Militarist Empire of Austria upon Serbia, it is certain that the workers of all countries likely to be drawn into the conflict must strain every nerve to prevent their Governments from committing them to war.

Everywhere Socialists and the organized forces of Labour are taking this course. Everywhere vehement protests are made against the greed and intrigues of militarists and armament-mongers.

We call upon you to do the same here in Great Britain upon an even more impressive scale . . . Down with class rule! Down with the rule of brute force! Down with war! Up with the peaceful rule of the people!

That was on 2 August 1914. Austria and Germany were at war with Russia; France was virtually bound to join in against Germany;

---

* Henderson had become Secretary of the British Section of the International for purely tactical reasons – to keep Hyndman out.

Britain was not yet involved. On the 3rd, Grey made a long speech in the Commons setting out the case for British participation. The two central questions were our obligations to France and to Belgium. We had no contractual obligation to support France, but through a naval division of labour the French fleet was concentrated on the Mediterranean and the British fleet on the Channel and the North Sea. France was therefore exposed to naval attack in the north, and Britain had a moral obligation to defend the French Channel coast. Britain was bound by treaty, Grey went on, to respect Belgian neutrality, which we must guarantee if the Germans should try to attack France through Belgium. The Unionists and Irish Nationalists indicated their support for Grey. Then MacDonald spoke, to say that our obligations to France were insufficient to justify going to war in alliance with Russian despotism. No less than fifteen radical Liberals spoke in broadly similar terms, against immediate participation, and Hardie made a short speech. He made only two points. The first was to criticize the Government for failing to provide against the destitution and food speculation that was bound to arise. He went on:

One word more. The decision of the Government has been come to without consulting the country. It remains to be seen whether the Government and the House of Commons represent the country on this question. So far as some of us are concerned . . . we shall endeavour to ascertain what is the real feeling of the country and especially of the working classes of the country in regard to the decision of the Government. We belong to a Party which is international. In Germany, in France, in Belgium, and in Austria, the party corresponding to our own is taking all manner of risks to promote and preserve peace.

These were brave words, but Hardie must already have known that his world was collapsing around him. By midnight that day, Germany had invaded Belgium. On the 4th, Britain declared war. The invasion of Belgium was the turning-point for almost all those who had been against war twenty-four hours earlier. Hardie and MacDonald remained opposed to participation; but they were in a tiny minority, a minority even of their own party. MacDonald resigned the leadership, to be succeeded by Henderson.

On 31 July, then, the resounding but hollow oratory of the Socialist International's manifesto had called on the working class not to take part. On 3 August Hardie still professed to believe that the workers would oppose the war. In fact, international socialist pacifism collapsed miserably at its first test. In every combatant country including Britain the majority, if not the whole, of the socialist party voted to support its national government. In so doing, they were only reflecting the views of the voters who supported them. The idea that the working class was anti-war was pure fantasy, and moreover had been shown as such during the Boer War. But this was an aspect of harsh reality that Hardie was unable to face. So far as one can tell, he seriously believed that the notion of an international general strike against war, which he had put forward in Copenhagen in 1910, was a viable proposal. One of the difficulties for a man in Hardie's position was that he was insulated from working-class opinion as a whole, unless he was prepared to endure the psychological cost of investigating it. It was all very well to rouse vast demonstrations in Brussels or Trafalgar Square to passionate opposition to war. But speakers at demonstrations are preaching to the converted. Almost everybody in the labour movement with whom Hardie was closely associated was against the war. Robert Smillie, for instance, said on 2 August that he would be glad to pledge the Scottish miners against the war. But the army of socialist pacifists was truly a stage army. The Scottish miners had opinions of their own about the war, and they were not Robert Smillie's opinions. Hardie, Smillie, even the leading members of the Merthyr I.L.P., represented nobody's views but their own. This divorce from reality was the more unfortunate as it obscured the pungent criticisms being made by Hardie, MacDonald, and others about Sir Edward Grey's secret diplomacy. Britain's obligations to Belgium were one thing; her obligations to France were quite another, since they arose out of military conversations which had been going on ever since 1905, but of which Parliament had never been fully informed. Later in the war, criticisms of secret diplomacy were to make some impact; in 1914, however, they were lost in the great surge of patriotic emotion.

Within forty-eight hours Hardie was exposed to the full force of working-class patriotic frenzy. He honoured a long-standing obligation to speak at a meeting in Aberdare on 6 August. The Aberdare valley had always been the less friendly part of Hardie's constituency; but Hardie was obviously shaken by the degree of hostility to him. The *Merthyr Express* contrasted the 'feeble cheers' of his supporters with the 'tremendous roar of thousands of voices in the remainder of the hall'. Initially Hardie got a hearing as he explained his reasons for not cancelling the meeting: 'Whatever else I may be my constituents know there is no trace of the coward in my blood (Applause).' Before long, his remarks were drowned by continual shouting and singing of *Rule Britannia*, the National Anthem, and *Sospan Fach*. Hardie had no further chance of a hearing after he had said, 'Surely we are nearer to Germany in thought and feeling than we are to Russia.' He was escorted back to the home of a local supporter, where he was staying, by a large disorderly crowd shouting 'Turn the German out!'

'And so', said the *Aberdare Leader* with inspired bathos, 'an exciting experience for Mr Hardie came to an end.' 'Shattering' would have been more appropriate. It was not so much that Hardie was threatened with violence – he later claimed that the interruptions at the meeting were made 'in a fairly good temper'. Rather, the Aberdare meeting abruptly and unmistakably showed Hardie that all his dreams of socialist internationalism were so many castles in the air. C.B. Stanton, the syndicalist, ostentatiously withdrew from chairing the meeting, saying 'Although a Socialist, I am a Britisher.' The South Wales miners, after an appeal from the Admiralty, were working for an hour longer every day to supply fuel for the Royal Navy, according to a report in the *Merthyr Express*.

A few days earlier Hardie had written in the *Merthyr Pioneer*:

> The task of standing for our principles will be no easier than during the Boer War. But that must not deter us. The I.L.P., at least, will stand firm. . . . The cause of International Social Democracy must be proclaimed as the one and only hope for the world. Keep the Red Flag flying!

But after Aberdare, Hardie was not the man to repeat a campaign like the anti-Boer War agitation. He said melodramatically, 'I understand what Christ suffered in Gethsemane as well as any man living.' Ramsay MacDonald met him when he returned to London: 'He was a crushed man, and, sitting in the sun on the terrace of the House of Commons, he seemed to be looking out on blank desolation. From that he never recovered.'

Hardie's standing in his constituency was not, indeed, irretrievably damaged. The Rector of Merthyr attacked Edgar Jones and others who abused Hardie in his absence at recruiting meetings. In October Aberdare was partly compensated for by a meeting in Merthyr addressed by Hardie and MacDonald where the audience was not at all hostile. What had gone beyond recall was Hardie's will to fight back. After the Merthyr meeting, Hardie arranged to travel home in company with Glasier because he was afraid to travel alone on trains and be exposed to the insults of 'patriots'. 'I felt strangely moved by this timidity on his part,' Glasier wrote. 'It was so unlike his pro-Boer days. Dear old Hardie!'

One consolation was that the I.L.P. was solidly anti-war. Ramsay MacDonald's speeches opposing British entry and his resignation from the leadership of the Labour Party reunited him with Hardie after the rift which had lasted since 1910. In the remaining months of activity left to him, Hardie did what he could to oppose the excesses of 'patriotic' frenzy. For suggesting that Grey should have discussed peace proposals submitted by the German Ambassador on 1 August, Hardie was called a coward on the floor of the Commons. In November 1914 Hardie suggested that 'atrocity stories' – that the Germans were melting down the dead bodies of war victims for fat, or raping Belgian nuns and tying them to the clappers of the bells of their own convents – were completely baseless, as of course they were. His erstwhile colleague Edgar Jones asked the Government to censor Hardie's writings as a consequence. In January 1915 Hardie was one of very few people to report on the strange Christmas truce on the Western Front in 1914, when Allied and German troops sang carols to one another and exchanged Christmas presents before returning to their trenches to slaughter each other. Unlike raped Belgian nuns, Christmas truces were not thought to improve British morale.

In February 1915 Lloyd George attacked British engineering workers for excessive drinking, which was allegedly harming the output of munitions. Hardie was one of the first to rebut the attack, and he drew blood in the form of a sharp reply from Lloyd George. It was not long, however, before Lloyd George found that his allegations were not only untrue but impolitic at a time when the cooperation of the men's leaders was needed, and they were quietly dropped. Hardie's last campaign ended in partial victory.

A Victorian melodrama would have it that Hardie was dying of a broken heart; and it would not be too far from the truth. In seven days Hardie had seen the beliefs of a lifetime about international cooperation destroyed, and it had an equally destructive effect on his health. Early in January 1915 Hardie had a stroke, a more serious repetition of the seizure of 1907. He continued indomitably on his round of speeches and meetings, but it began to become as clear to himself as to everybody else that he was not fit for it. In what was to prove his last speech in the Commons, on child labour in agriculture, he apologized for his lack of 'physical exertion'. That was on 25 February, about the same time as Lord Morley met him in the Commons and spoke to him with concern about his health. Morley, with John Burns, had resigned from the Government on the outbreak of war. After twenty years of stormy disputes Morley, Burns and Hardie ended their political careers all on the same side – ironically in support of one of the cherished dreams of the old, Gladstonian Liberalism: no entanglement in continental wars.

In March, Hardie was writing bravely to friends in Merthyr saying he felt much better, and was recuperating on a diet of raw cabbage and onions: 'If you never want to die start out on that diet.' But at the

I.L.P. conference in April, Hardie's illness was only too plain. He spoke only once, in tired and hopeless denunciation of the Tsar of Russia. Hardie's journalism was petering out, after all the millions of words he had written about socialism ever since his first efforts in the *Ardrossan and Saltcoats Herald*. His last contribution to the *Labour Leader* was in March 1915, and his last weekly article in the *Merthyr Pioneer* was on 24 April. The same day he apparently had another stroke, and was whisked off to Caterham Hydro in Surrey, where it was officially stated that he had a 'recurrence of an old complaint, coupled with a nervous breakdown'. Frank Smith moved in to act as his secretary and to fend off visitors. Outside Hardie's family only a few close friends found out how ill he really was. Sylvia Pankhurst was one of these, and her book *The Home Front* contains some poignant scenes of Hardie's last months. The saddest is perhaps her record of a card she received in July from Caterham:

Dear Sylphia,
    In about a week I expect to be gone from here with no more mind control than when I came.
Love.

Hardie could no longer remember how to spell her name.

Soon afterwards he was moved to stay for a short time with T. D. Benson, Treasurer of the I.L.P., at Manchester. Benson warned Bruce Glasier that Hardie's mind had deteriorated, and Glasier decided he could not face up to a meeting with him just then; he would wait till he could see Hardie at Cumnock.

He never did. Hardie was moved to Cumnock, and enjoyed some lucid intervals. He was even able to visit some of his family on holiday in Arran, but in mid September he was taken to a Glasgow nursing home, where on 26 September 1915 he died of pneumonia. He was fifty-nine. Like Lady Macbeth, he died in the midst of battles raging elsewhere, and his death was largely ignored. Not a word was said in tribute to him in the House of Commons of which he had been a member for eighteen years. *The Times* offered a brief and somewhat grudging obituary.

He never caught the ear of that assembly [the Commons] and was an ineffective leader of the independent group which owed its existence in great measure to his unflagging energy. He . . . did not at any time gain the complete confidence of the working class. The Labour Party disappointed his hopes. He was out of tune with the more moderate views of the trade unionist majority for a considerable time, and his views ceased to have any influence in the councils of the party with the coming of the war . . . The bitter passions which he aroused in his life were in great measure forgotten before his death.

Hardie was buried at Maryhill Cemetery, Glasgow, on 29 September. The service was rather confused and undignified. A minister gave a 'ghastly malapropos' – Glasier's phrase – eulogy about Hardie's work for the Evangelical Union church. 'Hardie might have been a grocer merely. It made me wild', wrote Glasier, who then stood up and 'said a few confused words about his being the greatest agitator of his day'.

To all obvious appearances, his day was done. An official Labour candidate was put up to succeed him at Merthyr, only to be defeated by the same C.B. Stanton whom we first met as an enthusiastic syndicalist. Stanton was now a leading exponent of annihilating the Huns, and beat his official Labour opponent by 10,286 votes to 6,080. The worst of the war was still to come, with the appalling slaughter of the Somme in 1916 and Passchendaele in 1917. By the time it was all over, three quarters of a million British citizens had been killed, and a higher proportion in France and Germany. Russia had had a socialist revolution, but not of a sort that Keir Hardie would have welcomed for very long. The world after the war was very different from Keir Hardie's world. But, now that time has put these events into perspective, nobody would dismiss his career as off-handedly as did most commentators in 1915. It remains to us to look more closely at the sort of man Keir Hardie was, and the impact he had on politics and society in his time – and after.

8

THE MAN
AND
HIS WORK

The previous seven chapters have dealt almost
exclusively with Hardie's public life. This is largely inevitable. If it
had not been for his public life, biographies of him would not be
written. And Hardie was much more a public man than most politicians of his time. Rosebery bred horses; Balfour wrote articles on
philosophy; Asquith played bridge. But Labour politicians did not
have the time or the money for gentlemanly relaxations. And no
Labour politician was more singleminded than Hardie. Even *The
Times* in its obituary acknowledged that the Parliamentary Labour
Party 'owed its existence in great measure to his unflagging energy'.
Almost all his waking hours were taken up with politics and political

journalism. Hardie was hardly ever off duty, and very few people saw the private face of Keir Hardie.

But we cannot fully understand him without some assessment of his personality. The private Keir Hardie was much more complex than the public man. In some ways Hardie's personality was much what we would expect, given his upbringing; in other ways it was quite unexpected. But in more aspects than not Hardie acquired and retained the moral views of an earnest, late-Victorian Scots artisan. His very reserve was part of this. Hardie, like most men of his generation, was not one to display emotions in public, and, since surviving letters and documents which give any insight into his private feelings are so meagre, it is often hard to guess Hardie's true feelings. His puritan morality was likewise in character. Ramsay MacDonald, who knew Hardie's mind better than most, again and again referred to the Covenanting traditions he inherited. In an obituary tribute MacDonald wrote: 'If Hardie had ever written a historical introduction to a history of the Labour Movement, he would not have begun with the Reform Bill or any such insignificant superficiality, but with Airds Moss, the Declaration of Sanquhar, and that time and such happenings.' But the Covenanting tradition did more than simply mould Hardie's political outlook. As MacDonald continued, 'his very shortcomings' were those of the Covenanters. For Hardie the boundary was too vague between rightness and righteousness, and between righteousness and self-righteousness. He was too ready to let fly with his tongue at political opponents while sublimely confident of the rightness of his own views. In one sense this was his greatest strength, because it gave him reserves of stamina which forced him to persevere where any normal man would have given up in despair. But it did not show him in an attractive light to those who found themselves on the wrong side of him.

It is only natural, too, that a Covenanting Scot should have shared his generation's frigid repressiveness on matters of sex. According to Tom Johnston, the editor of *Forward*, 'a smutty story caused him to leave a railway carriage'. But he seems to have had more than one amorous affair during the years of separation between husband in London and self-effacing wife in Cumnock. A dozen or so letters relating to a brief but passionate affair in the summer of 1893 have come to light. Hardie fell deeply in love with Miss Annie Hines, of Oxford, daughter of a self-taught socialist and atheist chimney-sweep who led the local branch of the Fabian Society. But, however passionate, Hardie kept up his guard. Initially he shrank from meeting Miss Hines in case they were observed together. Before long, though, he was writing 'Make what arrangements you please sweetheart, and I will prove a willing slave.' It was too late; Miss Hines broke off the affair and Hardie was left mourning his unrequited love. He was getting neither sexual satisfaction from his wife nor an adequate substitute for it from anybody else.

Hardie's sexual urgings may have been frustrated; his vanity certainly was not. It was part of his Covenanting self-righteousness that he had a very high opinion of himself, and there is no doubt that feelings of unjustified neglect encouraged him in some of his early political activities like the Mid-Lanark election and the challenge to Broadhurst in the T.U.C. Hardie was constantly posing for photographs of himself, especially in his Old Testament prophet guise, and a favourite form of money-raising for the I.L.P. was to sell these pictures at a penny or two a time, like the cigarette cards and pin-ups of later generations. Once in 1905, Hardie himself wrote to his wife on the back of one of these postcards. 'I am told this is having a big sale,' he said complacently. A striking example of Hardie's vanity emerges from a letter he wrote to David Lowe some time after 1900.

[I] Dined with Rosebery on Friday at the Welsh Parliamentary dinner and he found in the 'good Scotch face at the end of the table' the one and only thing which now bound him to Wales. He had a long steady look in my direction as he declared that 'Parliamentary courage, too rare a quality in our political life', needed to be held in check sometimes lest it do harm.

Hardie and Rosebery could scarcely have been more opposed in temperament, social class, or political views. But Hardie was not too proud to take dinner and compliments from Lord Rosebery. Hardie's vanity, his extremely high opinion of himself, was one of the things which made him a difficult colleague. But it must be said that this vice was very widespread among Labour politicians, who were without exception very self-satisfied at having got as far in politics as they had.* And, as we have already noted, Hardie's vanity came nowhere near the surpassing conceit of his contemporary John Burns. At the time Burns seemed the greater man, but who, other than historians and students, now remembers John Burns? Hardie has had posthumous revenge.

One facet of Hardie's character that did not reflect the puritan Covenanter was his attitude to formal religion itself. As we saw in

---

* An odd indication is the plethora of 'From . . . to' biographies and memoirs of Labour politicians of Hardie's generation. *From Pit to Parliament* (Hardie, by David Lowe); *From Workshop to War Cabinet* (George Barnes); *From Workman's Cottage to Windsor Castle* (John Hodge); these are only a few examples.

Chapter 1, his mother and stepfather were unusual Victorians. G. B. Clark, who knew David Hardie, recalled that he was a follower of Charles Bradlaugh and his policy of 'Atheism, Republicanism, and Malthusianism, which was once defined as the policy of No God; No King; and No Babies'. However, as we have seen, Keir Hardie was 'converted to Christianity' in 1878, possibly during a visit by the American revivalists Moody and Sankey. Clark averred that Hardie was 'one of the few leaders of the International Socialist movement who retained his early faith'. In his youth Hardie chose not the repressive and inherently conservative Presbyterianism that dominated contemporary Scotland and produced leading figures like Lord Overtoun, but the liberal doctrines of the Evangelical Union. Orthodox Calvinism relied on the doctrine of justification by faith: we will be saved not because of anything we do on this earth, but because we believe in God and Jesus Christ. This was only too liable to slide into the perverted beliefs of Robert Burns's Holy Willie or James Hogg's Justified Sinner* – men who believed that since God has preordained who shall achieve the Kingdom of Heaven, it does not matter what the elect (i.e. themselves) do on earth. Burns's lascivious drunken elder, Holy Willie, prayed thus to his Presbyterian God:

> Yet I am here, a chosen sample,
> To shew thy grace is great and ample:
> I'm here, a pillar o' thy temple
>   Strong as a rock,
> A guide, a ruler and example
>   To a' thy flock.—

Hardie had seen enough Holy Willies in his youth to have no use for this sort of religion. The Evangelical Union believed in the humane doctrine of justification by works: the commonsense view that good deeds make good Christians. These were Hardie's religious principles, in so far as he professed them in public – which was not very far. He was not a regular churchgoer, but he occasionally preached the social gospel from the pulpits of Merthyr and elsewhere. He claimed (notably in his Merthyr election addresses, where it was calculated to appeal to his audience) that his socialism was derived from the Sermon on the Mount; and, drawing the moral of that very practical piece of Christian doctrine, he added, 'The only way you can serve God is by serving mankind.'

For Hardie, Christianity was perhaps more a matter of ethics than

* See *The Private Memoirs and Confessions of a Justified Sinner*, by James Hogg (1824) – a little-known masterpiece, one of the most striking novels in the English language.

of religious inspiration. It was the ethical principles laid down in the New Testament which attracted him: he could not be called deeply religious, but he regarded the New Testament as a code of conduct by which people's actual behaviour should be judged. It is interesting that in 1900 he deliberately chose to affirm rather than take the oath at the opening of Parliament. Where others might have found comfort of mind in religion, Hardie had a curious attachment to spiritualism, and believed firmly (according to Philip Snowden) that he had lived in a previous incarnation. As his daughter Agnes said after his death, 'My father had some queer notions sometimes.'

Hardie once remarked that he was one of those unfortunate people who had never known what it was to be a child. Especially after Mary Keir married David Hardie, life was too desperate a struggle for young Jamie to have time for play. He probably had no close companions of his own age; his half-brothers were much younger, and he may have been an outlaw among other children because of his illegitimacy. When his stepfather was drunk he would angrily complain to his wife about 'the bastard'. It is not until Keir Hardie was well on in years that we see any sign of a playful nature. But in the right mood and the right company he could unbutton himself, and abandon his normal reserve. One of the happiest pen-portraits of Hardie has been left by W. J. Edwards, who was growing up in a socialist household in Aberdare in the early 1900s. In the Edwards household Hardie behaved like a favourite uncle; he sat down to a hearty tea (eating twice as much as anybody else) and led the singing of his favourite songs – *Jingle Bells* and *Annie Laurie*. Of his close friends, Bruce Glasier seems to have been the best able to tempt Hardie into a jovial mood. Glasier's diary records an amusing occasion near the end of Hardie's life, when they were both attending a Fabian summer school in Keswick. Hardie led the rousing singing of a number of traditional Scots songs in the presence of Sidney and Beatrice Webb, who in Glasier's words 'sat through it all as if witnessing for sociological purposes an Indian orgy'. If Hardie had been closer to Glasier, say, and less close to the austere and colourless Frank Smith, the sunny side of his nature might have been exposed more often to the outside world.

Unfortunately these moods were usually all too short, to be superseded by a temper of gloom, suspicion and backbiting. In 1902 Hardie said, 'My work has cut me off from communion with my fellows. I have few friends and cannot, somehow, enter into the healthy and legitimate light side of life.' As we have already seen, Hardie never had any totally unswerving political ally except Frank Smith. Glasier was the next closest, but Hardie and Glasier sometimes fell out, as over the *Labour Leader* in 1903 and 1904. And from about 1910 onwards Glasier usually sided with Ramsay MacDonald in disputes between him and Hardie. Philip Snowden, the fourth leading member of the I.L.P., had a prickly enough personality of his own to guarantee that he never really became a close friend of Keir Hardie. Hardie's Covenanting temperament was, again, partly to blame. Seeing other people's points of view was not one of his strong points, and political disputes tended to become personal as Hardie would cast doubt on the good faith of his opponents. Throughout Hardie's career we see examples of people whose hostility to him was based on personal dislike, not political disagreement. Chisholm Robertson, John Burns, Ben Tillett and Robert Blatchford are cases in point. Blatchford said Hardie was the only person he had ever tried and failed to like. Such dislikes were sometimes exacerbated by Hardie's occasionally curious attitudes to money matters. There was never the slightest suspicion that he was dishonest, but he had a way of regarding as his personal property what others thought rightly belonged to the I.L.P. as a whole, and after his death there were some awkward discussions over the Kippen bequest. The Misses Kippen, two elderly Scots ladies who had made donations to the I.L.P. through Hardie from 1893 onwards, made a bequest jointly to Hardie and John Redmond of the Irish Party, for the use of their respective parties. In 1915 the I.L.P. had to wrest its share from Mrs Hardie, who claimed it for herself.

In small things, then, Hardie could be petty, vain, even unscrupulous. This was not the Keir Hardie who inspired affection, even reverence, in thousands of households; whose portrait supplanted Mr Gladstone's on working-class walls all over Britain. What was it about Hardie that inspired such loyalty?

Hardie had a unique ability to gain the trust of audiences in the right place. He was not a natural orator; David Lowe thought that making speeches was 'torture to soul and body' for him. His style was not for the House of Commons. A supercilious lobby correspondent described one of Hardie's speeches during the Balfour administration.

Mr Keir Hardie, stodgy Socialist, was speaking in grim, sullen, despondent Doric ... Here was none of the rugged riotousness of tongue we get from John Burns. Mr Hardie is as morose and chill as the Galloway hills. He is solemnly, terribly, in earnest ... He spoke like one who felt he was talking to a blank wall. The House listens to him because of the touch of tragic earnestness in his style. But it never does more than listen; he is not persuasive.

But the same style was ideal for audiences in Scotland, the West

Riding, or South Wales. W. J. Edwards recorded the impact of Hardie's speeches on himself and his friends:

Keir Hardie's great strength lay in the fact that he and his gospel were indivisible. A more glowing personality of infinitely greater charm could have uttered the same words and even with greater force; but without Hardie's sense of mission, without Hardie's character which had not the slightest interest in personal gain, without his essential virtue and purity of mind, such a man could have had no lasting effect on the people of the valleys.

As we have noticed, the missionary style went down best with audiences accustomed to being preached at from evangelical pulpits. Hardie never really made an impact in Anglican or Catholic Lancashire, nor in godless London. But whatever the context, what shone through Hardie's countless speeches and writings was his directness and honesty. He said exactly what he meant, meant precisely what he said. Hardie had no radio, no television, not even any mass-circulation newspapers through which he could project himself. His appeal necessarily depended on sheer force of personality, and his personality infused all his speeches. Nothing else had the impact of personal contact, and it was the need for personal contact that drove Hardie on his murderously intensive rounds of public speaking encounters, from addresses to striking Lanarkshire miners in 1879 down to his last anti-war speeches in 1914.

Hardie's moral courage often showed up to best advantage in his speeches. He was never afraid to speak up for a wildly unpopular view in a totally hostile context. We can see notable examples from all through his career: his attack on Broadhurst in the T.U.C. in 1887; the Royal Baby speech in the Commons in 1894; the speech in the Cambridge Union in February 1907; the Aberdare meeting in August 1914. Nobody was less afraid to face a hostile audience; and Keir Hardie moderated his views for nobody. Unlike many of his colleagues, he was not softened by the parliamentary embrace. He did not regard the Commons as the best club in the world, a place to conduct gentlemanly debate tempered with profuse expressions of personal respect for one's opponents. That was no way for a Covenanter to behave, and Hardie's parliamentary speeches were often harsh attacks on middle-class indifference to the plight of the unemployed, or on the misbehaviour of employers or policemen, and they jarred in the atmosphere of the Edwardian House of Commons. As the lobby correspondent we have quoted saw, Hardie's style commanded attention, but it was not persuasive. None the less, these are sometimes the occasions on which we see Hardie at his best, and his conventional opponents at their worst. 'I've been in a wild beast show at feeding time', wrote a West Ham journalist after the Royal Baby speech.

I've been at a football match when a referee gave a wrong decision. I've been at rowdy meetings of the Shoreditch vestry and the West Ham Corporation, but in all my natural life I have never witnessed a scene like this. They howled and yelled and screamed, but he stood his ground.

Undoubtedly there was something in Hardie's temperament which made him relish this. He was never cut out to be in a majority, and this partly explains his growing restlessness in the Parliamentary Labour Party after 1906. Once he had ceased to be alone in a hostile world, he was no longer so content. The *South Wales Daily News* devoted a rather shrewd editorial to a discussion of Hardie's and MacDonald's anti-war meeting in Merthyr in October 1914. If a vote had been taken, according to the writer, MacDonald and Hardie would have been in a 'sorry minority'.

That, however, would not have affected them so much as the discovery that they were in a majority ... They must be in the right with only two or three; for them truth is always with very small minorities; when a lot of people join in, Mr MacDonald and Mr Hardie move on.

As a description of Hardie's temperament (for it fitted him much better than MacDonald) this was very perceptive. Hardie more than once said that he felt his work was done after 1906, and in a sense he was right. As the Labour Party became more important, Hardie became less so, as should be evident from Chapters 6 and 7. Once the party had been launched, Hardie was not the man to steer it through parliamentary shoals.

But this only highlights the achievements of his earlier years. In 1893 Keir Hardie did more than anyone else to found the I.L.P., and in 1900 he did more than anyone else to found the Labour Party. These are his greatest achievements, and are unquestionably his, whatever claims others may have to a share in them. At first it is hard to see what Hardie's unique qualities were. He was not the best propagandist for socialism. Snowden was a better speaker; Blatchford a better journalist. He was not the best administrator, or backstairs intriguer. Here Ramsay MacDonald and David Shackleton were the experts, compared to whom Hardie was an amateur. None the less, Hardie had considerable ability both as a propagandist and as an organizer. But, first, last, and always, he had staying power. This was his greatest strength, and it sprang from his personality. Once convinced that he was right, nothing would deflect him from his path. He

could brush off an amount of failure and ridicule that would deter
almost anybody else. Truly he was a 'dour, dogged fellow', in John
Burns's phrase. Blatchford and Champion, for instance, had none of
Hardie's perseverance. If they could not follow up success in one
sphere, they would go away and try something else instead. And other
politicians hung back to see what success Hardie's lonely crusade
would have before risking making fools of themselves by joining him.
Ramsay MacDonald and Arthur Henderson were both clear cases:
wary politicians who would not join Hardie until they were convinced
that his idea would succeed. Unlike Hardie, MacDonald was careful
to keep his route of retreat open, at least until 1900: if independent
Labour representation was a failure, he would be able to slip back into
orthodox Liberalism without too much loss of face. From 1893 to
1900 it was Hardie who bore the brunt of the vital negotiations to
bring trade unionists round to the side of the I.L.P. After 1900, and
especially after 1906, the day of the pioneer gave way to the day of the
bureaucrat and the organization. Keir Hardie's party became the
party of MacDonald, Shackleton, and Henderson.

Keir Hardie did not make the Labour Party a mass movement.
True, there were substantial sections of the working class to whom
Hardie was a prophet to be revered. But there were still larger numbers whom his message could not reach. Some parts of the country, as
we have pointed out more than once, provided much more fertile
ground than others for the I.L.P. message. Labour support, however
measured, was still very patchy by Keir Hardie's death. In terms of
seats, the Labour Party seemed to be unable to break out of the en-
claves it secured in the Gladstone–MacDonald pact. In the elections
of 1910 the Liberals pursued a quite deliberate policy of 'containment'
of the Labour Party. There were very few three-cornered fights; and,
ominously, where there was one, the Labour candidate was usually
soundly beaten by the Liberal. The Labour share of the vote in 1910
was less than 8 per cent. During Keir Hardie's lifetime the Labour
Party never emerged beyond the status Hardie envisaged for it –
namely that of a pressure group 'second in importance only to . . . the
Irish Nationalist Party'. Even by this humble criterion, it did better
than the larger Irish Party. It had one major triumph in the Trade
Disputes Act, and a number of lesser successes. But it was not, by
1915, a major party. Over most of the country it was the Liberal
Party which most deserved the title of 'the working-class party'.
Many more working men voted Liberal than Labour, and this usually
remained true even in the few cases when they had to make a choice
between the two.

It was the First World War that changed all this. It is the final irony of Hardie's career that the cataclysm which destroyed him also saved his party. In 1916 the Liberal Party split, damagingly, when Lloyd George ousted Asquith as Prime Minister. Lloyd George formed a coalition with the Conservatives which continued after the war until 1922; and the anti-coalition Liberals under Asquith were decimated in the General Election of 1918, when they were reduced to 28 seats. The Liberals never recovered from the First World War. But the Labour Party was immeasurably strengthened. As we have seen, few Labour M.P.s joined Hardie and MacDonald in opposition to the war. But the pro-war majority had enough tolerance and good sense not to hound their colleagues out of the party. Arthur Henderson joined the Cabinet in May 1915 and a number of other Labour M.P.s had their first experience of Government posts. The Press and the Civil Service were pleasantly surprised to find that working-class M.P.s made as good ministers as any and notably better than some. In 1917 Henderson resigned again from the Cabinet, which had not allowed him to pursue peace negotiations with the socialist parties of other combatant countries. Again the Labour Party was more or less united; the appalling carnage of 1916 and 1917 induced a mood of war weariness that benefited the Labour Party. In 1918 the party, though almost submerged by the renewed patriotic fervour for hanging the Kaiser, got 63 seats, thus driving Asquith's Liberals into third place. In 1922 the Labour total rose to 142 against 116 for both factions of Liberalism together; in December 1923 Labour got 191 seats, and Ramsay MacDonald formed the first, minority, Labour Government the following month.

Thus the First World War was vital for the rise of the Labour Party. At the same time as it split the Liberals, it put Labour for the first time into the role of a party of Government. This went far beyond Hardie's vision of what the Labour Party could or should do. Nevertheless, Hardie's role was quite indispensable. Without Keir Hardie there would have been no Labour Party. Without Taff Vale, or the Gladstone–MacDonald pact, or MacDonald's work as Secretary, or Henderson's conduct of the party during the war, the Labour Party would never have been in a position to form a Government in 1924. Hardie was not responsible for any of these things. But if he had not taken the first step, none of the rest would have followed. Only Hardie's single-mindedness – a characteristic not shared by his early colleagues – ensured that the party was in any position to benefit from the reaction to Taff Vale, and thus set out on the voyage outlined above.

In perspective, then, Keir Hardie's life work was by no means so totally destroyed in 1914 as he thought. This is true not only of his work of party organization, but of his views. When Hardie died, John Burns wrote: 'I once told him that he would be known as the leader who never won a strike, organized a Union, governed a Parish, or passed a Bill. Baron Cumnock in the Duchy of doctrinaire Barren . . . He must be judged less by his achievements than by his aims, and to his credit they were exalted.' It was magnanimous of Burns to make this lofty concession. And Hardie has been vindicated by the achievement of many of his aims, and the general acceptance of his views. Many would now agree that he was right about the Boer War and, to some extent, the First World War. The frenzied patriots whom that war threw up, men like Pemberton Billing and Horatio Bottomley, are mercifully forgotten for the most part, and Hardie's criticisms of secret diplomacy were widely accepted, not just in the Labour Party, after about 1917. On colonial and Indian affairs Hardie was many years ahead of his time. He was almost the only British politician of his day to protest at the treatment of black South Africans. And his views on India were thought so scandalous that they provoked a tremendous uproar – yet only forty years later India was given sovereign independence.

On the home front most of the causes sponsored by Hardie, in their time novel and controversial, are now beyond political dispute. Often, indeed, reform came from quarters other than the Labour Party, but many of Hardie's objectives have now been achieved. The 1911 system of sickness and unemployment benefit was greatly expanded, after the Beveridge Report of 1942, into the 'Welfare State' as we know it today. The 'right to work', one of Hardie's favourite campaigns, has re-emerged with a new vigour since the occupation of the yards of Upper Clyde Shipbuilders by the workers in 1971. It would be a brave politician today who dared to poke fun at any Right to Work Bill as Herbert Samuel did in 1909 when he wrote that the Labour members might as well introduce a 'right to be happy' bill giving everybody the right to be happy and instructing local authorities to find the means. The legal position of trade unions as secured in 1906 has been maintained, after a disastrous period of experiment from 1971 to 1974. Only one of the causes for which Hardie fought is still not on the political agenda: the tradition of Hardie's republicanism has been continued by a few solitary campaigners, notably his son-in-law and biographer Emrys Hughes. But the Royal Family has been entirely unscathed by the attacks of successive generations of radical individualist M.P.s; and, since the few Labour M.P.s who share Hardie's republican views are elected by working-class voters overwhelmingly loyal to the Royal Family, this situation is unlikely to change. The last crusade of nineteenth-century radicalism remains unfought.

Hardie was not a profound thinker; but his contribution to British socialist thought was perhaps all the more important for that. A combination of idealism and robust common sense made him an anti-Marxist. Marxism, Hardie complained, did not 'touch one human sentiment or feeling'. And classes had an awkward way of not behaving as Marxists said they must. 'Take child labour: here we have the "Bourgeoisie" actually legislating in advance of the opinion of the "proletariat", although the latter stand to gain and the former to lose from the change.' Hardie always deplored the arguments of advocates of 'class war'. His reasons were interesting. Socialism entailed the common ownership of the means of production – but this was not an end in itself, only a means to a better way of life based on cooperation and fraternity rather than competition and envy. Feelings of brotherhood, Hardie argued, 'can never grow out of a propaganda of class hatred. Life is already barren enough without our voluntarily adding to its bitterness.'

A creed of socialism based on Robert Burns was not only, in Hardie's view, more humane than one based on Karl Marx, it was also more likely to gain working-class support. 'For twenty-one years', Hardie said in 1901, 'the S.D.F. has based its propaganda on the class-war theory, and the result is dismal failure. How could it be otherwise? Mankind in the mass is not moved by hatred, but by love of what is right'. The language might be sentimental, but the observation was shrewd. It was Keir Hardie's vision of socialism, not H. M. Hyndman's, that attracted thousands of working-class followers in South Wales and the West Riding. And it is Hardie's vision of socialism which has been shared by most members of the Labour Party throughout its lifetime. Philosophers and economists may regret its lack of precision; Fabians and sceptics may note that Hardie was better at describing the good life under socialism than at explaining how to achieve it. But in a world more complicated and (perhaps) more depressing than Hardie could have dreamed of, we could do worse than attempt to live up to his vision

That Man to Man the warld o'er,
Shall brothers be for a' that.—

BIBLIOGRAPHY

   This list is divided into two sections. Section A, *Further Reading*, suggests some possible sources of information for readers wishing to find out more about Hardie's life and times. Section B, *List of Sources*, shows what sources, published and unpublished, have been used in the preparation of each chapter. Full references are given on the first mention of any book, or collection of papers, and an abbreviated version on each subsequent mention. Books are published in London unless otherwise stated.

Section A : Further Reading

There have been many previous biographies of Hardie. Only the following are of any value. The first three are by personal acquaintances, the latter two by modern scholars.

W. Stewart, *J. Keir Hardie* (1921). The official life, commissioned by the I.L.P.

D. Lowe, *From Pit to Parliament* (1923). Covers Hardie's early life.

E. Hughes, *Keir Hardie* (1956). Emrys Hughes married Hardie's daughter Agnes.

K. O. Morgan, *Keir Hardie, Radical and Socialist* (1975). An excellent, scholarly biography.

F. Reid, 'Keir Hardie's Conversion to Socialism', in A. Briggs and J. Saville, eds., *Essays in Labour History 1886–1923* (1971). Covers Hardie's life up to 1887.

Most of Hardie's own works are now very hard to obtain. The following, however, may be obtainable in some libraries.

From Serfdom to Socialism (1907). Hardie's statement of socialist principles.

India: Impressions and Suggestions (1909).

Keir Hardie's Speeches and Writings, ed. E. Hughes (Glasgow, n.d., *c.* 1928). A useful collection.

A number of memories and biographies of Hardie's contemporaries are useful for the light they shed on his relationships with his close colleagues. Three of the most important are:

Lord Elton, *The Life of James Ramsay MacDonald (1866–1919)* (1939). The best of many lives of MacDonald, but it ends in 1919.

Philip (Viscount) Snowden, *An Autobiography*, 2 vols, (1934). Snowden's memoirs, written in his old age after his break with the Labour Party.

L. Thompson, *The Enthusiasts* (1971). An excellent biography of John and Katherine Bruce Glasier.

There are now an enormous number of works on the political history of Britain during the years of Hardie's active career. A selected list is given below; many have bibliographies of their own to take the interested reader still further.

F. Bealey and H. M. Pelling, *Labour and Politics, 1900–06* (1958).

N. Blewett, *The Peers, the Parties, and the People: the General Elections of 1910* (1972). There can be very little left to say about the 1910 elections after this massive work.

K. D. Brown, *Labour and Unemployment 1900–1914.* (Newton Abbot, 1971).

H. A. Clegg, A. Fox, and A. F. Thompson, *A History of British Trade Unions since 1889*. Vol. I, 1889–1910 (Oxford, 1964). A standard work, with good coverage of trade-union and Lib-Lab politics.

G. Dangerfield, *The Strange Death of Liberal England* (1935). Brilliant but unreliable.

R. C. K. Ensor. *England, 1870–1914* (Oxford, 1936). Not yet replaced as the standard history of the period.

E. Halévy. *History of the English People in the Nineteenth Century*. Vol. 6: *The Rule of Democracy (1905–1914)* (1934).

W. Kent, *John Burns: Labour's Lost Leader* (1950).

K.O.Morgan, *Wales in British Politics, 1868–1922* (Cardiff, 1963).

H.M.Pelling, *Origins of the Labour Party*, New edn. (Oxford, 1965). An important study.

H.M.Pelling, *A Short History of the Labour Party* (1961).

P.Rowland, *The Last Liberal Governments*. Vol. 1: *The Promised Land, 1905–10* (1968). Vol. 2: *Unfinished Business, 1911–14* (1971). A very full narrative history.

Section B: List of Sources

CHAPTER 1. EARLY YEARS

Hardie papers in the National Library of Scotland, MS. Dep. 176.
William Small papers, National Library of Scotland, MS. Acc. 3350.
Ardrossan and Saltcoats Herald.
The Miner.
Trades Union Congress: Annual Congress Reports.
Reid, 'Keir Hardie's Conversion'.
T.B.Aldrich, *The Stillwater Tragedy*. 2 vols. (Edinburgh, 1886).

CHAPTER 2. MID-LANARK TO WEST HAM

Glasgow Weekly Mail.
Scotsman.
Glasgow Herald.
The Times.
Irish National League papers, National Library of Scotland, MS. 1809.
The Miner.
J.G.Kellas, *The Liberal Party in Scotland, 1885–1895*, Unpublished Ph.D. thesis (London, 1962).
T.W.Moody, 'Michael Davitt and the British Labour Movement 1882–1906', *Transactions of the Royal Historical Society*, Fifth series, III, 1953.
T.U.C. Reports.
West Ham Herald.
Stratford Express.
West Ham Guardian.
Hardie collection, West Ham Public Library.
Papers formerly in the possession of Francis Johnson, transcribed by Dr H.M.Pelling (cited as Johnson MSS.)

CHAPTER 3. MEMBER FOR WEST HAM SOUTH

Parliamentary Debates, 4th series (Cited as Hansard).
I.L.P. Annual Conference Reports.
Pelling, *Origins*.
I.L.P.: Minutes of the National Administrative Council.
Labour Leader.
R.Blatchford, *Merrie England* (1894).
Clegg, Fox and Thompson.
West Ham Herald.
Stratford Express.

CHAPTER 4. OUT OF PARLIAMENT

H.D.Lloyd papers, Wisconsin State Historical Society (microfilm).
Labour Leader.
I.L.P. Conference Reports.
J.K.Hardie, *Lord Overtoun: Chrome, Charity, Crystals and Cant* (1899).
J.K.Hardie, *More about Overtoun* (1899).
Clegg, Fox and Thompson.
Labour Representation Committee: Conference Reports.
Johnson MSS.
Labour Party papers, Transport House Library.
K.O.Fox, 'Labour and Merthyr's Khaki Election of 1900', *Welsh History Review*, II, 4 (1965).
Merthyr Express.

CHAPTER 5. THE YEARS OF THE L.R.C. 1900–1906

Bealey and Pelling.
F.Bealey, 'Negotiations between the Liberal Party and the Labour Representation Committee before the General Election of 1906', *Bulletin of the Institute of Historical Research*, XXIX (1956).
Labour Leader.
I.L.P. Conference Reports.
Hansard.
Johnson MSS.
Hardie MSS, Edinburgh.
Labour Party MSS.
Merthyr Express.
W.J.Edwards, *From the Valley I Came* (1956).
Sir R.B.Martin, 'The Electoral "Swing of the Pendulum"', *Journal of the Royal Statistical Society*, LXIX (1906).

CHAPTER 6. THE LIBERALS IN OFFICE 1906–10

Bealey, 'Negotiations . . .'.
Rowland.
Johnson MSS.
Pease papers, bound as 'The Infancy of the Labour Party', British Library of Political and Economic Science.
Hansard.
Clegg, Fox, and Thompson.
Labour Party: Annual Conference Reports.
I.L.P. Conference Reports.
Labour Party MSS.
The Times.
Blewett.
Merthyr Express.

CHAPTER 7. LAST YEARS

Hansard.
Merthyr Express.
Blewett.
Rowland.

E. Larkin, *James Larkin*, (1965).
I.L.P. Conference Reports.
Thompson, *The Enthusiasts*.
Merthyr Pioneer.
E. S. Pankhurst, *The Home Front* (1932).
The Times.
Forward.

CHAPTER 8. THE MAN AND HIS WORK

Forward.
Hardie MSS, Edinburgh.
Edwards.
Kent, *John Burns*.
Hardie, *Speeches and Writings*.

INDEX